Stephen F. Kelly was born and brought up on Merseyside. Educated at Ruskin College, Oxford, and the London School of Economics, he was for many years a political correspondent with *Tribune*. In 1978, he joined Granada Television, working on programmes such as *World in Action* and *What The Papers Say*. Now a freelance writer and television producer, he devotes most of his time to writing about football and labour history. He is a regular contributor to many newspapers and magazines, and is also Fellow in Media at the University of Huddersfield. He is currently working on a football anthology, *Not Just A Game*, to be published by Headline later this year.

Graeme Souness

A Soccer
Revolutionary

Stephen F. Kelly

HEADLINE

First published in 1994
by HEADLINE BOOK PUBLISHING

First published in paperback in 1995
by HEADLINE BOOK PUBLISHING

10 9 8 7 6 5 4 3 2 1

ISBN 0 7472 4377 8

Printed and bound in Great Britain by
Cox & Wyman Ltd, Reading, Berks

HEADLINE BOOK PUBLISHING
A division of Hodder Headline PLC
338 Euston Road
London NW1 3BH

For
Judith, Nicholas and Emma

Contents

Acknowledgements

This book has been written without the co-operation of Graeme Souness, though not through choice. Unfortunately, shortly after I approached him for an interview, he resigned as manager of Liverpool Football Club. For obvious reasons he then felt that he did not wish to participate. I understand and respect those reasons, but hope that what I have written is a fair account of his years at Ibrox and Anfield.

There are, however, many who have helped in the preparation of this book, but there are those who, for one reason or another, have asked to remain anonymous. To them goes my deepest appreciation for their enormous assistance. Without their recollections and insights, this book would not have been possible.

Of those happy to have their help placed on record, I would, in particular, like to thank Jim Gardiner who read the manuscript, making many suggestions as well as corrections. Needless to say, any mistakes which remain are entirely my fault and mine alone.

Among the many other people and organisations I should like to thank are Alder Hey Hospital, Jeff Anderson, Stephen Boulton, Hugh Cairns, the staff of Chorlton

Acknowledgements

Library, Companies House, Stuart Cosgrove, the FA Premier League, the Football Association, the Football League, Andrew Fox, Steve Hale, Brian Hall, Dave Hill, Don Jones, the *Liverpool Daily Post and Echo*, Dermot McQuarrie, Mainstream Publishing, the staff of Manchester Central Library, Denis Mooney, the late Sydney Moss, Murray International Holdings, Bill Murray, the Scottish Football Association, Les Rawlinson, Sandy Ross, Jim White, John Whittaker, and the editor of *Through the Wind and the Rain*.

I should also like to express my appreciation to Denis Mooney and Sheila Casey for their kind hospitality during my visits to Glasgow as well as for the considerable assistance which they have given me.

I should also like to thank my publishers, and in particular editor Ian Marshall, whose enthusiasm and advice kept me going through some of the bleaker moments. I am also grateful to my agent John Pawsey, as well as Anthony and Marjorie Rowe Jones and my mother Mary Kelly, for regular supplies of newspaper cuttings and even more regular bouts of baby sitting.

But above all my deepest appreciation goes to my wife Judith Jones and children Nicholas and Emma who have been forced to endure my dark moods and enforced absences during the time it has taken to write this book.

Stephen F. Kelly
May 1994

A Great Hope fell.
You heard no noise.
The Ruin was Within.

Emily Dickinson

CHAPTER ONE
The Godfather

There is an aura about Graeme Souness. He is imposing. When he strides into a room, heads turn. You are in the presence of the distinguished, the fortunate. People pay attention, waiters scurry, tongues wag. Even journalists freeze at asking embarrassing questions while friends are careful not to overstep their mark. Souness carries an authority about him like others carry a wallet; some might call it arrogance.

You can love him or hate him but he rarely inspires mere indifference. Ask a few ex-first division forwards and they will talk about his vindictiveness; ask those who have served under him and they will complain about his ruthlessness; ask David Murray of Rangers and he will tell you about Souness' revolutionary zeal. But on Merseyside you would be hard put to find anyone who could say much that is complimentary about their one-time adopted son. Liverpudlians can be the warmest of people, but they can be equally vitriolic or scathing; cynical when it comes to southerners, Conservatives or anyone just that bit too flash. As far as they were concerned, Graeme Souness slotted into at least one of those categories. The feeling was pretty much mutual. It was hardly surprising when he once confessed to a journalist that he didn't like scousers, they were always whingeing. And yet Graeme Souness is a hard man to pin down. He does not fit comfortably into any slot. The trouble with Souness is that he is also likeable.

He's a handsome man with a gaunt sad face, a punch-drunk nose, a rough old Scottish smile and Tuscan blue eyes that talk as much as his lips. He doesn't look like a football manager. He's suntanned, fit, with no sign of the statutory limp of most ex-professionals. He likes to keep in shape, enjoys a daily massage and usually sports a designer suntan and a pair of Raybans. With his straight back, he cuts a dashing figure in his Italian suit. He is immaculate, never sloppily dressed. There is a touch of the Godfather, a young Michael, seizing his unexpected opportunity to take over the dynasty. Maybe not quite as ruthless and ambitious as young Michael, but he could easily be the new Padrone, the Ibrox and Anfield Godfather without the Mafia connections.

It's not hard to see why the Italians worshipped him so much. He looks at ease in the sun and warmth of Italy where style and a touch of arrogance are the rule rather than the exception. One journalist remembers spotting him stepping out of a car outside Sampdoria's elegant stadium. 'The crowd raced over to see him, pushing and shoving just to get a glimpse. He looked so classy; smart car, jacket over his shoulders, a woman on each arm, the sun beating down on him. The kids loved him. He was at home.' That same journalist spotted him a few years later in a record store in Glasgow. 'He had two minders diplomatically standing a short distance away, watching carefully as he flicked through the record racks. Outside it was grey and drizzling. I felt sorry for him.'

Souness is no ordinary manager. He would never have served his apprenticeship in the lower divisions. Not for him the Darlingtons, the Doncasters or the Dumbartons of this world. Souness was always destined to arrive and remain at the top. You would never spot him slopping out the showers, humping the kit around or mucking in as most managers do at less fashionable clubs. Nor could you ever imagine him kow-towing to some trumped-up, self-elected club chairman. Souness is his own man. That's what you pay for. Never a reformist, never a yes man, always a revolutionary.

Even as a player Souness embarked on his career at the very highest level, serving his apprenticeship in the hallowed surrounds of White Hart Lane before exalted spells at England's and Italy's finest. In between came a brief, learning curve with Middlesbrough, under the guidance of the enigmatic Jack Charlton. And finally came his time as a manager with two of Britain's top clubs. That was part of his aura, the surroundings fitting the man. Trophy rooms, glistening with gold and talk of money, his natural background.

As a player he showed the same kind of authority. Rarely did his shoulders drop, or his socks dangle untidily around his ankles. If he did get weary, then he never showed it. You could always spot him; upright, leaning gently backwards, chin raised, barely needing to swivel his head or raise his eyes as he poked the ball forward. It was the style of the arrogant, the man confident of his abilities, frightened of no one.

As manager, he was a stark contrast to his Anfield predecessor. Dalglish was the austere professional, fun if you knew him, but a man of few words, privately complicated, even insecure, but not really one of the lads in search of a good night out. Souness was the more fun-loving, wickedly brash, the more worldly, the more publicly complicated, the man who liked a glamorous dame on his arm, a good suntan and a stylish Armani suit. Dalglish was the man who liked to remain off stage, the actor manager; Souness a man who liked to be centre stage, the star attraction.

They were much the same as players. Dalglish

beavered furiously and methodically with touches of genius and a toughness belying his fine array of skills. Souness strutted about the park like a peacock, pecking at his opponents here and there. At times he almost overstepped the bounds of legality. He bruised more than a few shins, broke the occasional bone and always caused headaches wherever he strutted. One journalist dubbed him 'Renoir with a razor blade'. It was an apt description. Opposition terraces loathed him, opponents feared him but how they envied him; they would all have loved a Souness in their side.

Here was the combination of artist and general. When Souness was on the field there was no mistaking who was in charge. He controlled the play, the pace, the passing. In his time, no other player dictated the pattern of the game as he could. From the edge of one penalty area to the fringes of the other Souness was the boss, pushing his troops forward, pulling them back occasionally, but never hauling up a white flag. He would rather die. It was his territory and nobody was allowed to dispute that. If they did, then it was at their peril. The word was 'don't get on the wrong side of Souness'. It was much the same whether he was a player, manager or simply Joe Public. He was a winner. That was the way everyone described him and that was the way he wanted to be known.

Archie Gemmill once labelled him 'a chocolate soldier', then waspishly added that 'if Souness was made of chocolate he'd eat himself'. It summed up his arrogance perfectly. Even Souness admits that there was more than an element of truth in the description. 'Archie was 90 per cent right,' he says. 'Maybe I was a bit vain and thought the world revolved around me, but it was my way of motivating myself.' As ever, Souness could rationalise his behaviour.

In another age he might have been a screen idol, a swashbuckling hero, clashing foils on some stone spiral staircase, before diving headlong into the castle moat and sweeping a glamorous maiden off to his hideaway. A Clark Gable, an Errol Flynn, a matinee star of the two and sixpences. But in the nineties Souness found his screen part in the boardrooms of soccer's fiefdoms. He slotted into the majestic mahogany background of Ibrox as if he had always been destined for the role. And the slumbering giant of a club was suddenly and dramatically awakened. In 1986 Souness and Rangers were meant for each other. In 1991 it seemed also that Souness and Liverpool might have been made for each other. But it was not to turn out that way.

At Ibrox he signed the club's first batch of Englishmen, spending like there was no tomorrow; then he recruited Rangers' first black player. As if that wasn't enough he then challenged a hundred years of sectarianism by escorting the first ever Catholic through the doors. Jaws dropped, eyebrows were raised, Scotland was agog. But Souness never flinched. 'I don't give a monkey's,' he insisted. 'Are they good enough? That's all that matters.' It was fighting talk. It didn't endear him to the King Billy traditionalists of the terraces. But there was no doubting that it was not before time. Souness was perhaps the only man with the ambition and courage to have done it. It was a social revolution that had every tongue in Scotland chattering, from the factory floors to the university seminar rooms. Even today, years later, and long after Souness deserted them, they will readily admit that Souness changed the face of Scottish football, ending the years of insularity.

But the revolution that Souness engineered at Ibrox could not be repeated at Anfield. It never needed it. Where drastic measures were desperately called for in Scotland, only the merest of tinkering was necessary in England. Souness failed to comprehend that and with it his costly soccer revolution collapsed. It was reformism

5

that was needed at Anfield, not revolution. If you want a revolution by all means call for Graeme Souness, but if you want something else, Souness isn't your man.

He is a man increasingly more at home in soccer's boardrooms than dressing rooms. He is an achiever, a man with a wider perspective than most managers, a man who knows how to manage money, a man with a vision of what football should be about. Souness would never be content simply with training, selection and transfers. His horizons have been stretched by Italy and a lucrative spell on the board at Ibrox where his influence was able to extend well beyond the football field. He is comfortable with wealthy industrialists like David Murray where profits, style and ambition are paramount. He is the first of a new breed of super manager, involved from the boardroom to the dressing room. Rich as well. His wife claims he told her he is worth £8 million. But if all that makes him sound flamboyant and unapproachable, it would be conveying a wrong impression. There is much more to him. Above all, he is also a charmer. He can be hospitable, welcoming half-strangers into his company, lavishing his friendship upon them. His cold stare soon gives way to a warm smile. Journalists, players, managers, even referees, will all testify to his generosity.

The former Celtic and Scotland manager Jock Stein once watched him walk into a hotel bar where the Scotland team had assembled. Suddenly there was a buzz about the place. Stein turned to a colleague. 'Class, the man's got class,' he observed. 'There's no substitute for that. He's got it on and off the park. You won't push that man around.' Scottish soccer writer Archie MacPherson reckons 'he was indisputably the most significant figure I have met in football since Stein'.

Brian Hall, the former Liverpool midfielder and now Community Officer with the club is fond of reminding people how generous Souness could be to those less fortunate, particularly children. He tells a particularly revealing tale.

> We once had a letter from a woman whose child had cystic fibrosis and was very ill. The little boy was a fanatical Liverpool supporter but had never been to the club. We decided to help out. We hired a helicopter and brought the lad up to Melwood, our training ground. Graeme organised it all. The helicopter landed at Melwood one morning, on the pitch, and in the middle of training. Now that might not sound very much but at Liverpool it is sacrilege even to think of putting a helicopter on the training pitch or to even interrupt training. But Graeme did it. And as the lad came off the helicopter Souness had organised a guard of honour for him, all the players were lined up to applaud him off. The youngster spent the day with the team, visiting Anfield as well, with Souness even returning to Anfield to have a further chat with the boy. A month later the young lad died. It was just one of many examples when Souness would put himself out to help people.

It was a different picture from the confrontational, hard-tackling demon that was often painted in the papers.

Souness may be a paradox but he is undeniably a winner, ever the optimist. Few could rival his competitive edge, his burning desire to win. It was an instinct that drove him to success on the football field and a glittering array of honours. It also brought him success in football management as Rangers captured three Scottish championships. But it also heralded its disasters. His marriage failed, he was forced to endure major heart surgery and his reign at Anfield ended in disappointment and humiliation. His ex-wife Danielle says it was always football first with him. 'It was his temperament which was to blame because he would never accept defeat.' There was something of a man occasionally walking a thin tightrope between madness and sanity in him. Others simply claim that he paid the price for his own arrogance and commitment.

The swashbuckling hero of our film is a man of many parts but he is essentially a man of change: fearless, visionary, strident, committed. He knows what he wants. He arrived at Rangers and at Liverpool preaching revolution. In Scotland never was change more essential. At Anfield it was to be a different story. And when he left it was to face a dark void. Since he was a teenager Souness had always known where he was going. From Spurs to Middlesbrough, to Anfield, to Sampdoria, to Glasgow and then back to Liverpool. His destiny had been mapped out. But suddenly as he walked out of Anfield he was no longer a man in demand.

CHAPTER TWO
One Step Backwards, Two Steps Forward

Edinburgh is a grand city, not just the grandest in Scotland but as princely and bourgeois as any in England. Like Bath, York or Oxford, it is steeped in its own history and culture. It has witnessed the crowning of monarchs, court plots, assassinations and even the odd street battle. It has also been the scene of artistic triumphs, a world-famous tattoo and a festival that has no rival throughout Europe. This is the Edinburgh most of us know — majestic, engaging, cultured.

But, like any stylish, royal city, Edinburgh has its grimmer aspect. Tucked away from public view, far from the elegance of Princes Street which Defoe called the 'largest, longest and finest street for buildings . . . in the world' or the well-trodden cobbled backways around the castle; far from the arrogance and pomp of Holyrood and its court, there is another Edinburgh, an Edinburgh nobody wants to acknowledge or boast about to visitors. On the council estates of Niddrie, Pilton, Muirhouse and Broomhouse you could be a million miles from the wealth and splendour of the Princes Street shops. In places Edinburgh is a city that has more in common with Glasgow and the

Gorbals than one would ever have dreamt. In these areas, housing problems, poverty, drugs and crime are rampant. There are no jobs, no prospects, not much to look forward to if you are young. You are sucked into its abyss, with little hope of escape. Thirty years ago breaking free was difficult enough but at least someone with determination and a smattering of talent might have been able to make the break. But it's different today. Had Graeme Souness been born into the 1980s generation, even he might not have been able to shake himself free of its grip. As it was, Graeme Souness was born in a different era.

It was May 1953, just a couple of days after Stanley Matthews had finally picked up that longed-for winners' medal at Wembley. They were auspicious sporting days. Sir Gordon Richards was about to bring home a popular Royal Derby winner, Edmund Hillary and Sherpa Tenzing were set to make their final assault on the summit of Everest and the shy young Elizabeth was about to be crowned Queen. Later that summer the Aussies would be hung, drawn and quartered by Hutton, Bailey and May. Though not so far away in the November mists lay an embarrassing lament for English football at the hands of the Mighty Magyars.

None of this probably mattered much to the folk of Edinburgh who had plenty of problems and ambitions of their own. They were no doubt more swept up by Hibernian's assault on the Scottish League title which they had just lost on goal average to Rangers. Coronation fever belonged elsewhere. Even then, loyalty to the English crown was not unquestioning. But it was not enough to stop Scottish football promoting a Coronation Cup, the pride of Scotland against the best of England. Celtic, Rangers, Aberdeen and Hibernian represented the north, with Manchester United, Arsenal, Newcastle and Tottenham fighting the Royalist cause. The English were expected to win comfortably but to the astonishment of many, including one suspects the Scots as well, it turned out to be rather different. It was as unpredictable as Scottish football can ever be. In the end, Scotland triumphed with Celtic beating Hibs in an all-Scottish final played at Hampden in front of a 117,000 crowd. The English, humiliated and embarrassed, had fled the lowlands long before Celtic and Hibs walked out at Hampden.

The Edinburgh of the fifties was an even more elegant city than that of today. Austere, perhaps, but without the drugs and violence that are now so generic. Formal, undoubtedly, but without the neglect that the nineties have wrought. There were few high-rise blocks casting their grim, destructive shadows over the thoroughfares. There was even a hint of majesty and pride that is all but gone today. There was certainly poverty, though perhaps not so apparent as it is now. What poverty there was lay well hidden from public gaze. People put on their best for public viewing, instilled in their children a fear of the law, and regarded education as a passport to a career. But most of all there were jobs and that was, and remains, the crucial shaping difference between the two eras.

The Souness family were not part of the grand Edinburgh of the fifties. On the contrary, they were poor, hard working, living in one of those prefabs thrown up after the war as temporary emergency accommodation but which you can still spot in many parts of the country even to this day. His father Jimmy was a glazier, his mother Elizabeth managed the home, though she did occasionally have a job. Football was in the family. His brother Gordon played with Hearts for a couple of seasons.

Souness' education was formal, just what you would have expected at a Scottish school of the late fifties and early sixties. Sport was an important part of the curriculum

11

and the young Souness was soon showing the kind of ability that another past pupil at Carrickvale had shown. Dave Mackay, the infamous Spurs defender, had attended the same school ten years earlier leaving as indelible a mark on the teaching staff as he did on many a forward's ankles. Mackay was to become a role model, the first outside influence in Souness' life. Even then his teachers were likening his style to the aggressive tackling that the Hearts and Tottenham man had shown during his school days. Years later the two would team up at White Hart Lane where the lessons would be spelt out in more detail.

Football was a way of life at the school in much the same way as it was at most other Scottish state schools, particularly those in Edinburgh and Glasgow. Souness was soon showing potential, playing for Tynecastle Boys Club, Edinburgh Secondary Schools, then finally for Scotland Schools. He trained with his local club Hearts and even had a spell working out with Celtic on a regular basis but neither clubs took out an option on him, something they would both regret in the years ahead.

Playing for Scotland Schools provided a platform for all young footballing talent north of the border, and the annual tussle with England was the kind of occasion that draws scouts from all over the land. A few years earlier a skinny young lad from Glasgow called Kenny Dalglish had been displaying his precocious talents for the schoolboys and now it was the turn of Graeme Souness who was chosen to represent Scotland in the fixture played at White Hart Lane in March 1968. Watching from the stands that day was none other than Dave Mackay, the Tottenham captain, who saw in the youngster something that must have reminded him of himself. Mackay recommended Souness to the Tottenham manager Bill Nicholson.

But it wasn't always so easy. Even in those days Souness showed the occasional flash of arrogance that was to dog so much of his early career. After playing for Scotland Schools at White Hart Lane, they went on to play Wales in Cardiff. This was to be followed by a fixture against Northern Ireland and a further game against England. But Souness never got to play in the final two games. By then he had deserted his Scottish schoolmates, walking out on them when he was asked to wear a number ten shirt in training. Souness retorted that he always wore number four for the Scotland team and consequently would only wear a number four in training as well. It seemed illogical and irrelevant, though to a proud fifteen-year-old it was interpreted as a threat to his position. The schoolmaster in charge told him not to argue about it but to put on the bib for training and get on with it. Souness refused and was then told to either put it on or get dressed and go home. Astonishingly, he got dressed and went home. Ironically, some years later Ally McCoist would do the same when confronted by the school-masterly Souness.

That any professional club should have pursued an interest in him after that is perhaps surprising but they did and in their dozens; his talent must have been undeniable. Even West Bromwich Albion gave him a trial while Nottingham Forest, Wolves and Burnley led the pack from England. In Scotland, Glasgow Rangers were said to be interested. Hibernian, the club that he was training with, also had a word. Earlier favourites, Celtic and Hearts, were keen but it was Spurs who eventually snapped up his talents, tempting him south with the promise of style and ambition. No doubt the thought of Dave Mackay played a part as well. Even then Souness had horizons beyond the Tweed. He was sixteen and more than ready to leave the sobriety of Edinburgh for the bright lights of London. It was May 1969.

Tottenham Hotspur have always been one of England's finest, a club steeped in its dedication to attractive

13

football, a name synonymous with talent and a commitment to the passing game. They may have had their share of tough traditionalists like Mackay and Maurice Norman but they had also boasted a plethora of artists; giants such as Danny Blanchflower, Cliff Jones, Jimmy Greaves, John White, Alan Gilzean and Alan Mullery. These were the men that any young lad looked up to and although some of them had by 1969 moved on, their influence was still close enough to touch. Their ghosts would haunt and inspire Tottenham forever. Think of Spurs and you think of Blanchflower and Mackay. It was hardly surprising that they should leap at the chance to sign the young Souness.

The glory days of the Double might also have been a decade past but even in the early seventies Spurs had a side to match most in the Football League. Goalkeeper Pat Jennings was at the height of his career, defenders Joe Kinnear, Cyril Knowles and Welsh captain Mike England were a match for any attack. Elsewhere there was World Cup-winner Martin Peters, England striker Martin Chivers, another England man Ralph Coates, and youngsters Jimmy Neighbour and Steve Perryman, while Alan Mullery was nearing the end of his Spurs days. The names still trip off the tongue. White Hart Lane was an impressive place to learn your trade.

Tottenham manager Bill Nicholson had few doubts about his new signing. 'Souness is very skilful but, of course, is young and has a lot to learn. Still, there is every possibility he will come through to senior football in the near future,' he told anyone willing to listen. Nicholson was trying to be encouraging as well as polite. In hindsight he perhaps ought to have tempered his enthusiasm; instead he was stoking the fires of ambition and impatience. A year later, and having had chance to digest Souness' ability, he was going even further. 'I really think this boy will be another Mackay. For his age he has

14

wonderful control,' he told the papers. It all went to Souness' head.

You could hardly blame him, or any youngster, for that matter. Most seventeen- or eighteen-year-olds are vulnerable to praise and over-enthusiasm. It doesn't take much to imagine the young Souness – impatient as he was, ambitious and full of self-confidence – relishing the accolades, suddenly sprouting six inches, his self-esteem boosted yet again. Not only that, but his team-mates began to look up to him. The boss had called him a future star. Little wonder Souness was soon acting like one. Some team-mates despised him, calling him arrogant. Others saw him as a role model. Even first teamer Martin Chivers invited him to his home and took him under his wing. In the close harmony of the apprentices' dressing room Souness soon became king among the would-be knights.

The apprentices spent all their time together. It was a gang, much like any other, but with a few differences; most of this gang shared digs together, were fit and healthy, had a bit too much cash burning a hole in their pockets, were envied by those of their own age and admired by most girls. What's more they had plenty of time on their hands for fun. It was little wonder they got up to trouble. But then wouldn't any gang of lads in those circumstances?

Not that there was that much trouble. It was really just a matter of attitude. And Souness had too much of that. The worst had been his sending off in the 1970 replayed final of the FA Youth Cup after a tussle with Coventry's Dennis Mortimer. Souness had already pushed his luck in the earlier game with Coventry and there is little doubt that there was a running feud between the two youngsters. Perhaps Souness' biggest sin was to commit his offence right in front of the directors' box where the club's directors were given an especially fine view. In their report the Football Association described his behaviour as 'persistent infringement'. Spurs went on to win the trophy, but they did not like embarrassments like that at White Hart Lane. Nicholson and coach Eddie Baily always emphasised that style and courtesy were just as important as victory, especially to the apprentices. Souness was reprimanded and a winners' medal never appeared.

By 1970 Souness was old enough to sign professional forms and was on the verge of the first team, or at least he reckoned he was. There were arguments, chiefly with Baily, a White Hart Lane institution and a member of the famous push-and-run post-war Tottenham side. An abrasive man, Baily was not inclined to take too much of Souness' youthful audacity. Instead he believed in that modern footballing idiom, workrate. Souness didn't; he seemed to think that you either had it or you didn't and, as far as he was concerned, he had it. And wasn't it time Tottenham recognised this and gave him his opportunity in the first team? But the opportunity did not come. 'He was impatient, arrogant and tended to be flash; he wanted success and he wanted it yesterday,' is how Pat Welton, the youth team coach at White Hart Lane, remembers him. The craving for immediate success would haunt him for much of his life.

Frustrated, perhaps even a little homesick and fed up with the heavy cockney accents of north London, Souness packed his bags and fled back to Edinburgh. It was an unusually honest thing for one so self-confident to do. But he was soon back, in fact almost before his absence had been noted. The club ticked him off, accepting that this was par for the course with youngsters living so far away from home. It was quietly forgotten, at least until it happened again. This time it was different.

Souness had been home during the 1970 close season and had struck up a romance with a young girl, a pretty

16

dark-haired civil servant, Julie Ingram. It was his first serious romance. Returning to London later that summer Souness was now more unsettled than ever, but on top of that he was pining as well. And there is nothing worse, no one more headstrong, than a pining, lonely teenager. Edinburgh, Julie and first team football seemed a million miles away. There was only one option. Souness had to get away from White Hart Lane. He went to see manager Bill Nicholson, not of course telling him about Julie, merely insisting that he wanted first team football and wanted to leave. Nicholson, not always the most sympathetic of men to such impatient demands, especially from eighteen-year-olds, told him to forget it and concentrate on his training. The mighty roar of Nicholson might have terrified most youngsters but it never worked with Souness. It only made him all the more determined. He packed his bags and went, catching the next train to Waverley. But whereas the previous escape north had been quietly resolved, this time Souness was to find himself the focus of Parliamentary questions. The club pleaded with him to come back to London but Souness was adamant. He was staying put.

Within days the press had seized on the story and any hope of a peaceful resolution quickly disappeared. Souness was under contract and Spurs did not take kindly to the breaking of a contract. They slapped a two-week ban on him and promised to renew it every fortnight until his contract expired two years later. Again it was hardly the kind of attitude to adopt with Souness. The issue soon came to the attention of Tam Dalyell, the maverick Labour Member for West Lothian. Dalyell wrote to the Secretary of State for Employment, Robert Carr, seeking clarification on employment contracts and the rights of employers. He even raised the issue on the floor of the House of Commons asking a Parliamentary question. But the reply offered few options, if any. The laws

17

governing employment were firmly balanced in favour of employers. The affair dragged on. Souness consulted the Professional Footballers' Association but was advised to go back to Spurs. And his parents, understanding at first, now began to lean towards resolving the row.

On 16 September Spurs were due in Scotland to play a first round Texaco Cup tie against Dunfermline Athletic. It seemed the ideal opportunity for all parties to meet up. By then Souness' determination was on the wane. He had even taken a job but had soon realised that football was far more preferable to manual labour. Spurs had not backed off. Many another club would have immediately placed him on the transfer list and been glad to be rid of him. But not Tottenham. There may have been a principle involved but they still wanted to hang on to their man. Unfortunately, Souness failed to read the significance of this. He returned, reluctant, his respect for Tottenham gone for ever, his spirit elsewhere.

He laboured for a few seasons more, making little headway. His only breakthrough came in the UEFA Cup a year later in 1971/72 when he was named as substitute for the first round tie in Iceland against Keflavik. Souness came on as a replacement for Alan Mullery, but even though Spurs had beaten the Icelandic amateurs 6–1 he never played again for Tottenham. After Iceland it was back to life in the reserves and the Football Combination.

Whether Souness would ever have made the final break into regular first team football at Tottenham will always be open to debate. There is every reason to think that he would have done but the early promise had by now given way to anonymity, his confidence battered and bruised. Souness needed an opportunity, but with so many other talented youngsters knocking on the door, there was a long queue of impatient apprentices. Spurs prided themselves on their home-grown products. Although they were always ready to drive the transfer market upwards paying out huge fees, as they did for Martin Peters, Ralph Coates and Martin Chivers, the emerging youngsters were just as important. Spurs had won the FA Youth Cup in 1970 and many from that side had by 1971 been promoted to the reserves. There they joined a plethora of talented home-grown players all ready to line up outside the first team door, keen, impatient and demanding. They included lads like Jimmy Neighbour, John Pratt, Steve Perryman, Jimmy Pearce, Terry Naylor, Barry Daines, Tony Want, Nigel Clarke and Phil Holder. Souness was just one of many. Some had already tasted the good life and many of those in the wings would eventually get their chance but it did require patience. Others, like Souness, would never get a real opportunity, and for them patience would be in short supply. Those at Tottenham at the time remain convinced that Souness would eventually have had his chance, but he would not wait. When Souness arrived at White Hart Lane he had joined a Tottenham side still at its height. But over the next six years it would slip into steady decline, eventually ending in relegation in 1977. Manager Bill Nicholson had achieved all that he could and would make way for Terry Neill shortly after Souness had left.

Souness would no doubt have made a fine figurehead in the Spurs midfield, sculptured in the traditions of Mackay and Gilzean. He may even have kept them in the first division. Who knows? But it was not to be. Just when it was least expected, the call came from elsewhere. He was in Scotland at the time, back home for the Christmas break when he received a message that Tottenham wanted to talk to him immediately. Typically, Souness thought it might be a call for first team football. It wasn't. It was to tell him that Middlesbrough had made an offer for him; Spurs were ready to accept and it was up to him. The Londoners didn't want him anymore. But it didn't bother Souness too much. He was to go to Middlesbrough immediately to talk to them. Within twenty-four hours Souness was a Middlesbrough player. It was January 1973.

When Graeme Souness enlisted with Middlesbrough, the only thing he knew about the city and the club was that it was closer to Edinburgh than London. That had to be good. It may have seemed like a step backwards to be joining a second division club but there are times in life when one has to take a step backwards in order to move two steps forward. At least they seemed to want him at Ayresome Park. Manager Stan Anderson talked enthusiastically about the club, as did his assistant Harold Shepherdson. What's more, Middlesbrough were not willing to pay £32,000 for Souness to sit in the reserves. They wanted him in the first team. Now, not next year. It did not take much to convince Souness that a move was in his best interests though, ironically, within weeks of him signing, Stan Anderson would quit. Souness was his last signing and probably the best he made in his entire managerial career.

Although Middlesbrough nestles on the edge of the North Yorkshire moors, it hardly ranks as a county town. It's an industrial centre; shipbuilding, steel, heavy engineering, full of working men's clubs and bingo halls. Or at least it was until the Thatcher revolution tore the heart out of its industries and gave it one of the highest rates of unemployment in the country. The football club hardly ranks among the elite of British soccer either. Yet over the years it has spawned its fair share of talent. The club may have won little other than the second division championship but it can list among its favourite sons names such as Wilf Mannion, Brian Clough, Steve Bloomer and George Camsell. When Graeme Souness arrived in January 1973 Middlesbrough were trapped in division two, hanging on to the place they had earned since coming out of the third division in 1967. They had acquitted themselves fairly well but had never been able to make that final burst into the promotion places. Manager Stan Anderson had tried all that he could, finally deciding shortly after signing Souness that there was no more he could do. He quit, much against the wishes of the board, leaving Harold Shepherdson in charge until a successor could be found.

Graeme Souness made his league debut on a cold winter's day back in London, at Fulham, coming on as a substitute in Middlesbrough's 1–2 defeat. It may not have been the best of starts but Stan Anderson had laid the foundations for a team that would soon battle its way into the higher division. After his abrupt departure, the managerial chair stood empty for some months as the directors carefully considered the candidates. There was no immediate hurry; Middlesbrough were out of the FA Cup and out of league contention. It was not until the end of the season that they fixed their sights on someone, a young man just ending his playing career.

Jackie Charlton was a legend. A tall, unmistakeable gangly figure whose presence in the Leeds United and England defences had made him one of the most respected defenders in world football. Charlton had just ended his playing days with Leeds. He had made no secret of his interest in football management and Middlesbrough were quick off the block to offer him his first opportunity. As the soccer season drew to a close, Charlton waved goodbye to Leeds and years of success and motored the short journey up the A1 to Middlesbrough. It was to be the start of a new career that would take the football missionary to all four corners of the world. But first of all, he would take undistinguished Middlesbrough to the top of the second division and promotion.

The side that Charlton inherited was largely the one that he would take into the first division. He made one simple adjustment, selling the former England international Nobby Stiles to Preston while signing the ageing Celtic and Scotland star Bobby Murdoch on a free transfer. The burly Murdoch was to bring a wealth of experience and calmness to the Middlesbrough midfield which coupled neatly with the driving ambition and enthusiasm of Souness. Charlton understood Souness. 'If you want to be successful with the girls,' he told him, 'the best thing is to be successful on the football field.' Souness knew what he was saying and worked doubly hard at his task.

By the end of his first season in charge, a season that had not looked too promising in late September after only three wins in their opening seven fixtures, Charlton had turned Boro into the runaway champions of the second division. They had notched up the highest number of league points in their history, their longest unbeaten league record, their best defensive record and the biggest ever points margin in the division. Every player except the goalkeeper had been on the scoresheet. Souness, with 35 appearances, had struck seven goals, even slamming in a hat trick in the penultimate game of the season as they thrashed Sheffield Wednesday 8–0 at Ayresome Park. By any accounting method Charlton had been a phenomenal success.

Souness had also come to the attention of the Scottish selectors, picking up an Under-23 cap with an appearance against England in March 1974 to add to his schoolboy and youth caps. Six months later he would pick up his first senior honour when he pulled on a Scottish shirt to face East Germany at Hampden. It was to be the first of more than fifty appearances for his country.

And so Souness kicked off the 1974/75 season as a first division player. It might have been Middlesbrough's first season back in the higher division for just over twenty years, but Charlton's blend of commitment and efficiency worked yet again as Boro ended the season in seventh place, an impressive performance for a newly promoted side. Like all Jack Charlton's sides, Middlesbrough were a difficult team to beat. In the midfield Graeme Souness and David Armstrong had moulded as solid a link between attack and defence as anyone in the entire league, while behind them Willie Maddren and Stuart Boam gave them the confidence to move forward. Upfront John Hickton was the target man, effective rather than spectacular, with Alan Foggon sharing the goals. Late in the season Terry Cooper, Charlton's old team-mate at Elland Road also signed up to bring even more experience to the first division's newest side. Souness struck seven goals in his thirty-eight league appearances and hit the same number the following season although Middlesbrough's season was not as rewarding as their first in the upper division. They finished in thirteenth place but enjoyed a useful run in the League Cup, reaching the semi-finals before losing to Manchester City. A year later they had managed one spot better and had reached the quarter-finals of the FA Cup only to be beaten by Liverpool at Anfield.

Souness had become the playboy of the Eastern coast. Craig Johnston remembers him as something of 'an institution' at Middlesbrough. 'Always immaculately dressed, he drove around town in a silver Mercedes sports and squired women who could have stepped out of the pages of *Vogue*.' But for one reason or another, Souness' international career had taken a surprising nosedive. After his initial three appearances in 1974, which seemed to herald further honours, he was surprisingly ignored for the next couple of years and by then he would be a Liverpool player. There seemed no apparent reason. He had acquitted himself well, had even behaved himself, but when the squads were listed, there was no place for Souness, G. It hurt. But at that time it was often the case that the Anglo Scots would be ignored in favour of the

Scottish League players. To this day Souness insists he should have had at least a dozen more caps.

By the autumn of 1977, Souness' days at Middlesbrough were drawing to a close. It was no secret that European champions Liverpool had been tracking him for months, holding a magnifying glass to his every performance. His old pal Phil Boersma had heard through the Anfield grapevine and had tipped Souness the wink. Other things at Ayresome Park were also conspiring to end his days with Middlesbrough. Jack Charlton, after months of speculation, had finally quit at the end of April 1977. He'd always promised that he would stay for only four years. The new man taking over was John Neal, the former Wrexham boss. Souness and Neal did not always see eye to eye. The new manager, thoughtful and engaging in his own way, had none of the carefree, slap-happy style of Charlton. You knew where you stood with Big Jack. Step out of line and he would crash down on you. Big Jack had done it all – World Cup winners' medal, league championship medal, European Cup final and countless other honours. You could hardly argue with his pedigree. What's more, he had even proved himself as a manager.

Neal was more considerate, a total contrast to Charlton. He was the kind of manager who would gently cajole his players, encourage them, listen to them, try to see their point of view. He had none of the pedigree of Charlton. Most of his days had been played in the lower divisions or even in non-league football. Never capped, he had never experienced the world's great soccer stages or known the tensions of first division football. Neal was the kind of manager more equipped to be managing a second division outfit on a shoe string. He was out of his depth with a man like Souness. He was undoubtedly good for some players but not for Souness. What Souness needed was a kick up the backside. Charlton had given

him that and it had worked. Under John Neal Souness'
form became inconsistent, the style of a man whose mind
is straying. Souness hankered for the bright lights, the
glamour, the bigger stage. Middlesbrough was a minor
repertory company, what Souness wanted was the
National Theatre. Middlesbrough might have provided
first division football, and under Charlton there had been
plenty of excitement but there was never any real
ambition inside Ayresome Park. Even Charlton would
have acknowledged that Middlesbrough was a club that
was never going to go very far. They had reached their
zenith and Souness had higher ambitions. His international career, after its promising start, had also petered
out. Scottish managers don't come to Ayresome Park.
Souness knew that if he wanted more caps he needed to
be with a top-class side. There was only one solution.
He slammed in three transfer requests, but they were
all rejected.

Neal's reaction was predictable. 'Souness has been
doing more talking than training,' he sniped as he
promptly dropped his rebel midfielder. But he could
barely do without Souness' influence. The Scot was soon
back; a turning point was approaching. On New Year's
Eve 1977 Middlesbrough played Norwich. Sitting in the
stands were two visitors, one a friend of Souness, the
other, Tom Saunders, the Liverpool scout, development
officer, an ex-headmaster. Souness heard of their presence
and decided to put on a special performance for them
though it was to end in total disaster. Nothing went right,
the Middlesbrough crowd who had never really taken to
his awkwardness ('Too big for his boots,' they would say)
heckled his every move. Finally as the two teams trooped
off the pitch following a 2–2 draw he tore off his shirt
and hurled it at the crowd. It was not a sensible thing to
do, yet with that gesture he sealed his fate and Souness
had played his last game for Middlesbrough. He

suspected that Liverpool would lose interest but they didn't. Rather it was Middlesbrough who lost interest, John Neal finally deciding that they would be better off without his whining, pushy ways that were clearly upsetting others. Souness could go.

Leeds were also rumoured to be interested, and when Souness was summoned to a hotel in the Leeds city centre to discuss a possible move, he travelled across Yorkshire more than half-convinced that he was about to become a Leeds United player. No doubt Elland Road would have been a stage that would have suited his talents well but there is also little doubt that he would never have matured there into the player he was to become. But when he arrived at Leeds it was not a contingent from Elland Road awaiting him in the lounge but Bob Paisley, the Liverpool manager. Souness had his wish. The deal was done, almost without consideration of salary and financial terms. Souness was on his way to Anfield, leaving Middlesbrough £352,000 the richer, the biggest cheque they had ever received.

CHAPTER THREE
The Chocolate Soldier

Graeme Souness joined Liverpool in January 1978. He was seen as a replacement for Ian Callaghan, who after a record-breaking 800-plus appearances in a Liverpool shirt spanning twenty years, was set to bow out of the game. Yet they were not similar players; Callaghan was more of an orthodox winger, sprightly, inventive, a good runner, boundless in his enthusiasm. Souness was a ball winner, strong, aggressive, a driving force in the midfield who could defend just as readily as he could attack. Souness would give a new dimension to Liverpool.

He had joined an impressive club. The season before, they had captured the European Cup for the first time in their history as well as the League championship and had come within a whisker of lifting the FA Cup, going down undeservedly to Manchester United in the final. But now Kevin Keegan had gone, off to Hamburg for £500,000; John Toshack was reaping the legacy of years of injuries; Ian Callaghan had reached the end of his career; Joey Jones, the popular Welsh defender, was also pushed aside; and, although Tommy Smith was soldiering on valiantly, his days were clearly numbered. Paisley was instituting a major reorganisation of his squad, rebuilding his team with younger players and a dash more flair.

It was a brave move on Paisley's part. Most managers would have been tempted to live with those men who had just carried Europe's greatest prize back to Merseyside. But not Paisley. He recognised that many of those who had brought glory to Liverpool in the seventies were getting on a bit. It had really been Shankly's team, but now Paisley was about to impress his own style and his own methods on Anfield. The Liverpool side that had won so much was about to be torn apart. Into the line-up at the beginning of the season had stepped Kenny Dalglish, a British record signing at £440,000, a straight replacement for Keegan. Alan Hansen, a tall, slightly stiff-limbed young lad from Partick Thistle and now Graeme Souness had also been recruited. Three Scots who over the next six years would form the backbone of a Liverpool side that would go on to ever dizzier heights of glory.

From the start, Souness was drafted into the side, making his debut at West Bromwich Albion as Liverpool notched up their fourth consecutive victory. Souness was an immediate success. But the success was as much off the field as on it. He was about to grow up. He was no longer a talented player among lesser mortals, frustrated by his environment. Now he was just one of a dozen or more outstanding players. And nor was he with a club that lacked ambition or pedigree. Liverpool were the foremost club in the Football League, the most feared side in European football. This was not a club that tolerated whingeing and complaining. Souness' rebel days would have to end. He had to prove himself now. There was no automatic place; one poor game and there was always somebody on the sidelines just as good as you, and more than eager to pull on your shirt. To survive you had to apply yourself.

Tommy Smith remembers having to teach Souness a simple Anfield lesson from the start.

The first day in the dressing room, he asked if he could borrow my hairdryer. 'Yes,' I said and gave it to him. The second day after training he asks the same. 'No problem,' I said and lent it to him. Then the third day, he comes to me again. 'Can I borrow your hairdryer, Tommy?' 'No, you bloody can't,' I said. 'You get paid enough money, go out and buy your own like everybody else here.'

Souness wasn't quite a convert from the start. His hotel drinks bill during his first two weeks at Anfield had topped £200. Peter Robinson sent for him. It had all been marked down as lemonade and orange juice. 'You'll go "pop" if you drink that much lemonade,' pointed out a wise old Robinson. 'In future you pay for your own lemonade!' In his first few months at Liverpool he was, by his own admission, burning the candle at both ends. He was drinking, clubbing, and generally enjoying life but eventually he began to realise that his priorities had to be Liverpool Football Club and his own career.

With a side showing so many changes it was hardly surprising that Liverpool's form spluttered in the league. Liverpool were never really in contention. Nottingham Forest were runaway leaders and although the gap was narrowed as Liverpool set about their traditional end-of-season spurt, Forest had left just enough in reserve to cruise home. Liverpool ended their campaign with nine wins and three draws from the final dozen games, a sign at least that Paisley's new format was beginning to take shape. Defeat in the league, however, was to have its compensations as Liverpool embarked on retaining their European trophy and bringing Souness his first major honour. Having been signed after the European qualification date, Souness was ineligible for Liverpool's quarter-final clash with the Portuguese champions Benfica. But it made little difference; Liverpool were still

formidable enough to slip comfortably through both legs
for a place in the last four. They found something for
Souness to do on those evenings. They put him in charge
of the team kit. Just as important as any other job at
Anfield, they told him.

The semi-finals, however, were not quite so comfortable. Souness eventually made his appearance coming on
as a substitute for Steve Heighway. In the end it made
little difference; Liverpool lost 1–2 to Borussia Moenchengladbach, the side they had beaten in the previous year's
final. The omens did not look promising but in the second
leg at Anfield in front of 51,500, Liverpool crushed the
Germans once more, by 3–0. This time, Souness did a
little more than look after the kit, masterminding Liverpool's triumph and playing as impressive a role as
anyone.

Their opponents in the final were Bruges, the Belgian
champions, managed by that astutest of European
coaches, Ernst Happel. Nobody had much doubt that Liverpool would win, especially with the match scheduled
for Liverpool's second home, Wembley. Bruges came to
defend, reluctant to trespass beyond the half-way line,
rolling the ball between their midfield and defence,
making Liverpool do all the running. The strategy was
simple, prevent Liverpool from scoring at all costs and
hope to win the penalty shoot-out. But the combination
of Souness and Dalglish was to put an end to that tactic.
It was Souness, in the sixty-fifth minute with a delicately
squeezed pass into the path of Dalglish, who set up the
goal. And Dalglish, with all the aplomb and confidence of
a master craftsman, chipped the ball beyond the helpless
Jensen in the Bruges goal. Dalglish and Souness celebrated fittingly. Shocked by Liverpool's effrontery, Bruges
finally broke free of their defensive shell to launch a wave
of attacks but they had left it too late. Thompson cleared
off the line and on more than one occasion Liverpool

threatened to break away and increase their score. But in the end it stayed at 1–0. Liverpool had become the first British side to win a second European Cup. Souness had picked up the first of many medals he would win with Liverpool but, perhaps more importantly, he and Dalglish had signalled their arrival on the world stage.

Souness' impact at Anfield inevitably led to further international honours. Just a month after signing for Liverpool he was back in the Scottish squad, pulling on the blue shirt of his country for the first time in three years as Scotland took on Bulgaria at Hampden in World Cup year.

The following season Souness began to mature into the player he had always threatened to become. The steely authority was now supplemented by delicate passing and quick thinking. Souness was the conductor orchestrating every Liverpool move, pushing the ball forward, pulling his defenders back, stretching his men on the flanks, barking out his orders. He had found his natural home in a side so packed with talent that he was at last able to express himself freely. There was never really any doubt that Liverpool would take the title. They won 10 of their first 11 games, drawing the other. They blasted seven goals past Tottenham at Anfield in what many still regard as the finest ever Liverpool performance. By the end of the season they had won 19 of their 21 home games, drawing the other two while conceding just four goals. Away from home they lost only four fixtures, conceding 12 goals. Their total of just 16 goals against set a new record for the Football League, as did their haul of 68 points. Souness missed just one league game, netting eight goals for himself.

Was this the most polished of all Liverpool sides, a team dedicated to attacking football but with a defence as mean as a fox on a wintry night? Outside of the league, however, Liverpool were not quite as commanding. In the

European Cup they were unfortunate to draw Nottingham Forest in the first round and were surprisingly beaten, though Forest went on to prove their worth by winning the trophy. Liverpool were also knocked out of the League Cup at the first hurdle, while in the FA Cup they took Manchester United to a semi-final replay before finally collapsing at Goodison Park.

'The 1978/79 season was sensational and I am tempted to say that the team was the best I have ever played in,' wrote Souness some years later. That was some praise.

The 1979/80 season campaign was almost a repeat, although Liverpool kicked off as if they were suffering a hangover from the previous season's exertions, managing only two wins in their opening seven fixtures. But by Christmas they had clambered up to their rightful spot at the top of the table and eventually lifted the title, just two points ahead of Manchester United, the only side to put pressure on them the whole season. But again there was no success in the European Cup as Liverpool crashed to yet another first round exit, this time at the hands of the highly entertaining and skilled Georgians of Dynamo Tbilisi. It was a bitter disappointment, especially as Nottingham Forest went on to retain the trophy, equalling Liverpool's earlier achievement. Liverpool came across the jinx of Nottingham Forest yet again as they reached the semi-finals of the League Cup only to go down to the side that had become their only serious rivals. In the FA Cup they also popped up in the semi-finals, but again tackled a side that had long held a spell over them, Arsenal, and after a marathon four matches eventually lost 1–0. At the end of a long, painfully exhausting season there was scant reward, other than their inevitable league title, of course.

It was perhaps little wonder that Liverpool's form in the league should slump during the 1980/81 season, particularly towards the end of the campaign, when their minds were firmly focused on the European Cup and the League Cup. Liverpool had never won the League Cup and the accepted word was that they had little interest in the competition, preferring instead to concentrate on the other more rewarding honours of the game. But with the league soon beyond their reach as the other competitions sapped their concentration there was a serious danger that they might finish up out of Europe altogether the following season. By the end of January they had been knocked out of the FA Cup, beaten by neighbours Everton. To be certain of a place in Europe they needed to capture the League Cup, or better still, the European Cup.

As it was, they would win both, with their first League Cup arriving on April Fools' Day. A couple of weeks earlier they had drawn 1–1 at Wembley with West Ham United, but in the replay at Villa Park, Liverpool edged West Ham aside to add another new trophy to their already crammed showcase. Although Souness had graced Wembley for the first game, injury ruled him out of the replay. But it would be in the European Cup that Liverpool would once more show their true mettle. In the first round, Souness even slammed in a hat trick as they ran riot among the Finnish part-timers, Oulu Palloseura, notching up ten goals in the process. The second round brought Liverpool face to face with the Scottish champions Aberdeen, who boasted that this would be a British championship decider and one the Scots would win. The Scots did win, but not the Scots of Aberdeen. It was Liverpool with their Scottish contingent of Souness, Dalglish and Hansen who emerged in triumph, winning 1–0 at Pittodrie and 4–0 at Anfield. In the last eight Liverpool drew the Bulgarian champions CSKA Sofia in what, on paper at least, looked a tricky tie. What's more, CSKA had already knocked Nottingham Forest out of the competition. Facing East European opposition was never easy as

Liverpool had found to their dismay over the years, and especially as the crucial second leg would be in Sofia. But surprisingly the tie turned out to be comparatively effortless, thanks mainly to the resolute Souness. It was Souness who got the scoring under way with a 16th-minute goal. Sammy Lee added a second on the stroke of half-time but in the second half Souness conjured up a memorable performance as Liverpool overwhelmed the Bulgarians. Surging forward from the midfield he struck another two, to make him the first player to score two hat tricks in one season in the European Cup while Terry McDermott added a fifth. Souness' performance had been majestic, perhaps his best yet for Liverpool, as he controlled and co-ordinated almost every Liverpool move. It was also a goalscoring performance that would have made any international striker proud and it was one that brought him to the attention of admiring continental coaches.

In the last four, Liverpool drew the German champions Bayern Munich, one of the most glamorous names in European soccer. The days of Franz Beckenbauer and European Cups had long since disappeared, but the Germans could still muster a side with household names such as Breitner, Hoeness, and Rummenigge. Souness skipped the first leg, still suffering from a back injury and after a goalless draw must have wondered if they would have any chance in Munich's Olympic stadium. The Germans were already making plans for the final in Paris. But on a warm spring night, with Souness deep in the heart of the midfield, Liverpool gave a gallant display, though with Dalglish limping off after just nine minutes, it seemed a different destiny awaited them. As it was, Bob Paisley tossed on unknown reserve winger Howard Gayle, whose maverick runs took the Germans totally by surprise. Gayle had not figured in their plans. They knew nothing of him, had never seen him play and certainly could not cope with his instinctive running. Liverpool even took a vital lead with seven minutes remaining and although Bayern struck an equaliser there was virtually no time left for them to find a winner. Liverpool were through to their third European Cup final. Souness called it a memorable moment. Typically, he could not resist poking his head around the Bayern dressing room door to make some wry comment about their plans for Paris. Souness, always one to make the best of the moment, showed no fear or respect for anyone.

The final between Liverpool and Real Madrid was billed as a personal duel between midfield maestros Souness and Real's Ulrich Stielike. Stielike, the iron man of European football, faced a challenge for his crown from the young pretender Souness. It was to be a battle royal. From the start, Souness was subjected to some of the most brutal punishment any Liverpool man has probably ever had to endure. The intent was to intimidate, weaken his resolve, and frighten him. The Spaniards knew that Souness' ability to control the midfield would be crucial. If he could be distracted from his task, then their own job would be that much easier. But Souness was not one to be bullied. If anyone was going to do the bullying, it would be him. From the start, Real's tackling was in the X-certificate category. Camacho, in particular, showed that Real had more than one assassin in their line-up, blasting in his tackles at every opportunity. After thirty minutes of enduring a barrage of punishment Souness had had enough. It was time to dish out some medicine of his own. Graeme Souness and Liverpool were not going to be intimidated; they could be just as brutal as Real.

The target was Camacho, but in the process of slipping Camacho with what Souness describes as 'a little nip' he was himself stalked by Stielike. There was a crunching of bones that left Souness limping. It was perhaps just desserts for him, but it was enough to calm the enthusiasm of Camacho at least. It was perhaps not what the game of football was supposed to be about, but with the European Cup at stake it seemed justifiable, especially if you were waving a Liverpool flag and more especially if the opposition were cultivating such tactics. Without Souness' intimidatory tactics Liverpool might well have folded. As it was, Souness' tackling in the midfield was crucial and with nine minutes remaining Alan Kennedy stole down the left and drilled a ball into the net from the narrowest of angles to give them a satisfying victory. It was a win that established Liverpool among the elite of European clubs who had won the trophy three times but, what's more, it established Graeme Souness as the most feared and respected midfielder in European football.

Souness was a star. In the Anfield dressing room they nicknamed him 'Champagne Charlie'. Not for him a pint of bitter after the game but a glass of chilled champagne. They said that when it came to the toss-up before a game, Souness didn't use a coin. His team-mates claimed he didn't know what a coin was. Instead, they joked that he used a gold American Express card. Souness loved the wisecracks; it was part of his style. After his first European Cup triumph he was spotted arm-in-arm with the former Miss World, Mary Stavin, and found himself splashed across the front pages, one arm around Miss World, the other arm around the European Cup. There may have been nothing in the romance stories but Souness revelled in it. He was creating an image and his team-mates looked on in envy. 'He was always Champagne Charlie to the lads in the dressing room,' says Mark Lawrenson, 'but take it from me when the chips are down and you are relying on real men to get you out of trouble the first person you should look to is Graeme.'

Eventually, he calmed down, a quiet word here and there from Paisley and, of course, meeting and then settling down with Danielle Wilson, the daughter of a wealthy Liverpool family. The Wilsons had made their money out of the airline business and a stake in the Army and Navy Stores. They met in 1978 and were married within two years. Danielle had been married before and had a daughter, Chantelle, from her first marriage. She and Souness would have two children of their own, both boys, Frazer and Jordan.

Souness even starred in Alan Bleasdale's *The Boys From The Blackstuff*, face-to-face with the maniacal Yosser Hughes. 'I could have been a footballer,' says Hughes scathingly, 'but I had a paper round.' Souness looks him in the eyes. He may have had only four lines in reply but they were spoken with enough panache to impress both Alan Bleasdale and actor Bernard Hill. It was a memorable performance. And it all added to the image of Souness the screen idol. There was something of the Yosser Hughes in Souness. He was Yosser Hughes made good.

Over the next three years, Souness would lead Liverpool to three successive league titles, the first club to achieve the distinction since a pre-war Arsenal. If Liverpool had been the most successful English club since the mid-sixties, they were to dominate the English game totally during the eighties. In 1982 they retained the League Cup, beating Tottenham Hotspur 3–1 at Wembley. The following year they added another League Cup, their third in succession, to their growing list of honours, this time beating Manchester United 2–1 in the final. Then, in the 1983/84 season, Liverpool reached a new pinnacle even by their own standards as they clocked up their third successive league title, their fourth successive League Cup and their fourth European Cup. Three trophies in one season was a distinction no club had ever achieved. Only the FA Cup evaded them. That season was also to be Souness' final one as a player at Anfield.

It had been a season of highlights, perhaps none more so than a memorable League Cup final against their greatest rivals Everton with Souness scoring the only goal of the game in the replay at Maine Road.

Souness' part in Liverpool's success story was central. He was the pivot around which the side revolved. Dalglish may have represented the flair but it was Souness who provided the drive, control and consistency. When he was absent, it showed. He limped off injured at Brighton in the fourth round of the FA Cup and Liverpool went down in the shock result of the season. There were not many defeats or draws that campaign but it seemed that the presence of Souness was always the determining factor. By then Bob Paisley had retired to be replaced by his long-time side-kick Joe Fagan. Souness had been close to Paisley, ever grateful for the influence and the advice he had passed on. But he also had a special affection for the poker-faced Fagan. Mark Lawrenson spotted it: 'He recognised that Joe was somebody special, to be treated with respect, and while that applied to the rest of us as well, Graeme was prepared to go out on the pitch and die for Joe. Bob Paisley had made him captain during his time and I think Graeme felt he had something to demonstrate to Joe when he became manager. Call it loyalty or commitment, but whatever it was, Graeme was determined to help Joe in every possible way in his first season in charge.'

Everything Liverpool and Souness touched seemed to turn to gold and with his last kick of a ball in a red shirt, the Liverpool midfielder converted a vital spot kick as Liverpool went on to win a penalty shoot-out against AS Roma in the final of the 1984 European Cup. His final task as the Liverpool captain was to lead his team up the steps of Rome's Olympic stadium to receive the European Cup. 'It was my proudest moment in football,' he insists. That fourth European Cup victory meant that only the famed Real Madrid had won more European Cups than Liverpool. It wasn't just the Football League that Liverpool had come to monopolise but the whole of Europe as well. Liverpool were the undisputed masters, the most feared side on the continent; the club and their players the envy of all Europe. And yet, given that Souness was leading this all-powerful combination, he still felt it was time to leave Anfield.

The lure of continental football, and Italy in particular, was to prove too much of a temptation to him. But at least he was honest. When he went, he admitted that the money and the financial security that it would bring for his family were paramount. Years earlier Kevin Keegan had abandoned Anfield for the spoils of German football, linking up with Hamburg and talking about the need for a fresh challenge. It had not gone down well with the Kop who saw Keegan's flight as an act of appalling betrayal. And the return of the one-time hero with his new club Hamburg in his very first season had been greeted with derision and cries of 'Judas'. But there were differences with Souness. For a start, Souness was not the one breaking new ground. He had given Liverpool more than six and a half years' service; he was already on the wrong side of 30, having just reached his 31st birthday and even the most optimistic would not have betted on his serving many more years of first team football. There were none of the accusations that had accompanied Keegan, none of the ill feeling. He simply went quietly and without fuss. You half expected it of Souness. Yet, ironically, whereas Liverpool were able to plug the gap left by Keegan without much upheaval, the gap left by Souness would stand vacant for many more years.

Souness also had the Latin temperament. He revelled in the sunshine, the villa life and the Gucci gear. He almost seemed hand-made for Italian soccer. You might equally have been able to imagine him at Barcelona or Real Madrid but you could never have imagined him settling for the smog and discipline of Hamburg. If he was going to the continent then it had to be Italy. The lifestyle, the players, the spotlight and, above all, the money appealed to him.

The idea came indirectly from Trevor Francis. A friend visiting the Francises in Genoa returned, ecstatic about the lifestyle and the wealth. Souness admits that 'the seeds were being sown'. Liverpool were hardly enthusiastic at the prospect of losing so important a man but knew that they could hardly stand in his way. Souness would make up his own mind and if he wanted to go, then they should facilitate his easy passage and negotiate the best deal they could. By the end of the summer, Souness was on his way, joining the Genoese side Sampdoria, a club that had a British tradition stretching back to the fifties when they had signed Eddie Firmani, the Charlton Athletic forward. Life was made easier by the fact that the former Birmingham and Manchester City star Trevor Francis was also a firmly established Sampdoria player. It was also made easier by the salary. Souness went into his discussions with Sampdoria knowing precisely how much he wanted – double what he was getting at Liverpool. He was determined not to settle for less. Finally they got around to talking money. 'Well, here's what we're prepared to offer you,' suggested the man from Sampdoria. The figure was twice what Souness had in mind. In his astonishment he immediately agreed. It was not until he was outside that he realised he probably could have squeezed even more out of them had he haggled a little. For once, his famed composure had let him down.

The Italians would come to adore his style. Whereas Liverpudlians had been suspicious of his arrogance, in Italy they embraced it. For them, style was the name of the game. In Liverpool they were unaccustomed to that attitude. It even showed in the kind of football Liverpool played. It was a functional game, rarely filled with excitement and spontaneity. They were not a side associated with elegance or over-endowed with breathtaking skills. Nobody hung onto the ball longer than was necessary. It was the team that counted, with loyalty and commitment the priorities. At Anfield no single individual was ever bigger than the club.

All along, the Kop had never really taken to Souness, not in the way that they idolised Dalglish or Ian Rush. Certainly they appreciated him, but love him, no. There were no tears when he went. They just wondered how they would ever replace him. In Italy it would be different. If it was style you wanted, Souness was your man. They were made for each other. On the terraces at Sampdoria they sang 'Champagne Charlie'. They would never have sung that from the Kop.

CHAPTER FOUR
The Sleeping Giant

Souness enjoyed two fruitful years under the Italian sun. His only regret was that he had not gone earlier. And nor was his stay without success. With Souness in the midfield, Sampdoria, the club with an English tradition, climbed to fourth, their highest-ever place in the Italian league. And in that same first season they also won the Italian cup, qualifying for Europe on two counts. Souness was the toast of Genoa and was even chosen to represent the pick of the league against champions Verona. Here, it seemed, was a team capable of serious challenge to the title, but his second year was to be a disappointment. Injuries hit the squad, transfer deals never worked out and some strange team selections left Sampdoria struggling on the fringes of the relegation zone for the first half of the season.

Not that this had any influence on what was to happen. Souness still had a year of his contract remaining and although he had been linked with a return to English football he was more than prepared to negotiate an extension to his Italian contract. But at 33 years of age he knew that he could not play on much longer at such a high level and there can be few, if any, levels higher than the Italian Serie A. He had already begun to think about his future and had expressed an interest in management to more than one colleague. His old pal Kenny Dalglish had by then taken over as manager at Liverpool, as Souness had always suspected he would, and Souness saw no reason why he should not finish up in football management himself. He figured that, like Dalglish, he could begin as a player-manager but the thoughts had barely taken a hold in his mind when he received a phone call from a Scottish journalist. What he was told came as a complete surprise. It seemed his name was being mentioned in Rangers circles as a possible replacement for Jock Wallace. Souness was speechless. 'Why me?' he might have yelled. He had never even thought of managing a Scottish club, let alone Rangers. He had not even lived in Scotland since his teenage days. He had imagined that his future would be far less salubrious, probably somewhere in the basement department of the Football League. But here was an offer he could barely refuse. He had even joked about getting the job in an interview on Scottish Television in September 1985, saying: 'I'd still like to be player-manager of Rangers one day!' It was not long before talks were arranged and not long before pen had been put to paper.

That most erudite of journalists, James Cameron, once claimed that nobody ever set out deliberately to be a journalist, a judge or a politician. They simply stumbled into it by chance. He might well have said the same of football management.

Youngsters ballooning a ball about the park never boast of becoming a football manager. Rather they dream that one day they will be a whippet of a winger or maybe a cat-like keeper. And even those lucky enough to be given a chance in the professional game think only of their immediate careers, not of what might happen in later life. And although a football career is one of the shortest imaginable, thoughts beyond retirement are pushed to the back of the mind. Injuries may lie around the corner ready to strike down the most famous and the most talented, destroying their playing careers but rarely is more than a second thought given to the consequences. Football is a day-to-day business where horizons rarely stretch beyond the next game.

In this high-tech world of multi-skilling, footballers are not even trained or equipped for much else other than kicking a ball about a field. There was a time, before inflated salaries, when players struggled along on a minimum wage, when they were urged to train in some other profession, something to do when their careers came to an abrupt and early end. Tom Finney became a plumber, Billy Liddell an accountant, others opted for the life of a publican. But sadly today's players think no further than their next wage packet. Careers end in confusion with no direction, little motivation and hazardous uncertainty. Denis Law remembers how it took him more than a year to adjust from the institutionalised structure of football to the independent life of an ordinary family man where he was forced to deal with the incidentals of life. 'One day I was a footballer with the club catering for my every need; the next day I was sitting at home, nowhere to go, and the years stretching out before me.'

The football club, all too protective at times, offers every imaginable facility for its players. When legal advice is needed a solicitor is available, when the car breaks down it goes back to the sponsor's garage, travel arrangements are cared for, house removals paid for and arranged. The institutional life caters for the footballer's every whim. But it is also a trap. The retiring footballer is more like a prisoner being released from gaol after years of incarceration where release brings with it complications and frustrations. The art of living has been forgotten and has to be learnt all over again.

There are no qualifications for football management, no degrees, no HNDs, not even a GCSE. And, anyhow, most noted football managers would probably have failed the entrance exam in the first place. And yet it requires a list of abilities and talents that far exceed most occupations. It is a bizarre business for any young man. You could hardly call it a profession. There is no more insecure an occupation anywhere. A manager one day, Wembley on the horizon; on the dole the next. And while there are no formal qualifications for the job, there don't seem to be any necessary informal qualifications either. What makes a good football manager is anyone's guess. A career in the game, the more esteemed the better; an ability to articulate your views; an understanding of tactics; a talent to inspire and motivate; the ability to spot and nurture skill; a financial wizard in the transfer market; and an aptitude for man-management. And yet having decided that your candidate has all these qualities he may still fail.

To have been the captain of England's World Cup-winning side would, on paper, seem an admirable qualification, but in the case of Bobby Moore it proved to be of little value. The same could be said of Bobby Charlton, while Lawrie McMenemy and the great Herbert Chapman barely played the game at all. And when it comes to intelligence and verbosity, some of football's finest managers have never been able to string more than a few words or thoughts together. Bob Paisley was as uncharismatic, as ordinary and as inarticulate as imaginable. And yet. . . . But even with a pedigree as long as your arm, there is one other vital element. Luck. No matter how experienced the manager, no matter how successful his past career, without the added ingredient of luck you can fail. Souness was to enjoy considerable fortune when he was playing and at Rangers as well, but the day he arrived at Anfield his luck ran out.

Graeme Souness was always a natural for the management game. Even as a player he carried a field marshal's baton in his knapsack. His arrogance underpinned his authority. He was the automatic choice to become Liverpool's captain. Commanding, decisive, and with a warm seducing smile. He had 'street cred', the sort of man to have on your side rather than against you and although he may not have been as popular as others, you always felt that he was the man who could take tough decisions. His authority was legendary, it oozed out of him. He was undoubtedly one of the finest Liverpool chiefs of all time, ready to go where others feared, leading from the front and always setting an example. There may have been moments in his early Anfield career when his attitude was not quite what it should have been but a few threats from Paisley eventually saw him straight. Responsibility was the key and once Souness was handed that responsibility his career never looked back.

Even as a youngster he had been an awkward customer, self-assured and cocky; he was the sort that either finishes up in a remand centre or on millionaires' row. Fortunately Souness chose the latter path but he could so easily have made a wrong turning, wasting away his talents and ending his career in an alcoholic haze. Football is littered with those, particularly Scotsmen, who chose the wrong route. Souness, however, was probably always too wise to fall into that trap. He always knew what he wanted. He was just too impatient, something that would haunt him everywhere from Tottenham to Anfield.

Not surprisingly, Souness had flourished in Italian football. It suited his style and style was the key word in Italy. He had an open mind, ready to take on new ideas, new cultures. He was the ideal student; receptive, inquiring and motivated. All he needed was the tuition. His marriage to Danielle had partly provided that. With her wealthy, *nouveau riche* background, she had access to places that might otherwise have been barred to the average footballer and these were readily opened for her husband. Souness was on a learning curve: Anfield, European competition, Italy. The revolutionary was in the making. By the time he arrived in Glasgow he was even ready to tackle the cultural backwardness of religious sectarianism.

For a club so steeped in ancient prejudices, the home of Glasgow Rangers Football Club is unusually futuristic. It may be a monument to Protestant loyalism but it is equally a stylistic challenge to the old order. The restoration of Ibrox Park had begun long before Graeme Souness had ever been thought of as a possible manager in this loyalist quarter of Glasgow, but it was largely his influence and his vision which would help fill and eventually transform the ground into one of the most exciting football stadiums in Europe. It was a stadium that could compare with any in Britain and with all but a few on the continent. And yet, it would be this juxtaposition, this conflict between tradition and the contemporary, that would haunt Souness throughout his Ibrox days.

Jock Wallace's reign as manager of Glasgow Rangers came to an abrupt end in 1986 as his club crashed to defeat against Tottenham Hotspur in an unimportant end-of-season friendly. But it wasn't just one match which decided Wallace's fate. It had not been the best of seasons for Rangers. For that matter, it had not been the best of seasons for many years. Celtic were champions, Rangers were not even in the top three and nor had they made the final of any of the cup competitions. Rangers were in more than decline – they had struck rock bottom. Gates were tumbling, enthusiasm was on the wane; they were the laughing stock of Glasgow and much of Scotland, with even Aberdeen, Dundee United and the two Edinburgh clubs challenging their traditional authority. Bill Struth would have turned in his grave. Somehow, they were being left behind as the old order changed and despite a grandiose stadium taking shape, it seemed they might never become part of the new order.

The decline had begun in the late sixties as Celtic, vibrant under the leadership of Jock Stein and his assistant Sean Fallon, took everything before them. Boasting the likes of Danny McGrain, Jimmy Johnstone, Billy McNeill and David Hay, they picked up the Scottish title nine years in succession between 1966 and 1974 and in 1967 had become the first British club to win the European Cup. Throughout the period Rangers were always second best, even in the domestic cup competitions, forced to watch in envy as Celtic trod the international stage. These were among the worst years in Rangers' history and in a city that is so fervent about its football, it was a humiliating experience for the men in blue. When Celtic went through their rebuilding process after the resignation of Jock Stein, Rangers had a sporadic burst of success. They won three titles in the four seasons between 1974/75 and 1977/78 but success was to be short-lived. Eight years barren of league titles followed. There was some success in the cup, but it was the league that really counted. In the gloomy years of the sixties they had at least always been second best. Now they were not even that.

Jock Wallace's departure was inevitable. Rangers were developing a smart and expensive new stadium and although they were a rich club they did not have a bottomless pit of spare cash. They could ill afford to see so many empty seats. At some games the crowd was down to as little as 15,000 with average gates just over 25,000. But worse, they had not won a league championship since 1978 and the championship was something Rangers fans regarded as their birthright. In October 1983 they had sacked manager John Greig, a Rangers legend, who had stepped straight from the dressing room into the manager's chair. Jock Wallace, his replacement, was as fanatical a Rangers man as any who had gone before him. It was his second stint as manager. He had been Greig's predecessor, making way for the Rangers captain in 1978 under mysterious circumstances. During his spell as manager, Wallace had taken the club to two trebles before his sudden departure. Now Wallace was gone again. And into his shoes stepped the stylish, enigmatic man of the eighties, Graeme Souness.

Rangers fans will tell you that they can still remember where they were the day Souness was appointed. The announcement came like a bombshell, sending shockwaves bouncing across the city. Telephones buzzed, office workers gossiped and on the factory floor you could tell a Rangers man by the smile on his face. But there were the doubters. Rangers had broken with tradition. Souness was not a Rangers man. He had never had anything to do with the club. He had never played for them, not even had trials. Souness was an Edinburgh lad, an East coast man and as a youngster he had trained with Celtic. What's more, he had played all his football south of the border and in Italy. There was also another question mark. He might have been a Protestant but he was married to a Catholic. It was also pointed out that Souness wore a gold cross around his neck. When Graeme Souness joined Rangers he must have wondered what he was getting himself into.

The decision to break with tradition went back further. Six months previously, a bitter boardroom coup, described by one football writer as 'one of the most savage bloodlettings in the history of the Rangers board', had dramatically altered the balance of power at Ibrox. The instigator was Lawrence Marlborough, the wealthy grandson of the former Rangers chairman John Lawrence who had ruled Ibrox during the sixties and seventies. His grandson had inherited the family's substantial shareholding but had moved to America in 1983 to run the family business in Nevada. It was generally assumed, wrongly as it proved, that he had lost interest in the club. Marlborough had befriended a recently appointed director of the club, David Holmes, and through Holmes he began to master-mind a takeover of the club that would give him a majority shareholding. The key to their plan involved the shares of Jack Gillespie and once these had been secured Marlborough, through Holmes, ruled supreme. The next step was to rid the club of those who belonged to the old order. Directors were edged aside. Out went former chairman Rae Simpson, Tom Dawson and Jim Robinson while Jack Gillespie was promoted to vice chairman as reward for selling his shares to Marlborough. In came Hugh Adam, the man who controlled the lucrative Rangers pools, and then Freddie Fletcher, a man with no previous connections with Rangers but with considerable commercial experience.

The Rangers board began to take on a new complexion. Its previous directors may have all been wealthy men but they had run the club like a hobby. Money had been wasted, there were no tight budgetary controls and all that seemed to matter was beating Celtic a couple of times a year. They belonged to a past era. Marlborough, Holmes, Adam and Fletcher were different – they were wealthy but, with the notable exception of Marlborough, they were all self-made millionaires. They understood money, knew how to run a business and had a vision for the future. What's more, Graeme Souness was part of that vision.

The Souness who returned to Scotland, however, was a far cry from the young lad brought up in an Edinburgh prefab who had been all too keen to get away to the bright lights of London. He had escaped but was coming home a very different man. The youngster may well have had ambitions far beyond the Tweed even then but now he had the sophistication and the pedigree to go with it. Much had happened to him in the intervening years. He had won three European Cup-winners' medals, umpteen league championships, an Italian cup-winners' medal and had married a divorced heiress. Souness was no ordinary footballer, no simple soul from the rough side of Edinburgh. He was now a sophisticated millionaire, a man with a taste for the high life. Quite whether Scotland and this particular corner of Glasgow were ready for him was something which only time would reveal.

If Souness came back a changed man, he returned to find the Scottish soccer scene a far cry from anywhere else he had played. Rangers were down and out. Celtic may have been winning trophies but their football was parochial rather than international. Aberdeen and Dundee United were little better and they all played in a Premier League where teams faced each other four times a season. The league had become predictable and downright boring, because it had been designed to help the likes of Motherwell and Dundee rather than Rangers or Celtic. The Scottish game was in decline. Coupled with the miserable weather, open empty terraces and rusty old stadiums, Souness must have wondered if he had made the right choice. It was all a bit different from Genoa. But at least at Ibrox there was the potential. Money was no problem, the stadium was grand with a futuristic plan on the drawing board and a set of directors who talked with a glowing ambition and vision to match his own. Had Souness gone to Celtic, Hearts or Dundee he might have drowned in a sea of squabbles, debts and crises and never surfaced again. As it was, he had chosen well. As a child, Graeme Souness had admired Rangers from a distance. He may have been a Hibbies fan but, like every other kid in Scotland, he also held an allegiance to one of the two big Glasgow clubs. It was a mixture of religion, tradition and wanting to identify with success. The Hibbies may have had their moments but they were few and far between.

When Souness drove through the gates of Ibrox that first morning he found a picture of neglect. The reality was far different from the dream. It was a fine ground, even then, but attendances were miserable. Ambition might have been sky high in the boardroom but the reality in the dressing room was somewhat at odds with a playing squad at best described as mediocre. They hadn't won the Scottish championship or the Scottish Cup for years, only the Scottish League Cup had come their way; the silverware in the famous Ibrox trophy room was gathering dust. It was a cheerless welcome. In the weeks and months that followed, Souness would set about designing a revolution at Ibrox that would have repercussions throughout the Scottish game.

Souness' presence immediately set Ibrox alight. Ally McCoist remembers his first encounter with Souness the manager. 'It was the immediate presence of the man. He dressed immaculately; he looked fit and tanned and he spoke with firm authority. He said that he was used to success and he wanted to bring success to Rangers. Everyone on the staff would have the chance to show what they could do and he was looking forward to working with us as a team. Straight to the point – short and sweet.' Everyone was impressed, except perhaps Souness. Much needed to be changed if the sleeping giant at Ibrox was to be woken. Top of the list was staff. By the end of his first season Souness would have sold fifteen players and recruited nine more.

But it was one of Souness' earliest signings that turned out to be his most important. Souness had never been a part of Scottish football. He had never played there since he was a boy and although he knew many of the players from his international days, his knowledge was limited.

What he needed first and foremost was an assistant with a thorough working knowledge of the Scottish game. The man he chose was Walter Smith. Smith was nowhere near as exalted a player as Souness. He had been a resilient, almost unknown, defender with Dundee United and had remained with the club to become assistant to Jim McLean. Smith may have been short on honours and international caps but at Dundee United he had helped forge an effective side and was steeped in a knowledge of the contemporary Scottish game. Smith would also complement Souness' more aggressive, uncompromising dressing-room style. Outwardly tough, Smith was also a good listener, always ready to take a player's case back to the manager; always learning, never dogmatic. He could bend where Souness could not.

They agreed immediately on one fundamental point: Scottish football was in sharp decline. The traditions, crafted over the years, that had once made Scottish soccer so renowned and attractive had all but disappeared. The skill that had surfaced in men like Law, Baxter and Dalglish had now been smothered by the insularity of the Scottish game while the temperament that had created a breed like Bremner, Mackay and Big George Young had been replaced by open vindictiveness and aggression. It was all kick and rush. In his own days, Souness had been able to combine his considerable skills with intimidating physical strength. That was the way it used to be. But strength and stamina were all that seemed to count now and instilling the virtues of skill and excellence would take time. Smith knew the Scottish scene but could offer little encouragement. The players were simply not to be found. Both men agreed they would have to look elsewhere for their talent. They could do as a number of Scottish clubs had done in the past and look to Europe, particularly Scandinavia where players were cheap. But money was not really a problem. Then again, suggested

Souness, why not look at England? He knew the Football League as well as anyone. They nodded. England was the obvious target.

CHAPTER FIVE
The English Factor

The secret is that Graeme Souness is not a Scot at all. He's really an Englishman. He certainly carries all the trappings of one. There are none of the parochial tattoos that mark the Scot. Here is a man whose horizons have been stretched, a man who has always focused beyond the Tweed, a man who even tackles his spaghetti without a knife.

In Scotland they remember Graeme Souness mainly because he signed a Catholic for Rangers. That's typical. In England they remember his Scottish days for just one thing – the number of English players he poached. The English factor was to become predominant in the way Souness handled himself as a manager. Souness was not going to be stifled by traditional Scottish thinking. The Scots may have loathed the English but, as far as Souness was concerned, the English had dominated European soccer throughout the seventies and eighties, capturing seven European Cups, and ten lesser European trophies. English soccer had carried off more European trophies than any other European country. It was not to be ignored or discounted as the Scots believed.

Transfer traffic across the border had always been one

directional, with the posh English clubs swooping on the provincial lowlands to steal their up-and-coming talent. But it wasn't just the smaller clubs who were raided. Rangers, Celtic, Aberdeen and the Dundee clubs were just as susceptible, with stars like Dalglish, Macari, Strachan and Baxter, all big signings, tempted south of the border. There was little the Scots could do to hang on to their home-grown talent. Salaries were low, the honours were shared among a mere handful of clubs, and Scottish clubs never paid high fees for players. The big money, fat salaries, fame and fortune, the larger stage, all were in England. The likes of Dalglish were easily tempted away from Scottish football. If you wanted to be a star then you had to travel south, young man.

Once their English careers were over it was not unusual for a Scot to return home, back to his roots, the club where he had first flowered. There he would see out his final playing days. But spotting an English player in the Scottish league was as rare as spotting a giant panda on Glasgow Green. The occasional English player had of course tip-toed north but they were few and far between. In any season you could probably count them on the fingers of one hand. It was more than forty years since an Englishman had pulled on a Rangers shirt. But more to the point, those Englishmen who did venture north were largely unknown names, bought at giveaway prices, and usually past their sell-by date. Scottish clubs were not in the habit of sending their talent scouts down to Anfield, Highbury or Old Trafford. They could never have afforded the outrageous prices demanded even for reserve goalkeepers. Scottish football clubs are not rich. They survive by good housekeeping, low salaries, spotting local talent, and selling the occasional blossoming name to a big English club for some extravagant fee. Rangers and Celtic are the exceptions to this rule. The two Glasgow clubs have always been able to attract gates of more than 30,000 even for mediocre opposition, but their big stadiums, their wider scouting net and their recruitment of the best of Scottish talent kept even their balance sheets hovering between loss and profit. Rangers have always been the richest of the Scots, their bank balance primed by a lucrative pools system that today brings in as much as £5 million a year.

It was unknown for the Glasgow giants to venture south of the border with a fat cheque book. But for Graeme Souness, the nearly Englishman, it seemed a natural thing to do. A virtual lifetime in English football had shaped his views which were at variance to those of his fellow Scots. If the money was in the bank, why not spend it? That was his attitude. And if you didn't fancy any of the Scottish players for sale, then why not try an English club? He was quick to point out that Liverpool had only three English players in their 1984 European Cup-winning side and that even the Real Madrid side of the fifties was stuffed with foreign players including a Frenchman, a Hungarian and an Argentinian. The solution was simple: if you wanted to create a side capable of winning honours outside of Scotland then you had to attract the best players, be they English, Irish, Dutch or whatever. Celtic may have won the European Cup in 1967 with eleven Scots, but by the mid-1980s the game had become far more international. In 1986 there was no UEFA rule limiting the number of foreign players allowed for European competition. The world was your oyster, so why not scour the globe for the best you could afford? First stop: England and Watford. The revolution was about to begin.

Colin West was the first name on Souness' hit list. It was June 1986. Souness had only been there a few weeks and already he was poking his nose south of the border. It made sense as after all he had never played in Scottish football, barely knew the names or reputations of most of the players. And the last two years he had been away in Italy. At least he knew the English scene. The signing of West barely caused a ripple. West was not a big name and had only cost £200,000, chickenfeed even in June 1986. Souness' revolution had begun quietly but it was his next two signings that would really turn heads north and south of the border.

Start your building at the back was the Liverpool philosophy. It was not a bad way to begin. Rangers needed a goalkeeper and the Scottish league is not renowned for producing outstanding examples. Souness was already being forced to look further afield. The only one he had much knowledge of was Bruce Grobbelaar at Liverpool. He rang up his old pal Dalglish, but the Liverpool manager had no intention of selling Grobbelaar even if Souness was flush with money. He would have to try elsewhere. Souness looked no further than the England teamsheet. The first name was Peter Shilton. Souness contacted Southampton and was quoted a fee of £750,000 for a man who was even older than Souness. The Rangers manager politely declined. Next on his list was Chris Woods, four England caps and still young, Shilton's deputy and possibly the pick of the rest of the English keepers. Much to his surprise Norwich agreed and asked for a mere £600,000. The deal was struck. It was a good piece of business and over the years he proved to be one of Souness' better signings.

Next in line was a centre half. The obvious man was Terry Butcher. Ipswich had just been relegated and Butcher was looking to transfer his talents to a top club. Tottenham were favourites, already in discussion with him, while Manchester United hovered in the background. It seemed inconceivable that Butcher could be persuaded north of the border even if Rangers could foot the bill. The problem was compounded by the fact that both Souness and Butcher were away on World Cup duty with their respective international squads. But Souness got word to Butcher and received an early indication that he would at least be willing to talk. And talk they did. It needed just one visit to Glasgow and a few persuasive smiles from Souness to secure the deal and in July 1986 Terry Butcher formally signed for Rangers. He had cost £725,000, but Souness had had to track down David Holmes to his villa in Spain, the whereabouts of which was a closely guarded secret, to raise the fee. 'Give me another £50,000 and I'll give you the championship,' argued Souness. Holmes and Souness both delivered their part of the bargain. The English papers were agog; Tottenham were shattered. Knocked out of the World Cup by the 'hand of God', England were now losing their finest players to the ignominy of the Scottish league. The world was turning upside down. But Souness didn't care. He'd bought two England internationals for a little over £1.3 million. Before the season had even begun, Souness had typically put his mark on Scottish football. In his first game he was also to leave his mark on George McCluskey, but that was another story. If any Rangers fans had doubted the sense of appointing Souness, they only had to glance at the Scottish papers. It was Rangers, Rangers, Rangers. Celtic were relegated to a paragraph at the bottom of the page. Pride was restored, season ticket sales rocketed, and nobody could wait for the start of the season.

But Souness' spending was not to stop there, and nor were his raids south of the border. Before the year was out he had added Jimmy Nicholl to the squad at a cost of £70,000 from West Bromwich Albion; Graham Roberts from Spurs for a massive £450,000 and Neil Woods of Doncaster for £100,000. By the end of the year his spending had topped £2.1 million. There is no doubt that Ibrox had needed a clear-out. The players Souness inherited had by definition failed; new faces were needed and if Rangers were to make an immediate impact they were needed urgently. The Souness revolution had begun by sweeping away old prejudices about English players and by bringing big-name England internationals into Scottish football. There is no doubt that it was a welcome and innovative move by Souness. Generally, his early signings were inspired. Woods stood head and shoulders above any other goalkeeper in Scotland, while Butcher brought unrivalled organisation and strength to the Rangers defence. Graham Roberts, in his short stay, also helped further shore up a defence that would concede only twenty-three goals all season, just six of those coming at Ibrox.

The clear-out began immediately. In June alone, five players disappeared, all on free transfers. By the end of the year Souness had rid the club of more than an entire team – twelve players. By the end of the season three more had gone. In his first season in charge Souness had spent £2,275,000 and recouped a mere £530,000. But who cared about the money? At the end of the season he had something to show for his net outlay of £1.7 million – the Scottish league championship and the Scottish League Cup. It was Rangers' first league title since 1978. It was a small price to pay. What's more, he had brought the money back through the turnstiles as Ibrox was packed for virtually every game.

Success had not been immediate. Rangers started sluggishly, trailing Celtic by nine points at one stage. But as the team began to jell they soon caught their old rivals and the title was a foregone conclusion long before the trophy was officially handed over to team captain Terry Butcher. By then Ibrox was attracting gates of well over 40,000 for most games. Souness may have had his critics, those who argued that he was buying his way to glory, but given the huge gate receipts, the club was probably making an operating profit. What's more, there was silverware in the trophy room again, the fans were delirious, the club had shown that it was as big and ambitious as any in Britain and Ibrox was packed to the rafters. Whatever way you looked at it, there was no denying that Souness was good for business.

With two trophies safely stashed away, many expected Souness to ease up on the throttle for the following season. After all, his side had proved themselves and looked well capable of repeating the feat. But no. Instead, he applied even more pressure. The lesson he had seen at Anfield was to keep replacing; find new and better talent, never become complacent. It was a good lesson and it was a mistake many winning sides had made in the past as they simply relied on the same men, the same formula that had already brought success. But the Anfield formula was never to introduce sweeping changes. It was more subtle. The rule was: two in, two out, and always make sure that the two coming in are better than the two going out. It was a law that had served Liverpool well over the years, but it was one that Souness would ignore and that would cause him endless headaches. Even more disastrous would be the way he recklessly ignored the tradition when he returned to Anfield.

Even before the 1987/88 season had begun Souness had been wheeler-dealing in the transfer market. The money was burning a hole in his pocket. He was like a child with his Christmas money. Five new faces joined the club while five were shown the door. One of those going was Colin West. Signed twelve months earlier from Watford for £200,000, he was discarded and sold to Sheffield Wednesday for £150,000 despite the fact that he had played in all forty-four league games that season. It was to set a worrying trend.

Souness now began to cast his net beyond the shores of Britain and swooped to finally sign his old friend Avi Cohen from the Israeli club Maccabi for £100,000.

Souness had tried to make Cohen one of his first signings a year earlier but Maccabi had refused to release him. Cohen had been at Anfield at the same time as Souness but had never made much of an impact on Merseyside. Although he looked a stylish defender with his Beckenbauer touches, he had only made twenty appearances for Liverpool before returning to Israel in 1981. Six years later Souness reckoned he had a role to play at Ibrox. Cohen in fact would last just two seasons at Rangers, before returning to Maccabi on a free transfer.

The biggest headline-hitting new face, however, was another of Souness' old pals, Trevor Francis. Francis had played alongside Souness at Sampdoria. Now he was with Atalanta. Souness snapped him up for a bargain £75,000. A more expensive signing was yet another English player, Mark Falco, who joined the exodus north from Watford. This time the fee was £270,000. And there was also some money left in the purse for Ian McCall, the promising young Dunfermline player who cost £200,000. Five in, five out; Souness had already gone further than the Anfield formula. But even then he wasn't finished. In the autumn he was dealing again and this time with big money. First in, to nobody's surprise, was Richard Gough. The tall, robust defender had long been admired by Souness and had been expected to join Rangers the previous year. But Dundee United had refused to sell to another Scottish club. So instead, he went south to Tottenham. Now, a season later, he was returning home, a prize catch for Souness, even if the fee was his highest yet at £1.1 million. Having signed one veteran England international midfielder in Trevor Francis, Souness then decided on a second, Ray Wilkins. After a career in England with Chelsea and Manchester United, Wilkins had gone abroad, joining AC Milan. He had then wound up at Paris St Germain in the French league until Souness paid £150,000 for him. By the end of the season he had also added Dundee's John Brown to his squad for £350,000; the Dane Jan Bartram from Silkeborg for £180,000 and Ian Ferguson of St Mirren for another big fee, this time £850,000, plus Mark Walters of Aston Villa for £500,000. Walters was Rangers' first black player and one who would eventually follow Souness to Anfield.

It brought Souness' spending in his second season at Ibrox to almost £3.8 million. Added to the £2.2 million he had spent in his first season, he had now shelled out £6 million on new players in just two years.

But, of course, in that second season other players were sold. The most surprising departure was Mark Falco who had lasted just five months in the Ibrox hot house before Souness sold him to Queens Park Rangers, for £350,000. Falco had done the job he was bought for and that was it. Also off before he had the time to unpack his bags was Trevor Francis who took up an appointment as player-manager of QPR just four months after joining Rangers. Although the money was generally flowing in one direction – out – the manager did recoup some of his spending with the sale of Robert Fleck to Norwich for £580,000 and Dave McPherson to Hearts for £325,000. In all, Souness sold eight players in his second season, a total of twenty-three since he had joined the club. The Rangers of 1988 bore no resemblance to the club Souness had joined just two years earlier.

Souness' third season saw yet more signings, most of them English. By now the top Scottish clubs were reluctant to sell any of their men to Rangers even though substantial cheques were being waved temptingly in their faces. It was a paradox that had always faced Rangers, but antipathy towards Souness during his reign at Ibrox exacerbated their feelings towards the club that had now become their fiercest rival. Of the six players he signed that season five came from English clubs; only Tom Cowan, a £100,000 buy from Clyde, came from a Scottish club. The biggest signing was the Everton defender Gary Stevens at £1 million, closely followed by Mel Sterland at £800,000 from Sheffield Wednesday and Kevin Drinkell, a £500,000 buy from Norwich. But the most startling signing was surely Andy Gray, a man everyone knew was past his best when he had left Everton years earlier. Gray cost just £25,000, so it was perhaps not as foolhardy or reckless a signing as some made out at the time. He was bought principally as cover in case of injuries and although he quickly saw action, he was mainly named as substitute and made only a handful of full appearances before he was moved on at the end of the season. By then he had done his job and others had been bought to fill the gap. 'One thing was clear the minute I arrived in Glasgow,' says Gray, 'and that was that Graeme was in total charge. He could do what he liked.' Gray, at the end of his career, had seen enough of the footballing world to feel no bitterness. Others would not part on such happy terms.

Gray was not the only Souness purchase to be sold that season. Out went Jan Bartram, back to Denmark for £315,000 which at least was almost twice as much as Souness had paid for him in the first place. Arguably it was a good piece of business but the truth was that Bartram had had enough of Souness' dressing-room antics. He simply could not come to terms with the shouting and bawling that were part of the Ibrox order. Another feeling much the same was Graham Roberts. He, too, was off, back south to Chelsea for £475,000, glad to be away from the Souness stare and the rows that had erupted around him. Roberts had lasted twenty months.

Mel Sterland left quickly, too, having played just a handful of games, mostly out of position, and had disappeared before anybody had got to recognise him. He had been bought simply to help win the title. Once Trevor Steven had been signed in the close season there was no room for him. Avi Cohen also escaped back to his home in Tel Aviv, rejoining Maccabi, another unhappy man. By the close of the 1988/89 season six players had left, four of them bought by Souness himself.

At the end of that third season the ledger made exhausting reading. £2.675 million spent in the season and just over £1 million realised. As Souness entered his fourth year with Rangers, Ibrox was more akin to Fort Knox as the money was shipped in and out. A staggering £8.75 million had been spent on twenty-six players. Other Scottish managers looked on bewildered. Over at Parkhead they were weeping. And still the spending went on. Into his fourth season and Souness was at it again. It began almost as soon as the previous season had drawn to a close. The first to arrive was none other than Trevor Steven, the distinguished Everton and England midfielder, for £1.525 million and then a month later came the most sensational signing in the club's long Calvinist history, Mo Johnston. The former Celtic man cost Souness £1.25 million, plus a considerable headache. By the end of November 1989 Souness had added six new players to the squad, including Chris Vinnicombe from Exeter for £500,000 and Nigel Spackman of QPR for another half a million pounds. Souness' investment for the season topped a staggering £4 million, the highest he would spend in any one season at Ibrox, giving him a grand total expenditure thus far of £13 million in his time at Ibrox. And, of course, there were the usual exits, and again most of those were his own signings. Back to England went Mel Sterland, joining Leeds United and his former manager Howard Wilkinson for £600,000; Kevin Drinkell moved to Coventry for £800,000 while Ray Wilkins joined QPR on a free transfer. Ian McCall also left, joining Bradford, while two of his other signings – Jimmy Nicholl and Davie Kirkwood – ended up with Scottish clubs.

As usual the close season delivered the expected flurry of activity in the transfer market, this time almost a whirlwind trip around Europe. First stop was Monaco where the England international striker Mark Hateley was snapped up for a bargain £500,000. Abandoned by his country, cold-shouldered by all the big Football League clubs, Hateley jumped at the opportunity of playing his football back in Britain. He had a point to prove and leapt at Souness' offer. Next stop was Kiev where Souness agreed a fee of £1.2 million for Oleg Kuznetsov, the Ukrainian defender. Then it was off to Holland where Rangers secured the services of Pieter Huistra, the FC Twente attacking midfielder. He cost £250,000. And before August was over Souness had also recruited Terry Hurlock from Millwall for £325,000 and Brian Reid, his final signing, for £300,000 from Morton. The five men had cost him £2.5 million. They were largely paid for by the sale of Terry Butcher to Coventry for £500,000 where he took over as player-manager and Derek Ferguson to Hearts for £750,000. And that was it. Before the 1990/91 season had ended Souness had packed his bags and gone. There would be no more wheeler-dealing – at Ibrox any rate – leaving Scottish football all the poorer with the back page headline writers bemoaning his loss.

But the total bill was staggering. Over five seasons Graeme Souness had spent £15,375,000 on new players. In a similar period, Alex Ferguson had spent nearly £13 million at Manchester United, while Kenny Dalglish had spent almost as much. But it was the fact that nobody in the history of Scottish football had ever come anywhere near spending money on this scale before that truly marked out Souness' efforts. Celtic's spending was a fraction of this. Indeed you would be hard put to find anyone in English soccer who had spent so much in so short a time. Souness, of course, would argue, as would any manager, that you also have to take into account the amount recouped from players that have been sold. It was a fair point and in the case of Souness' five years at Ibrox he brought in £6,375,000 in transfer deals. But it still left a net transfer deficit of £9 million. A figure which should perhaps be compared with the price that he and David Murray had paid for Rangers back in November 1988, a mere £6 million. Souness would also argue, and again rightly, that it was money well spent. During his five years at Ibrox, Rangers did win three Scottish league titles (the 1990/91 title probably also ought to be attributed to Souness) plus four Scottish League Cups. Ibrox was packed week in week out, season ticket sales boomed and everyone beamed. It was probably a small price to pay for success. Some of the spending was also necessary. When Souness arrived at Ibrox, he and Walter Smith found a bunch of players who in his words 'would not have won anything'. Souness had to buy. He had to show ambition and bring the best to Glasgow. Substantial losses, however, were made on some players. The most notable was probably Mel Sterland, bought for £800,000 in March 1989 and then sold for £600,000 in July, a £200,000 loss over four months.

The turnover in players at Ibrox far exceeded the turnover anywhere else in British football. It was a revolution. 'Come the end of the summer break, you'd go back to Ibrox and never be quite sure who you'd find there,' said one player. 'Your mates would be gone, players you thought were good, you rated, and in their places would be all sorts of new faces. With all the chopping and changing it was difficult to get a settled side.' Richard Gough says it was like 'a revolving door', adding that 'sometimes you wondered just who would be in the dressing room when you arrived for training in the morning'. 'There were various reasons for the turnover in staff,' he argues. 'The manager was still trying to build the team he wanted and, bit by bit, he was getting it right. Sometimes though, if he felt that a player he had bought was not going to be right, then that player was moved on.'

But it was the signing of so many Englishmen that had made the headlines. Of the 37 players Souness brought to the club, 20 of them came from south of the border. He even recruited more players from the continent than he did from Scotland, signing nine from foreign clubs, compared with just eight from his own country. But what is perhaps of more relevance is that so many of the players that he signed, he then sold again. Of the 37 he bought, no less than 17 of them – almost half – were later moved on by him. Five of his signings lasted less than a year, with three of them – Mel Sterland, Mark Falco and Jan Bartram – remaining for less than six months. It was sometimes difficult to fathom what had gone wrong. Either the players had done the job they had been bought for or Souness did not rate them once they had arrived. Others did not like what they saw and were unable to cope with Souness' authoritarian attitude.

'If a player was not ready to conform to the code of conduct which Graeme had at Ibrox then he was on his bike,' says Richard Gough. 'Similarly, if anyone clashed with him about tactics or even questioned his approach to management then that player was on borrowed time from the moment he had challenged Graeme's authority.' Jan Bartram and Graham Roberts both had problems with the manager and ultimately it was a rift between Souness and Terry Butcher that brought about the captain's end as a Rangers man. Some players were simply recruited to do a specific job and were then moved on once the job was complete. Andy Gray, Mel Sterland and Trevor Francis fitted that description. Others such as Colin West, Mark Falco and Kevin Drinkell simply did not make the grade. It could hardly have been confidence-boosting for them.

All managers make mistakes, even the best. Bob

Paisley once spent £250,000 on Celtic youngster Frank McGarvey and while McGarvey could win a place in the Scotland side he never even made his debut for Liverpool. But Souness seemed to be making more than his fair share of miscalculations. To dispose of seventeen players he recently signed must raise some questions about his judgement. But at Ibrox, as long as the trophies were pouring in nobody cared. Fortunately, Souness had the money to make mistakes and experiment. When he came to Anfield the money dried up.

CHAPTER SIX
The Absentee Landlord

Lawrence Marlborough was being torn in two. It was the summer of 1988. Having purchased a controlling interest in Rangers, he was now beginning to realise that he may have taken on too much. The vast Lawrence building empire was expanding on the west coast of America. Business was good and running the company was a 24-hour-a-day job. There was little time for other projects, every effort had to be pumped into the American side of the business. When Lawrence Marlborough's grandfather John Lawrence ran Rangers in the sixties and seventies, he could afford to devote time to the club. He was 'Mr Rangers', a regular board attender, and always in his seat in the directors' box. Lawrence Marlborough had been out of the country since 1983 and his visits to Glasgow were infrequent, his trips to Ibrox even less frequent. In effect, he was an absentee landlord. When he purchased his controlling stake it was partly to secure a future for the club, a fitting memory for his grandfather. He had even anticipated that he might be able to play an active role but events had conspired against him. Time was now too precious. His life and interests, he was forced to admit, were in America and not in the south-west of Glasgow.

Although the day-to-day running of Rangers was left in the safe hands of David Holmes, even he was beginning to wonder if it was really worth it. Handling Rangers had proved a bigger task than either he or Marlborough had ever imagined. The club simply took over your life, back page news one day, front page news the next. Rangers were always in the spotlight. It had been a difficult season in many ways. Celtic had snatched the Scottish league title, leaving Rangers trailing in third place and although Graeme Souness was undoubtedly proving an enormous success, there had been some unsavoury moments as well.

The much publicised court case in April 1988 against Chris Woods, Terry Butcher, Graham Roberts and Frank McAvennie had cast a slur on the name of Rangers. The case had eaten up considerable time and energy, side-tracking everyone from other important tasks. Not only had there been unwelcome criticism from the courts but the unruly nature of the club's supporters had been thrown into question once again. After the famous Old Firm battle royal at Ibrox of 17 October which had ended in disarray and bad temper, Holmes and his Celtic counterpart Jack McGinn had been forced to meet behind locked doors to resolve the indiscipline that was becoming all the more acrimonious with every Old Firm clash. The papers had a field day. Holmes could do without it all. There were whispers around Ibrox that he had had enough. It was also said that without Holmes, Lawrence Marlborough would also throw in the towel.

David Murray is one of Scotland's most successful businessmen. In 1984 he was named Scottish Young Businessman of the Year. Murray made his money out of steel, not unlike Jack Walker in Blackburn. Walker had moved into football and would later strike up a partnership with Souness' predecessor in the Liverpool manager's chair, Kenny Dalglish. Born in 1951, just two years before Souness himself, Murray had a fairly obscure education. No university, no reputable business school, just a formal basic Scottish education. In 1976 at the age of 24 he formed his own company Murray International Metals and five years later turned it into Murray International Holdings. In that same year he was involved in a horrific car accident while driving his Lotus sports car home from a rugby game; both his legs had to be amputated. Such a catastrophe might have destroyed most men but not David Murray. 'It made me all the more determined,' he insists. Murray also suffered a second tragedy, the death of his wife from cancer at an appallingly early age.

By the time he was 30 he was chairman of Murray International Holdings and already on his way to becoming a multi-millionaire. Today he runs his empire from the aptly named Edinburgh headquarters, Murray House. He owns 90 per cent of Murray International Holdings, 11,208,500 shares out of a total of 12,725,707 shares. In 1992 his company paid him an annual salary of £469,000. His empire has operations in Scotland, Wolverhampton and Darlington – more than fifty companies – with an annual turnover exceeding £250 million. Not surprisingly, he's also a Tory with close connections to the party's hierarchy. Everything that Murray touches has turned to gold with one exception, the *Sunday Scot*. Murray had launched the new Scottish tabloid newspaper in 1990, perhaps seeing himself as another Robert Maxwell or Silvio Berlusconi, spanning the high profile worlds of the media and football. Next step politics, perhaps. But it was a disaster. The cynics labelled it the *Sunday Scud* and it quickly folded. It cost him £5 million.

Souness and Murray had struck up a friendship shortly after Souness' arrival in Scotland. They both operated from Edinburgh, and were soon regularly meeting on a Friday evening for a meal at Raffaelli's, a busy, upmarket

Italian restaurant in the city. Murray was football mad, an Ayr United fan, and liked to hear the gossip, the inside stories and Souness' opinion on players and teams. It boosted his ego to be on friendly terms with a man like Souness. Football was the source of their friendship, but Murray was also interested in basketball and had pumped money into a Scottish club. Murray and Souness had actually been introduced to each other by Alton Bird, the basketball player. Murray might not have taken up with most football managers. Not for him the brash gold medallion man with little between his ears other than a bladder of a football brain. Murray was a man with sophisticated tastes who was also immune to the west coast preoccupation with God's role in football. Good food, good wine and profitable spreadsheets were more to his liking. Football was merely a part-time interest. But with Souness he could meet on level terms. Both had made money and knew how to manage money. Football was not their only pre-occupation.

Murray had for some time been interested in purchasing a football club. He had looked about, had even thought seriously about buying Ayr United, his childhood team, but it had all fallen through in the end. With all his money he knew he could do better. Not for him some dreary first or second division outfit with its dreary ground and even drearier directors. What he was really interested in was a club like Rangers. He mentioned it to Souness in the summer of 1988. Neither man thought much more of it until some months later. By October it was becoming more apparent that all was not well at Ibrox, particularly at board level, and Souness' hunch that Lawrence Marlborough might be ready to sell if the right offer came along was beginning to look less fanciful and more like reality. Souness decided to mention David Murray's interest to David Holmes. Holmes took the message on board. There was no shock reaction, no flat denials that Rangers could ever be for sale. Holmes simply sat back and listened, nodding occasionally and taking in all that Souness was telling him. But for Souness there was also some self-interest. He had already mentioned to Murray that he might be prepared to put some of his own money into the club if Murray was ever in a position to take over at Ibrox. It would be a sound investment. Rangers could only get better and if they ever won the top European prize his stake would benefit. And besides that, as he admitted in his diary of a season, 'it should stop the knockers telling people that I am only at Ibrox until something bigger turns up'.

Holmes reported Murray's interest in Rangers back to Lawrence Marlborough in Nevada. It struck a chord with Marlborough and forced him to consider seriously his stake in Rangers. If he really wanted out then here was an opportunity. At the very least, he decided it was worth investigating. Marlborough and Murray met at David Murray's Edinburgh headquarters. After their meeting Marlborough indicated that he wanted to talk some more. The deal was a goer. By mid-November Marlborough had decided he would sell and, provided a financial agreement could be reached, he felt that Rangers would be passing into safe hands with Murray. All that was needed now was to fix the price. Further meetings were convened by both sides, with Souness, as a potential major investor, also heavily involved. The eventual price was agreed. Murray would take a 76 per cent stake in the club at a cost of £6 million. Souness would have a further 7 per cent holding valued at £600,000. Murray also agreed to take on board the club's £7 million debt. Everything was in place by 22 November. All that remained was for the final documents to be signed. So far they had succeeded in keeping their dealings and negotiations under wraps but just as the final papers were being prepared the news leaked out. Robert Maxwell, proprietor of Mirror Group

Newspapers and a man desperate to own a major football club, had got wind of the deal and had phoned up to express an interest. Maxwell wanted to buy Rangers as well. Nobody wanted that. It may well have been that Maxwell could have topped the Murray/Souness bid but nobody fancied the idea of Rangers falling into the hands of a non-Scot. The Maxwell intervention focused minds. With just minutes left to their deadline, all sides hurriedly initialled the legal documents.

Souness was delighted, brushing aside any doubts and warnings about going into partnership with someone who is also a friend. 'A casual remark made to a friend so many months ago has now flowered into a huge multi-million pound takeover,' he told reporters at the time. Murray was equally delighted. Souness warned him that the club would soon take over his life but Murray assured him that he was used to dealing with pressure and that he would be able to cope with the intense examination of everything on and off the field by the media and one half of Glasgow. Souness was later to chuckle at how indeed the club did come to take over his life.

The deal also cemented their growing friendship. Murray idolised Souness. In many ways they were not unlike. They were both self-made millionaires, both ambitious, stylish and both shared horizons that stretched beyond the parochialism of Scotland. Two extroverts, who enjoyed each other's company as well as the occasional fun evening. It was a marriage made in Ibrox.

Souness, thanks to his £600,000 stake in Rangers, was now the second largest shareholder and was appointed a club director. He could claim the unique distinction of being manager/player/director, almost certainly the first in the history of Scottish football, if not European football. In time his stake was to prove a wise investment, eventually netting him £2.4 million. As for David Murray, by 1992 he was boasting that Rangers was worth £34.5

million, excluding players. 'Not a bad wee return,' he reckoned, adding that 'it's not for sale, by the way.' Yet oddly enough David Murray does not officially own the club. Rather it is his company, Murray International Holdings, who control it through an 80 per cent shareholding in the club. But given that Murray has a 90 per cent stake in Murray International Holdings, he in effect has control of Rangers Football Club.

In the four years between 1988 and 1992, Rangers would spend £35 million. Of this amount, £26 million went on the stadium with £9 million net going on players. The overdraft had also risen from £7 million to £10 million but that did not worry Murray. 'I would rather be in debt and win something,' he said, 'than have no debt and win nothing.' Murray and Souness now owned not just a football team but also a magnificent stadium. As they signed the takeover documents they pledged to continue the work of turning Ibrox into not just one of the finest stadiums in Britain but one of the finest in Europe.

The giant Ibrox stadium, home of Glasgow Rangers since 1887, has suffered a chequered history. In 1902 it was the venue of soccer's first-ever disaster when old wooden terracing collapsed during a Scotland–England international, sending 26 spectators tumbling to their deaths 40 feet below. More than 500 were also treated for injury but after a short delay of 18 minutes the game resumed. Ironically, Rangers had not long since spent £20,000 on ground improvements including the building of stands and the fatal terracing. It was overcrowding that had caused the disaster as more than 80,000 struggled to watch the game. An inquiry later recommended that wooden terraces be replaced by solid concrete structures. As a result much of Ibrox was redeveloped and in 1928 Archibald Leitch designed a splendid typical Leitch stand on the south side. Today, that stand is a listed building. Gradually the capacity of the ground increased with regular pre-war attendances of over 100,000. In January 1939 a record gate of 118,567 had watched the annual Old Firm clash, making it at one time the second largest ground in world football.

But on 2 January 1971 came a second disaster as a tense crowd of 80,000 watched Rangers take on Celtic. This time sixty-six died as fans pouring out of the ground via stairway 13 suddenly turned to race back up the stairway when they heard the roar as Rangers scored a last-minute equaliser. The goal led to many more thousands deciding to leave the ground, only to collide with those racing up towards the top of the stairway. In the ensuing crush sixty-six spectators were suffocated or trampled on as people tumbled down the steep stairway. It was a horrific accident that had always been waiting to happen. It was almost inevitable: all it needed was the right set of circumstances. Following another inquiry the Government eventually introduced the Safety of Sports Grounds Act 1975 which severely curtailed crowd capacities at football grounds throughout the country.

Ibrox had suffered one disaster too many. In 1902, in those early days of soccer and large crowds, it was hardly surprising that tragedy should strike but not in 1971. Rangers was labelled a dangerous ground and something needed to be done. By the mid-seventies there was an additional problem. Rangers fans were by then among the most notorious in the country. Pitch invasions, riots, hand-to-hand fighting on the terraces, all had turned Ibrox into a battle scene on many occasions. It had an appalling reputation. Nobody in their right mind would go and watch a football match there. The stigma of a dangerous ground and some of the worst behaved fans in football brought an urgency to the situation.

Ibrox was already a tribute to Rangers' chairman Lawrence Marlborough when Souness first set foot inside the stadium. Good housekeeping, a lucrative pools scheme and a determination to make amends for the 1971 tragedy had all culminated in Rangers rebuilding their stadium. In 1977, six years after the disaster, they had unveiled a plan to transform Ibrox into the most modern and best equipped stadium in Britain. The ground would be completely transformed on three sides with the terracing knocked down and replaced by three magnificent new stands. Only Archibald Leitch's distinctive 1928 redbricked edifice, that housed the main administrative offices and trophy room, would remain. It was an enormous undertaking that would take many years to complete.

It was an ambitious decision but it was also a considerable risk. How would the fans react to seats when at times more than 100,000 of them had stood inside the o . ground? The atmosphere would undoubtedly decline, the cost to the fan would increase and Rangers would have to fill their stadium if it was to pay for itself. The danger was that they might end up like some English clubs with a magnificent stand but a team so poor that nobody wanted to pay to sit in it to watch them. And when it came to choosing between paying for a good team or paying to sit in the stands, the directors knew exactly which their supporters would opt for.

By 1981 Ibrox had been transformed from a drab, crumbling temple of Calvinism that could hold 100,000 spectators to a magnificent, ultra-modern vision of the future with 36,500 seats and a total capacity of 44,500. Only the enclosure under Leitch's old stand remained as a terracing, left to placate the die-hard bigots of Protestantism. But the gamble worked and, thanks to Graeme Souness' revolution, even more development would take place. In 1989 it was announced that work would soon begin on adding an upper tier to Leitch's splendid stand. A cantilever roof was also to be fitted along with 38 executive boxes, each seating 24 people. The Govan stand was to be revamped as well into a four-storey building with offices and 36 executive boxes. There were restaurants, a conference room and general office accommodation. It seemed bizarre to run a company from an office at Ibrox. But why not and what an address. What's more, it was all paid for out of the success of Souness on the field. The total cost of redeveloping Ibrox since the seventies was estimated at around £29 million.

Souness' vision and now Murray's money were dragging Rangers and Scottish football into the twentieth century. Souness had seen and played in the futuristic stadiums of Italy; grounds that were stylish, comfortable and exciting. Souness was of the breed who wondered why anyone should want to go and stand on a terrace in the cold rain or be forced to visit a toilet where the conditions resembled the Third World. Hot Bovril on a cold Saturday afternoon was not his idea of the future. Spectators were entitled to their comfort as well as decent facilities. Seats had already proved their value by helping to eliminate the hooliganism and violence that had marred the seventies when Rangers' reputation travelled before them. The Souness/Murray plan all along was to transform Glasgow Rangers into an AC Milan, a Barcelona, a Juventus. To put it among Europe's elite. They had the money, the crowds, now they had the stadium; and with Souness even more committed to the club than ever, the two men could set about their dream of turning Glasgow Rangers into one of the top clubs in Europe.

CHAPTER SEVEN
The Ibrox Revolution

Some years ago, long before Graeme Souness had been safely installed at Rangers, Liverpool Football Club were invited to Glasgow to open formally a new stand at Ibrox with a friendly against Rangers. It was December 1981. After the match the directors of both clubs gathered in the board room for their usual dram of whisky and canapés. The Liverpool directors were in raptures at Rangers' splendid new stand, but more significantly, the Rangers directors were in awe of the Liverpool team. The talk soon turned to the recent poor performances of Rangers.

'I don't suppose you have any players to sell,' inquired one of the Rangers directors, half jokingly. The Liverpool directors scratched their heads.

'Well, there is one player we might consider offers for,' they replied.

'Who's that?' Rangers asked.

'Howard Gayle,' answered the Liverpool contingent.

'Oh yes, he's quite impressive,' they replied. The Rangers directors then went into a huddle and emerged to ask, 'What religion is he, by the way?'

The Liverpool directors looked at one another. None of them had a clue and could not even guess at whether he was a Protestant or a Catholic. Gayle, of course, was black. Presumably the Rangers directors had spotted this yet it did not seem to concern them. Of far more consequence was Gayle's religion. The incident spoke volumes for the differing approach of the two clubs to footballing matters.

Govan is a quarter of Glasgow that is unmistakably Protestant. Its thoroughfares may be grand and imposing, almost European in style, but within its ordered streets there rings the distinct echo of Calvinism. The graffiti merely hints at it. 'No Pope here, Ulster Volunteer Force.' The word 'loyalist' is pervasive; it is part of the culture of the streets. What's more, it applies as much to the football club as it does to the Union Jack. This is the territory of King Billy, 1690, 'the sash my father wore', the land of No Surrender. To see Protestantism at its most vitriolic you need only to visit the loyalist bars, the Rangers clubs and just up the road the Freemason Lodges. This is where the vitriol is fermented. On match day outside the ground the King Billy flags flutter in the breeze, a bargain at £2 each from the street souvenir sellers. There is no compromise with Catholicism. Govan can be just as divided as Belfast. To an outsider the theology of the streets seems to belong to another era, to an age of the dinosaur.

And nowhere has it been more apparent than inside Ibrox, and especially when Celtic are the visitors. On the terracing beneath the south stand, known to Rangers fans as the Enclosure, the zealots gather to parade their religious trophies. Union Jacks waving jingoisticly in the wind, obscenities screeched and all the time the goading of Celtic supporters with a two-fingered salute and the cries of 'Papists'. It is not a pleasant sight. And nor is it just young, irresponsible kids but grown men as well; fathers, grandfathers, who all ought to know better. As Celtic race out on to the pitch, their players give a pronounced sign of the cross; the fans do the same. Inside Ibrox, the stronghold of anti-Papism, this is tantamount to heresy.

In Glasgow, religion and football are a fact of life, cunningly intertwined in the fabric of society. From the Catholic origins of Celtic with its vast Irish support to the loyalist established order of Protestant Rangers, there is no escape from football and God. At one time jobs, education and housing were also determined by creed, though thankfully those days have all but disappeared. Yet, oddly enough, Rangers was not always so vehemently Protestant. Its roots may have been in the Protestant community but it never had the links with the religious orders that Celtic had fostered from its beginnings.

Glasgow Celtic was founded by a Catholic priest, Brother Walfrid, in 1888, as a charitable organisation to help raise money for food, clothing and poor relief among the destitute Irish population. Since then the club has grown beyond all recognition but has never shaken off its Catholic Irish origins. They have always been an Irish club, worn the shamrock on their shirts and Republicanism in their hearts. Rangers, on the other hand, never cultivated its strident Protestantism until years later, and then only as a deliberate means to annoy their fiercest and oldest enemy and to capitalise on a potential money-spinner. It was almost contrived rather than natural. And it was particularly during the reign of its notorious manager Bill Struth that its devotion to the loyalist cause was finely tuned.

Glasgow Rangers was formed in 1873, founded by a bunch of lads from the Gareloch. They initially played at Fleshers Haugh on Glasgow Green and did not arrive at Ibrox until August 1887. At first relations with Celtic were friendly, matches would be followed by a social gathering, a few drinks and some music. By the turn of the century the two teams had taken over from the more famous Queen's Park, Vale of Leven and Renton to become the two biggest clubs in Glasgow and Scotland. Intense rivalry had superseded the old friendships, particularly on the terraces where 'bad blood' was said to disgrace their meetings. Their confrontations began to draw huge crowds and big gates meant big money. It became a simple formula; the more intense the rivalry, the bigger the gate; the bigger the gate, the more the proceeds. Glasgow historian Professor Bill Murray has plotted how 'the commercial potential of religious and national differences was apparent to both managements'. But that was not to say that at that time it was being cynically exploited. That would come later. Bigotry and business were about to go hand in hand.

Rangers may have been a Protestant club even before the turn of the century but only in as much as most Scottish clubs were Protestant. Celtic stood apart. Rangers had even signed three Catholic players between 1906 and 1908 in an effort to break Celtic's domination. But the problem was that any Catholic automatically wanted to play for Celtic rather than Rangers. The lines of demarcation were already becoming clearly drawn.

The shipyards of east Glasgow had long been Protestant strongholds and the arrival of the Ulster-based Harland and Wolff in Govan in 1912 only reinforced the Protestant grip on the community. Rangers had more than a nodding acquaintance with the shipyard employers. The club fixed players up with work at the yards when their playing days drew to a close or injuries brought a premature end to their careers. It was a relationship that worked two ways and the yards were only too aware that a winning Rangers was good for business all round.

It was the influx of Irish immigrants during the nineteenth century that had brought about the strain between the two communities. The Potato Famine of the 1840s and earlier poverty in Ireland had led to mass emigration from Ireland with the western ports of Liverpool, Manchester and Glasgow the nearest staging posts. Some arrived briefly on the mainland before seeking passage to America, Canada or Australia; most stayed, unable to afford the fare. At the beginning of the nineteenth century there were no more than 40,000 Catholics in the whole of Scotland. By 1827 their number had doubled to 80,000 and by the turn of the century it was reckoned to be close to 450,000. It was inevitable that there would be conflict and in the poverty of Glasgow the entrenched population of Protestants simply blamed the Catholics as jobs and housing became scarcer than ever.

The two communities were developing in parallel but always deeply divided. There were Protestant schools and Catholic schools, Protestant youth institutions such as the Boys' Brigade and the Scouts and Catholic youth clubs. There were Protestant employers and Catholic employers, Catholic ghettoes and separate Protestant communities. You could go for years without coming across anyone from the other side. At times there was open hostility, inflamed by the church on a Sunday and the terraces on a Saturday.

The architect of Ibrox's conversion to Protestantism was Bill Struth. Born in Edinburgh in 1876 he was a stonemason by trade but it was to be his devotion to physical fitness that would eventually map out his life. He had new ideas, a knowledge of physiology and understood the need for fitness in sport. He soon came to the attention of Clyde Football Club and under his ruthless training regime the 'Bully Wee' enjoyed some of their best days. It quickly brought him to the attention of Rangers and in 1914 he transferred his allegiance across Glasgow to become the club's new trainer.

Struth ruled with a rod of iron, often through a hierarchy of players and petty privileges. Only the most disciplined of players could ever hope to become part of that hierarchy. It was a form of psychological warfare. Behaviour had to be exemplary, dress always formal. Players were expected to strive for the highest level of fitness as well as total compliance to Rangers Football Club. Players were not allowed to use the subway or go to the cinema, freshwater bathing was banned and tennis forbidden. Religion aside, there was to be something of the Struth in Souness.

Struth was to rule Ibrox until he retired in 1954 and even then his philosophy and reputation would linger, haunting the club's corridors for many more years. Although Struth knew little of football tactics – he preferred to leave others to choose the team – during his time Rangers carried all before them, winning league championships and Scottish cups galore. They seemed invincible. Struth's dream was always to make Rangers the greatest club in Scotland, even if it meant signing a Catholic. But, of course, it never happened. Struth was a pillar of the Protestant community, as Orange as any man on the board. Struth was Mr Ibrox. He held a substantial shareholding in the club and engineered a boardroom coup that saw him emerge as a club director. By then he had become a football dictator.

There are still disputes about precisely how many Catholics have managed to slip through the net. Before Struth they could be counted on the fingers of one hand but all had kept their religious allegiances private. After Struth there were none although there may have been a question mark over one or two. Don Kitchenbrand in the mid-fifties was probably the only one although it was always emphasised that the skilful South African was lapsed and no longer a practising Catholic. Even the wives were vetted. The message was clear: Rangers did not sign Catholics. Of course, at an official level the club always denied this practice, though proving that it was a deliberate policy is not as simple as it may seem. The line was that, of course, they would sign a Catholic, provided he was good enough. It just so happened that none of them were. Really it was just a sop to FIFA. Even in 1976 following a serious riot in a friendly at Aston Villa, Rangers' manager Willie Waddell had made a public declaration that Rangers would sign a Catholic 'as soon as one good enough comes along'. Yet, in a city bursting at the seams with Catholics, Rangers never managed to find one of adequate promise or skill. It would take them another ten years.

Long after Struth had gone, the policy continued through his chosen successor, Scot Symon. Rangers was by then a bastion of Protestantism. Every July the annual Orange Lodge march would snake past the ground, pausing to salute the symbol of Calvinism. Celtic similarly held mass at Parkhead at the start of every season. Homage to Rangers or Celtic was more than support for a football team, it was support and devotion to a way of life. But all this was about to change when Graeme Souness made a move to sign a man who was not only a practising Catholic but a man who had recently played for their greatest rivals, Glasgow Celtic. Souness was about to face his biggest test as he engineered another step in the Ibrox revolution. The moment of truth had arrived.

Souness first had the notion of signing Johnston in early July 1989. For the best part of the summer it had looked as if Johnston was about to return to his former club Celtic. Celtic had sold Johnston to the French club Nantes in June 1987 for £1 million but after two seasons in French football there were whispers that Johnston would not be averse to a move back home. But just when it seemed that Johnston was set for a return to his beloved Parkhead, the deal fell through. It had dragged on for weeks as the two sides haggled over terms.

Johnston, confident that he would soon be a Celtic man again, had even been photographed clutching a Celtic shirt to his chest. It was a photograph that would come to haunt him.

During his time in France, Johnston had matured, learning to cope with the tight marking of continental football and the physical intimidation of foreign defenders. More importantly, he had discarded the pack who usually accompanied him around Glasgow, particularly to the wine bars and clubs. Souness had watched him play for Scotland and had been impressed with his new attitude. It suddenly occurred to him that, with Celtic now declaring their interest in Johnston at an end, the popular young player might be available for transfer to some other club. His protracted transfer to Celtic seemed to signal that he was not against a move, and Scotland was obviously near the top of his agenda. Souness would have to act quickly before any English clubs had the same thought. But there was one major stumbling block – Johnston was a Catholic.

Souness approached his assistant Walter Smith to test the waters. Smith smiled. He knew Scottish football but agreed that Johnston would be a valuable addition to their squad. It was clear what was on his mind. Within moments of Souness' first question to Smith, religion had raised its ugly head. The two men sat opposite each other for the next hour considering the religious question. How would Johnston react to an approach by Rangers, how would the fans respond? Would it be worth it? And on top of that Johnston was said to have quit Celtic in order to escape the unbearable microscope of Glasgow football that would splash you across the front pages if you had anything more intoxicating than a cup of tea or were seen out with a woman other than your sister.

For the past thirty years, perhaps even more, the first question posed to any new Rangers manager was 'Will you sign a Catholic?' The stock reply was 'Yes, if I find one up to our standards.' Of course, they never did. The fact that Celtic had managed to win the European Cup with Catholic players seemed to have escaped Rangers. Souness was asked the same question when he joined the club in April 1986. And he gave much the same response. But with Souness there was always a suspicion that maybe he meant it. At the time he was adamant. 'How could I have possibly taken on this task if I could not have signed Catholics?' he insisted, revealing a particularly important factor that most supporters were not aware of. 'I am married to one and share my life with one. I could not have returned to Italy and told my wife I had the job but there was a problem with Catholics.' At the time Souness and his wife Danielle were still living together. She was a devout Catholic as the Scottish papers were soon to tell everyone. Even that was to cause a few problems for Souness. Heaven forbid, a Catholic inside the tabernacle.

Souness did mean it as well. He was contemptuous of the parochialism and sectarianism. He might have been a Protestant himself but a Catholic wife, a couple of seasons in Italy, a lifetime of football in England, all were enough to have shifted his horizons beyond the religious divide. His years in Liverpool, where tolerance had overcome decades of similar divisions, would at least have taught him that there was another side to bigotry. Souness may have hailed from Edinburgh but most pundits will tell you that although Edinburgh football has its religious affiliations, it has none of the intensity and vitriol that taint the game in Glasgow.

In his first season at Ibrox, Souness had tried to sign the Oxford United midfielder Ray Houghton. Houghton was a Catholic boy from Glasgow, who had even opted to play for the Republic of Ireland. Houghton knew all about Glasgow football and to be a Republic of Ireland international playing for Rangers would have been more than unique. Souness approached Houghton but it didn't take the Oxford man long to reject the idea. When the whispers turned into backpage speculation, the hate mail poured into Ibrox and through Houghton's letterbox. No way was he going to be the first man through the sectarian barrier. A spurious excuse was made up about not being able to agree money but nobody believed it, especially given some of the big deals that would be agreed a short time later. Instead, Houghton signed for Liverpool.

Souness and Smith agreed that a Catholic had to be signed some time. A century of primitive tribalism had to end. Celtic, although they were predominantly a Catholic club, had long since broken with tradition by signing Protestant players. In Kenny Dalglish they had signed a Protestant who would normally have been expected to join Rangers. The young Dalglish had waited, expecting Rangers to knock on his door. Instead, it was Celtic's Sean Fallon who turned up and signed the young lad. The result of that deal was there for everyone to see.

Souness knew that it was no use signing a Catholic simply for the sake of it. The player had to be right for the club. It had to be a player of the highest calibre and with enough character to resist the torrent of criticism and abuse that would come raining down from all sides. It was no good making a token appointment just to satisfy the liberals. Whoever joined would set the trend for the future. If someone came and failed, then it could harm the cause of religious harmony, as well as Rangers Football Club, for decades. Future managers would tread warily at the prospect of signing Catholics, even if they were of world-class calibre. Mo Johnston fitted the bill. He was an outstanding player, a strong personality, likeable. But he also had the additional problem of having played with Celtic. In a city where Old Firm inter-club transfers were unknown, Celtic fans would be unforgiving. It was a double whammy. Johnston would become just about the most unpopular man in Glasgow. But before they could even approach Johnston, Souness needed first to discuss it with club chairman David Murray.

It was the installation of Murray as the club's new owner in the autumn of the previous year that really paved the way for progress. Murray, a self-made millionaire, shared Souness' vision of a club that could be talked of in the same breath as Real Madrid, Barcelona and AC Milan. Murray was astute enough to know that it would never happen as long as the religious divide continued to taint Scottish football. Sectarianism could only stifle progress on the field. Murray, like Souness, was not a Glasgow man and was largely immune to the religious bigotry of the west coast. Murray found the Glasgow preoccupation with religion baffling. He didn't run his multi-million pound international business on religious grounds. He employed the best people for the job, irrespective of their religion. It made business sense as well as common decency to employ people for their ability and not which church they attended on a Sunday. All the parts were in play; a new owner, a new manager, ambition and vision. All that was needed was the final go-ahead. Murray had no hesitation.

Souness' next move was to contact Johnston's agent, Bill McMurdo, to get an early indication of how his client might react to such a deal. If his response was going to be the same as Ray Houghton's then there was little point in taking things any further. McMurdo was surprised but thought that Johnston might just fancy a year or so with Rangers. McMurdo said he would get in touch with Johnston immediately and come back to them. McMurdo was not long in responding. The indications were favourable and a meeting was set up at Orly Airport on the southern side of Paris, venue for internal flights to and from Nantes. Secrecy was of the utmost importance. It was vital that the Glasgow press did not get hold of the story. If they did, it could scupper the deal. There would be an outcry. Souness wanted the whole deal sewn up before anyone had any inkling. Souness flew to Paris with Alan Montgomery, chief executive of Rangers, where the pair of them waited, trying to remain as anonymous as possible, for Johnston and McMurdo to arrive on a flight from Nantes.

Eventually the four of them met up and retired to a small café. Over a coffee and dark glasses the proposition was formally put to Johnston. Much to Souness' delight, Johnston was more than ready to sign. They discussed the religious question but Johnston did not seem unduly perturbed by it. Nobody knew quite what would happen and Souness could give no assurances. He could only guess at what the reaction might be from the Rangers fanatics. The four men reached a verbal agreement, shook on it and made their way back to their respective clubs and braced themselves for the bomb that was to fall. There would be a formal signing ceremony at Ibrox.

It was the *Sun* who broke the story, on the morning of 10 July 1989, splashing its exclusive across the front page of its Scottish edition. It was a sensation. Even south of the border, the news was greeted with incredulity. In Glasgow it was the biggest soccer story in decades. Not only had the ex-Celtic man finally turned down a return move to his old club, but he had crossed the city to join the Gers. That in itself would have been a big enough story without the fact that Johnston was the first Catholic to sign for Rangers in nearly a century. It was that simple fact which took the news from the back pages onto the front pages. You didn't need to be a football fanatic to know the significance of this story.

Later that morning the story was confirmed as Souness

introduced Johnston to the waiting press in the famous
Blue Room at Ibrox. Even then most journalists could
barely believe it. The deal had been formally signed with
David Murray just moments before. Johnston was now
officially a Rangers player. The cameras flashed. 'Rangers
are a great club,' Johnston told the gathered journalists,
'and I'm glad to have joined them.' Really? Is that the
way you felt when you were sent off playing against them
a few years ago? It was stretching credulity to its limits. It
was the greatest conversion since St Paul. More cameras
flashed, journalists looked at one another, microphones
were thrust towards the young man. One hundred and
sixteen years of tradition had been torn down. There
could have been a third world war about to break out but
it would have passed Scotland by. There was only one
story north of the border. Rangers had signed a Tim;
it was all you could read about in the papers for the
next week.

'The Mo Johnston story was phenomenal up here,' says
Jim White, Scottish Television's football correspondent.
'It was like an earthquake. People were staggered. I don't
think Graeme Souness thought about it in a conscious
way. He simply saw Mo Johnston and rated him as one
of the best strikers in Europe and knew that Rangers
could afford him. He wanted the best.'

One Rangers fan telephoned his brother on the west
coast of America. It was the early hours of the morning.
A half-asleep voice asked, 'What's the matter, has somebody in the family died?' 'No,' came the reply from Glasgow, 'it's worse than that, Rangers have signed a
Catholic.'

Souness later said, 'I would like to think that maybe
this decision will make it easier in the future for whoever
else becomes manager of the club. They won't have to
face up to the particular problem of religious discrimi-
nation which bedevilled my first three years at Ibrox.

This is now a thing of the past. Hopefully it will soon be forgotten.'

It was an astonishing admission by Souness that the religious question had 'bedevilled' his first three years in office. There had been no hint of it in any public statements but privately he was clearly being harassed. As far as Souness was concerned, the signing was 'a milestone' and indeed it was. But there was also something of the showman in Souness. It wasn't just a case of signing a Catholic, it was also the chance to put one over Celtic.

The reaction among Rangers fans was predictable. There was disbelief. Eventually most accepted the manager's decision but for many the presence of a Papist in the hallowed corridors of Ibrox was tantamount to treachery. Letters poured into the local papers, scarves were burned outside the ground, season tickets torn up and a sworn campaign against Souness initiated. In Belfast they burned effigies of the manager. And on the walls around Glasgow's east end the graffiti told its own story. 'Mo Surrender', 'Souness You Roman Bastard' and more chillingly, on the walls of Bellgrove station, 'Collaborators Can't Play Without Kneecaps'. Belfast, the IRA, the loyalist cause. Suddenly there was a nasty whiff in the air.

Johnston was forced into hiding. For a time he was holed up in Souness' luxury Edinburgh home while the tabloid press hunted him, high and low. His family were threatened, there was a failed arson attempt at Souness' Edinburgh home and a quiet Saturday night for Johnston in his favourite trattoria became impossible. The club were even forced to hire a 'minder' who tagged along wherever Johnston ventured. When he arrived for training the minder would be there, carefully watching, and when Johnston left, the minder went in tow. Such is the power of religion.

But even though Souness and company almost certainly underestimated the reaction that would follow the signing of Johnston, the outcry was largely hollow. Johnston was at least given a warm reception, if not a hero's welcome, when he appeared in the blue shirt of the Gers for the first time and, by the end of his first season, the Govan True Blues Rangers Supporters Club had even voted him player of the year. Another supporters club took a different attitude. They loathed the defiance of sectarianism, the compromise with Catholicism. As far as they were concerned, Johnston was a Tim and not a Rangers man. At the end of the season they wiped his goals from the record and placed Rangers in second place in the league instead of first. It was a small price to pay for loyalty.

The bulk of criticism was to arise at the club's annual general meeting, a month later. More than 2,000 gathered, the largest audience for years. Everyone had come to gloat at the expected confrontation. Demonstrations had been promised with talk of walk-outs, punch-ups and boycotts. Murray and Souness each explained the decision and then sat back to take the punches on the chin. The blows, verbal of course, came thick and fast. They have long memories in Glasgow and nobody had forgotten how Mo Johnston, as he was being sent off playing for Celtic against Rangers in the 1986 League Cup final, had turned to the crowing Rangers supporters and given the sign of the cross. But in the end it was only a small minority, and an insignificant minority at that, who were hurling the abuse across the floor. With Murray and Souness clutching the bulk of club shares the shareholders' meeting was little more than a sounding board and a rubber stamp. In the end the expected demonstration fizzled out and 116 years of bigotry had been cast aside. For the moment at least.

Inside the club itself there were no problems. Even the west coast players took to Johnston immediately. On his first day they laid a separate table for him, some distance from the team's usual table, and placed a little bread and water on it. Johnston saw the funny side. Ally McCoist is adamant that there was no ill feeling inside the club. 'Mo was totally accepted by the entire Rangers squad. There were rumours circulating that, just as some Rangers supporters objected to Mo's signing, so did some of the players. Nothing could be further from the truth. Even the true Blues in the team, lads like Ian Durrant and Ian Ferguson who had been life-long Rangers fans, loved him and still speak warmly of him today.'

Five years on, however, anyone could be forgiven for wondering what had happened to Souness' preaching of religious tolerance. Souness himself did not sign any more Catholic players, although it was reckoned that another leading Rangers player was a Catholic but that it was kept quiet. The experience may well have shocked him though it is unlikely that that alone would have deterred him. Perhaps it simply gave everyone cause for thought. Johnston went on to play 65 games for the Rangers, scoring 26 goals, and four months after his arrival was reported in one paper to have been spotted singing 'The Sash' at a Masonic Lodge bash. After the departure of Graeme Souness the flame-haired Johnston ironically followed his manager to Merseyside, signing for Everton. In the three years since Souness' departure from Ibrox, the expected floodgates have never opened.

If religious intolerance is one thing, racial intolerance is an altogether thornier problem. Rangers could perhaps be forgiven for never having signed a black player in their chequered history. After all, black players had never even really emerged in English soccer until the sixties. The immigrant populations that had sprouted up around the country during the fifties had largely homed in on areas such as the Midlands, London, the North West and parts of industrial Yorkshire while Glasgow, and Scotland in general, had attracted only a small number of immigrant settlers. What's more, those communities that did exist in Scotland tended to be Asian rather than Afro-Caribbean. And it was the Afro-Caribbean communities that were producing footballers rather than the Asian communities. The numbers of West Indians north of the border remained small and, as a result, the number of black players has always been significantly fewer than in England.

The first black player in Scotland is reckoned to have been John Walker of Leith Town who signed for Hearts in 1898. But Scotland's best known black player was probably Victor Kasule. Born in Glasgow, Kasule played with Hamilton Academicals, Meadowbank Thistle and Albion Rovers during the eighties as well as Shrewsbury Town in the English league. Kasule was criticised for what a number of managers described as 'his attitude', which was code for 'he has a chip on his shoulder'. Celtic had been the first Glasgow club to boast a black player, back in the early fifties, when the American Giles Heron had pulled on the green and white hoops. But he only lasted a couple of seasons. Then late in 1987 along came Mark Walters.

Souness had already signed a plethora of Englishmen, including Colin West, goalkeeper Chris Woods, Terry Butcher, Graham Roberts, Trevor Francis, Ray Wilkins and Mark Falco. Now he was about to sign Rangers' first black player in fifty years. An Egyptian, Mohamed Latif, played for Rangers during the 1930s while still a student in Glasgow. It was a neat progression, breaking down the barriers one by one. The English players, now a black player and finally tearing down the biggest barrier of all by signing Rangers' first Catholic.

Birmingham-born Walters had spent all his footballing days in the Midlands with local club Aston Villa. There he had picked up England Under-21 honours and looked to have a bright future ahead of him. He may have been a delicate-looking lad but he carried a deceptive turn of speed which Souness fancied might catch leaden-footed Scottish defenders on the hop. He agreed a fee of £500,000 with Villa, then tipped off Jim White at Scottish Television about the signing, adding wickedly 'he's different'. Walters was the first black player inside Ibrox. The Celtic fans dubbed him Jaffa, black on the outside, orange on the inside. The newspapers, more politely, said he was a black in blue.

Souness could not have signed Walters at a worse moment, just in time to make his debut in an Old Firm clash. It was New Year's Day 1988 and as Walters took the field he was predictably greeted with a chorus of abuse that ranged from monkey calls to being dubbed a 'hun'. As expected, it was accompanied by a barrage of fresh fruit. Much of it of course was hurled along with the abuse by Celtic supporters, but there were more than a few racists in the Rangers ranks as well. The club hardly helped, allowing Walters to be photographed on the Ibrox pitch, dressed in kilt, sporran and black bow tie. It was not in the best of taste, simply helping to underline that Walters was somehow different, out of the ordinary, and didn't he look funny in a kilt. If the fans didn't initially like the idea of a black playing in blue, they soon became used to it. Another barrier had been torn down and it was all credit to Souness. Walters was soon delighting with a trick or two down the flanks. And if his commitment to Rangers was ever in doubt it was dispelled in the Old Firm battle of Mad Sunday, 17 March 1991, when he was sent off, battling for the Rangers.

Englishmen, a black and then a Catholic; Souness' revolution had certainly changed the face of one part of Glasgow, if not the whole of Scottish football. Step by step he was chipping away at the traditions and age-old fears that had shackled Scottish soccer. He was preparing

Rangers for the future and now that he was a director as well as manager he could influence events off the field as well as on it. David Murray might have had the larger stake in Rangers but there was little doubting who was the real Mr Rangers.

CHAPTER EIGHT
The Leaving of Ibrox

Graeme Souness sat in the directors' box at Parkhead. He was watching Rangers face Celtic in the Scottish Cup. It was not a good afternoon. Rangers crashed out of the competition, losing 2–0 to their old rivals. That was bad enough but from a personal point of view there was another irritation. The Celtic fans sitting in front of him had spent most of the second half with their backs to the game. Instead of watching the play they had spent most of the afternoon yelling obscenities in his direction and gesturing at him as he sat, eyes fixed firmly ahead of him. They were barely concerned with what was happening on the pitch; nor were they a minority, nor even the lumpen proletariat of Parkhead's Jungle. They were smartly dressed men sitting in the stands and yet they still harboured the appalling prejudices of their religion. At that moment, in that single snapshot, Souness, like many intelligent men before him, must have realised that the Scottish game had its limitations.

It had been almost five years since Souness had arrived in the west end of Glasgow. During that time Rangers had leapt to the top of Scottish football and had remained there. By February 1991 he could claim three Scottish league championships and four Scottish League Cups. Ibrox was the pick of stadiums north of the border and one of the finest in Britain. What's more, it was virtually full for every home game. Gates which had slumped to below 15,000 before his arrival were now averaging more, than 40,000 with over 33,000 season ticket-holders. Gate receipts were staggering, with between £320,000 and £350,000 a week coming through the turnstiles. Souness had created a revolution in Scottish football that few could deny.

His successor Walter Smith is one of many who acknowledge Souness' crucial role. 'There is no doubt,' he has said, 'that without Graeme Souness this club would not be where it is today.' David Murray says much the same. Souness filled Ibrox with expectation. He plundered the English leagues, signing top quality English internationals and even raided the Serie A in Italy and the French league to bring superstars Trevor Francis, Ray Wilkins and Mark Hateley to the dusty streets of Glasgow. All the time he was adding new and further dimensions to Scottish football. No longer the underdog, eager to sell its talented youngsters to the English predator, Rangers themselves had become a predator, bringing a fresh pride to Ibrox and Scotland. If the England manager wanted to check on his players he now needed to visit Ibrox as well as Anfield, Old Trafford and Highbury. It was a neat reversal of one hundred years of history.

But more than that, Souness had dragged Scottish football into the twentieth century. As well as raiding south of the border he had broken with tradition by signing a Catholic. It may have brought the wrath of freemasonry and Calvinism down on him, but it was a necessary and undeniably brave act. He had also bought Rangers' first black player, breaking down yet more barriers of prejudice and intolerance. But there was another view. The chairman of one Scottish Premier League club is scathing of Souness. 'Some clubs will go bankrupt because of him,' he argues. 'Souness paid outrageously high wages and generally inflated the transfer market as well. None of us could compete.'

He cites the example of one player signing for Rangers. 'I'll double whatever you earn,' Souness told the player in an attempt to persuade him to sign. The player, who was actually on £250 a week, immediately claimed he was on £500 a week. Souness doubled it to £1,000 and the player promptly reached for pen. Rangers could certainly afford it but for the smaller clubs it was an additional pressure on their purses. Big crowds in Scottish football are restricted to the Glasgow giants. Average gates at Aberdeen, Hearts, Hibs and the two Dundee clubs are all under 10,000, barely enough to pay the wages bill, let alone anything else. It's easy to see why some of them felt pressured by the Souness school of spending.

But it was in Europe that Souness had hoped to notch up his greatest achievements. It had been his ambition to turn Rangers into another AC Milan, a club and team that could compete on equal terms with any of the great European clubs. But in five seasons of trying Souness had never managed to progress beyond the quarter finals of one of the major European competitions. Rangers did not achieve all that might have been expected. There were moments of individual glory, particularly against Dynamo Kiev, but generally their European campaigns were uninspired, smacking of fear and a lack of self-belief. In his first season they progressed uneasily past the part-time Finns Ilves Tampere in the first round of the UEFA Cup, even losing in Finland, before then beating Boavista of Portugal in the next round. In the third round they faced the Germans Borussia Moenchengladbach. It was always obvious that as soon as they came across any formidable opposition, they would crumble. And so it was, as Rangers lost their heads as well as their feet. Stuart

Munro and Davie Cooper were both sent off in an ill-tempered goalless second leg in Germany.

The following season they were in the European Cup, beginning impressively with a victory over Dynamo Kiev, winning the second leg 2–0 after losing 0–1 in Kiev. They then defeated Gornik Zabrze before meeting Steaua Bucharest in the quarter finals but went down 3–2 on aggregate. It was the only time they would reach the last eight of a European competition during Souness' reign.

In season 1988/89 they were in the UEFA Cup once more but managed only to reach the second round where they lost to Cologne. The following year, in the European Cup, German opposition was again their undoing as they went out at the first hurdle, soundly beaten by Bayern Munich. In Souness' final season, Rangers fared little better, this time going out at the second hurdle in the European Cup to Red Star Belgrade. It was not an impressive record and one that caused much soul-searching. If Europe was Souness' criterion, then he had failed.

The resignation of Kenny Dalglish as manager of Liverpool Football Club sent shock waves through the city of Liverpool. There had been nothing like it since the day Bill Shankly walked out on the club. It was so totally unexpected, and the reasons for Dalglish's quitting simply begged questions rather than provided any answers. Dalglish was the ultimate hero, a player who had brought glory to the club. Honours, international caps and trophies galore had swept his way. He had smashed goalscoring records both north and south of the border and was the highest capped player in Scottish history. He had been the perfect signing in the wake of Kevin Keegan's much publicised departure for Hamburg, perhaps the only player in Europe who could equal the professionalism, dedication and flair of Keegan. Keegan's departure, viewed with more than a touch of bitterness by Liverpool fans and a few players, was soon forgotten as the Kop took to its new hero. For thirteen years Dalglish had plundered the footballing fields of Europe in the red of Liverpool. Graeme Souness rated him the most consistent player in world football and it was undoubtedly Dalglish's dash and devilishness that inspired Liverpool to add another three European Cups to the one they had already won with Keegan. With Dalglish as their inspiration, Liverpool became the most feared club in Europe.

Then, in a surprise move on the eve of Liverpool's ill-fated European Cup final against Juventus at the Heysel stadium in Brussels, Dalglish was heralded as the new player-manager. For many his appointment came as a surprise. It broke with the club's well-known tradition of promoting the next in line from the bootroom. Bob Paisley had been Bill Shankly's assistant and in turn Joe Fagan had been Paisley's assistant. In the normal run of events it had been expected that Fagan's assistant, Ronnie Moran, would step up into the top job. But for once the old order was cast aside and in an unprecedented move for Liverpool Football Club, a player was suddenly promoted to player-manager. Dalglish was to be the first player-manager in the history of the club.

To begin your new job with thirty-nine people lying dead on the terraces was hardly the ideal start. Heysel cast a dark and depressing shadow over Liverpool Football Club that even to this day has never been fully erased. Liverpool fans stood accused, the finger of blame pointing directly at them. And inevitably some of the tarnish rubbed off on the club. Liverpool fans, for all their faults, had always been recognised as among the friendliest of travelling supporters. They may have had a reputation for thieving but they were not renowned for their thuggery. Into this abyss stepped Dalglish.

His naivety was apparent from the start. A shy, diffident spokesman, he found the glare of the world's press

and his new status more than he could cope with at times.
And yet, despite this inauspicious start that included
a lengthy ban from European football, Dalglish quickly
returned the trust put in him by going on to win the
Double. Only two other managers this century had previously achieved that honour and yet Dalglish had done it
in his first season. In his brief reign as manager Dalglish
collected three league titles and two FA Cups, coming
within a whisker of the Double on two more occasions. He
was without question not only one of the most successful
players the game had ever produced but had now proved
that he was one of the game's most astute managers.
What's more, he had with John Barnes and Peter
Beardsley forged a team that was one of the most attractive in post-war football. No longer could the backpage
critics accuse Liverpool of producing successful but boring
sides. Former England winger Tom Finney reckoned their
5–0 defeat of Nottingham Forest was the finest performance he had ever seen by any team anywhere in the
world. 'Something to rank alongside the Brazilians at
their best,' he insisted.

Dalglish was part of the Anfield furniture. If he had
shown his naivety after Heysel, never was he more
imposing than in the wake of the tragic horror of Hillsborough. In those dark days after the disaster that
left ninety-five Liverpool supporters dead, it had been
Dalglish who had held the club together with his
dignified words and sentiments. When people were
lost for thoughts and the city stood confused in the chaos,
Dalglish provided support, comfort and vision. And yet,
unknowingly, he had suffered as well, drained by the
appalling events as much as anyone else. Nobody but his
closest family circle were aware of just how much he had
been affected.

Then suddenly he was off, dramatically quitting the
club just as the season was reaching its climax, quoting

exhaustion as his reason. The decision had been fermenting in his mind for months. He had considered the possibility of quitting during the summer, but after a refreshing break had returned to his desk. But the nagging doubts and exhaustion turned out to have only been on temporary hold. Once the rough and tumble of the football season was under way, he felt himself being drowned again in a sea of problems and pressures. It was all too much and on the morning of Thursday 21 February 1991 at a regular meeting he held with the club chairman Noel White and secretary Peter Robinson he finally voiced his anxieties and took the dramatic decision that was to rock the world of soccer. An emergency board meeting was called that afternoon where Dalglish once again explained his dilemma.

He told the directors that during the week he could cope but as Saturday came round he found the pressures unbearable. 'I feel as if my head is exploding,' he told them. The board tried desperately to find a way out of the problem, even offering him the chance to take time off until the beginning of the next season. But Dalglish, typically, had made up his mind and was sticking with his decision. The following day a press conference was arranged and a weary-looking Dalglish this time tried to explain his decision to a shocked Liverpool public.

It was not just the city of Liverpool who were stunned but the entire football world. In the league, Liverpool were in pole position, they still had hopes in the FA Cup and looked set to add at least one more trophy to their collection. How could Dalglish resign in such circumstances? Dalglish tried to explain. He told a surprised press:

It is a decision that has taken me a long time to come to. The worst decision I could have come to was not to make a decision. I was putting myself under enormous pressure because of my desire to be successful. Basically it was just the build-up to matches and the aftermath that was a problem. I have been involved in football since I was seventeen. This is twenty years with two of the most successful clubs in Britain. I've been in the front line throughout this time, and it is as a result of twenty years' active involvement at the highest level that a person is pushed to the limit.

At the time few believed him. Only later would they acknowledge his frankness and begin to understand the torment and pressure that he had been suffering. There were some who pointed to Dalglish's ageing team and suggested that he could not face the daunting prospect of rebuilding the side. They reckoned he was getting out before the inevitable consequences began to show and the task took on impossible proportions. Although there was no truth in this suggestion, Dalglish's ageing side was to be at the heart of the club's problems over the next few years. Not simply because of the legacy which Dalglish had left but as much due to the over-zealous steps which his successor would take.

The search for a new manager began immediately. Not surprisingly, given that this was the number one job in British soccer, there was considerable press speculation. Assistant manager Ronnie Moran was immediately handed the task of looking after the side until a suitable candidate was found. And inevitably his name was among those suggested. Moran, however, seemed to be only half-interested, happy to help out loyally but not quite sure if he really wanted to take on the responsibility. He had witnessed at first hand the pressures that had overcome Shankly and Dalglish. Had he shown any inclination the job could have been his. 'Had he come to us and insisted that we made him manager, rather than to simply carry on as a caretaker manager, then he would have had the job,' argued the club's vice-chairman Sydney Moss shortly before his death. 'But he seemed to lack the motivation, determination and desire to be manager.' A fine soldier, perhaps the club's finest ever sergeant major, but not quite officer material.

Moran fell by the wayside, not helped either by a string of poor results that saw Liverpool dismissed from the FA Cup and begin to slide out of contention for league honours. It was hardly unexpected given the psychological shock of losing Dalglish. But it did little to help Moran's cause. Liverpool needed to make an appointment urgently and there was no lack of candidates. Yet Liverpool delayed. They were reported to be talking to John Toshack and one or two other names were being thrown into the ring. But it was all tactics. There was a very good reason for the delay.

Almost from the start the one name that cropped up on everyone's list was that of Graeme Souness. But Souness seemed also to be instantly counted out. In his book of the 1988/89 season *A Manager's Diary*, he had said of his job at Ibrox: 'I don't want to leave. Ever. Only failure will move me out of the manager's office at Ibrox.' He insisted that he was still happy at Rangers where he was not only manager but a director and extremely well paid. He had a substantial financial stake in the club, almost certainly the wealthiest in Britain, had a close friendship with the club's millionaire owner David Murray and was winning every honour in the Scottish game. Why should he leave Glasgow where his future was so secure? The press acknowledged that there seemed little sense in his moving to Anfield and quickly shifted its attention to the next candidate – John Toshack.

Souness might have been forgotten by Fleet Street but not by Liverpool. What the press did not know was that Souness and Liverpool had already been in touch through

111

a third party. Initially, Souness said 'no', he was not interested. The board was not altogether surprised and turned their thoughts to other contenders. Then a couple of days later Liverpool received a call from Souness. He had been thinking it over. He had decided that he was indeed interested and wanted to be their next manager. The board liked that kind of attitude. They needed a winner, someone like Dalglish, someone who knew the Liverpool style, someone the players would respect. Souness had proved himself north of the border and in his playing days at Anfield had been the most determined and one of the most successful captains in the club's history. They remembered that at Anfield. There were no dissenting voices on the board. Souness was the man for Liverpool and a meeting was quickly set up. Contrary to public and press belief, no other candidate was even seriously considered.

The meeting was held in the strictest secrecy. Given Souness' contract with Rangers it was crucial that no word leaked out. After all, he still had three years of a five-year contract remaining. At the meeting Souness insisted that he wanted, more than anything, to manage Liverpool Football Club. Glasgow Rangers might have been a big club but Liverpool were the club with the pedigree. He had enjoyed his happiest playing days with Liverpool and it would be an honour, the highest honour in the game, he argued, to manage them. With the prospect of Europe on the horizon he wanted to be there on the glory trail once more. The board had little need to persuade him. Within hours, a provisional secret deal was put together. Souness would come to Anfield but there was one strict condition. He would not come until the end of the season. He owed David Murray and Glasgow Rangers at least that much loyalty and did not wish to leave Ibrox until another Scottish championship had been clinched. To leave at the penultimate stage of the season with Rangers top of the Scottish league could have a detrimental effect on the players and might jeopardise their chances of winning the title. If that happened one half of Glasgow would never have forgiven him. Souness had no intention of leaving Scotland under a cloud. It was agreed that they would bide their time. Further secret meetings were convened where the financial package was ironed out.

Souness also had one other condition. He wanted to bring Phil Boersma, the Rangers physiotherapist, with him. Although Liverpool knew Boersma from his playing days at Anfield they were not altogether happy, knowing full well that it would not go down well with the current coaching staff. Noses would be put out of joint. Souness was insistent. It was not altogether unusual for a manager to want to bring his own assistant with him but it would be the first time this had happened at Liverpool. Yet nobody was prepared to say no. In the end the club agreed. All they had to do now was hope that they could keep the deal under wraps.

But of course it never turned out like that. It rarely does. Indeed, it was naive to imagine that it ever could. News was bound to leak out and on Tuesday 16 April it hit the back pages with a splash. There was little that Souness could do other than admit that the story was true. In Scotland they were furious; David Murray was livid. He felt betrayed. 'He's making the biggest mistake of his life,' he told reporters. He was also angry with Liverpool, slamming them for 'not having the decency to negotiate on a chairman-to-chairman basis'. They had dealt directly with Souness in secret talks. Murray had known nothing and was angry that both Liverpool and Souness should have gone behind his back. 'His feet are not going to touch the floor going out of here,' Murray confided to the Rangers captain Richard Gough. Murray even demanded compensation from Liverpool and in due

113

course milked Liverpool for every penny he could get. Liverpool, embarrassed at how the news had leaked out, stumped up £400,000. There was little that Souness could say. His friend Murray found it difficult to wish them well. Rangers had been left high and dry with a few crucial weeks of the season still remaining. It was Rangers who now had to set about the task of finding a new manager.

It was a bitter blow for Rangers although for the diehard bigots of Ibrox it was just about what you would expect from the man. 'Graeme Souness was the best thing that ever happened to Rangers,' said one player, adding that 'the second best thing was his going'. At Ibrox loyalty is a prized virtue. Souness had looked settled for life in that small corner of the city. When he arrived in England he only hinted at his reasons for leaving Rangers. 'Certain things happened this year at Rangers or in Scottish football,' he explained, 'that made me think seriously about my future there. I felt I had gone as far as I could with Glasgow Rangers or as far as I would be allowed to go.' He further hinted at problems with the Scottish Football Association but would elaborate no further.

Souness had almost quit in August 1987 after he had been sent off for fouling Billy Stark in a particularly venomous Old Firm game. Chairman David Holmes found him in a state of distress in the dressing room and Souness said he wanted to go. Later that evening, at Holmes' house, Souness was even more adamant. However, Souness turned up as usual on the following Monday, thoughts of resignation behind him.

There was no one, single, reason why Souness quit Rangers but a collection of frustrations. Much of it could be summed up in that one single snapshot as he sat in the directors' box at Parkhead, trying to ignore the taunts of a prejudiced minority. Their vision of football came to a halt at the M78 just south of the city. Glasgow football seemed all too preoccupied with events that happened off the field as much as on it. Had that been the only doubt Souness could have coped with it. But there were other things as well.

Souness had also crossed swords with the Scottish FA on one occasion too many. Rightly or wrongly, it seemed at times that the petty bureaucrats of the SFA were out to teach him a lesson. Another clash with them could lead to even more serious charges and disciplinary action. He was already on a touchline ban that seemed to have dragged on for ever. After the incident with tea lady Aggie Moffat at St Johnstone some members of the Scottish FA had pleaded with Geoff Brown, the St Johnstone chairman, to report the incident, much of which had been deliberately hushed up. Souness was walking a tightrope, which ultimately could have gone as far as a total ban from Scottish football. It was an unnerving tightrope to walk.

On top of all that there was the Scottish fixture list. The Premier League was hardly the most competitive in Europe. Take Celtic, Aberdeen and maybe Hearts away, and what you were left with was a glut of sides who would struggle to survive in the English first division, let alone the English Premier League. The only two clubs who would have a chance of surviving at the top of English football would be Rangers and Celtic. Playing the likes of Hamilton Academicals or Dunfermline Athletic, clubs he had once labelled the 'hammer throwers', four times a season was hardly conducive to top quality football. It only bred complacency on the field and off it. To succeed in Europe, Rangers needed demanding competition every week. They also needed a fixture list that left time for pause and consideration rather than the usual rush through 40-odd games a season. Rangers might go on to win countless more Scottish championships and Scottish Cups but in Europe, where Souness really yearned for success, Rangers would never make much impact. They might be able to compete off the field but on the field they were no match for the likes of Milan, Barcelona or Juventus.

Souness may have attracted some of the top names in English soccer north of the border but in general they were players at the wrong end of their careers. There were exceptions but Butcher, Spackman, Gray, Francis and Wilkins had all seen their best days in the English league. Souness may also have gone a long way to revolutionising the game in Scotland with the signing of Rangers' first Catholic player, Mo Johnston, but dismantling the religious barriers of Glasgow football had turned out not to be as easy as he first supposed.

Five years earlier, Souness had returned to Britain from Italy, a man with horizons widened and a vision of what might be achieved. He had unquestionably made giant strides in Glasgow. He may even have converted many to his ideals, but a substantial number remained, as ever, bigoted, spiteful and blinkered. Scottish Television reporter Jim White reckons Souness had had enough. 'I think he felt that he had gone as far as he could. He could see the insularity of Scottish football. He knew he would never win the European Cup with Rangers but he thought he could with Liverpool.'

Rangers' loss was Souness' gain. For a start there was a £250,000 a year contract with Liverpool, a hefty hike on his salary at Rangers. It made him the highest paid manager in British football. But far more than that were the shares. Souness had a seven per cent stake in Glasgow Rangers which he had bought when David Murray had taken over the club. The shares had given him an automatic seat on the board which at the time looked to secure his future indefinitely at Ibrox. Everyone assumed that when he tired of management he would step upstairs to some executive post as a general manager or overlord.

His stake amounted to 345,000 shares. At the time of his resignation each share was valued at £7. As he left Rangers Souness relinquished his shareholding and walked off with an estimated £2.4 million. It made Souness an extremely wealthy man and, after David Moores, probably the richest man at Anfield. How rich was anybody's guess but it certainly added up to a lot of Armani suits. Souness' wife Danielle told the *Sunday People* in May 1993 that he had boasted to her of having £8 million in the bank.

South of the border, however, there was general agreement that Liverpool had pulled off something of a coup. Souness was the right man for the job; he knew the Liverpool way, had gained managerial experience at the highest level with what some regarded as Britain's top club, and had also widened his horizons by playing in Italy. Most of the newspapers seconded the view that Souness was a winner. 'Only He Could Have Replaced Kenny,' ran the headline in the *Liverpool Football Echo*. Most supporters nodded and it was only the more astute follower of the game with Scottish connections who might have raised a few questions about his appointment. A note of caution was sounded in one of the club's fanzines *Through the Wind and the Rain*. 'I think my main apprehension with his appointment is that he will change too many things at the club as he strives to do it his way rather than on tried and trusted methods,' wrote someone calling himself Jimmy the Jock. But he added a serious question, 'Will he listen to Ronnie Moran for instance? I recall a comment he made in his Rangers days: "I don't listen to anybody – it's been to my detriment that".' Jimmy the Jock had a point. Over the next few years many would come to ask the same questions.

There were signs everywhere. You just had to spot them. Even in the month before he quit Rangers, six of his players had been sent off. Three of them, Terry

Hurlock, Mark Walters and Mark Hateley, had all been dismissed in the infamous Scottish Cup defeat by Celtic. At Dunfermline, Ian Ferguson had also been shown a red card while his £300,000 buy from Morton, Brian Reid, had been given his marching orders against Hibs. But only the brave voiced a dissident view. Winning the Football League would be a far different task from winning the Scottish League.

Souness was duly paraded before the cameras at Anfield. Although Liverpool were only five points adrift of the league leaders, he was under no illusions that he had a mammoth task ahead of him. 'I would say this is a harder job than when I first went to Rangers,' he told the papers, explaining that 'the standard of the team is higher here but the level of expectation is higher too.' He was quick to add, however, that 'our first priority is to see if we can win the championship this season.' The former Liverpool and England captain Emlyn Hughes was one who warned that Souness would face problems. He predicted major changes adding, somewhat caustically, 'and by golly it needs it'. Though quite why when Liverpool were second in the table was mystifying. 'His task will be even bigger than when Shanks took over,' he continued, adding, 'I weep for what's happening at my old club.'

Rangers midfielder Nigel Spackman was in the unique position of having played under both managers. It was Dalglish who had signed him for Liverpool and then Souness who had taken him from Queens Park Rangers to Glasgow Rangers. He had few doubts that Souness was the man for the job. 'I think he's a winner,' he told the local papers. 'He's a bit tougher than Kenny was in certain ways – he's not so easy-going. Kenny and Graeme are both their own men. Kenny used to be in work every day, but there were times when you might only see Graeme twice a week because he had other business like watching games abroad.' He added that 'Graeme has always used Liverpool as an example, saying how good their football is, and I think he's tried to instil that into the players at Rangers.'

Alongside Souness at the press conference sat bootroom evergreen Ronnie Moran and the new apprentice Phil Boersma. Moran smiled and made a short welcoming speech. 'I'll do everything to help,' he said. But there was little conviction in either his voice or his words. 'How did Souness compare with Dalglish when they were both here?' inquired one journalist. Moran hesitated. Souness was 'a man even more ruthless than Kenny Dalglish' he replied but declined to add anything further. His words were to prove right.

CHAPTER NINE
The Littlewoods Supermarket

The Anfield bootroom is the home of legends, a cubby hole where dreams have been conjured over the years. Wherever you go, managers have tried to recreate its mystical powers, though without ever really understanding what those supernatural powers were. Former Liverpool players, reared on its character, have often tried to build bootrooms of their own when they moved to other clubs but never with anything like the success of the original. Recreating it physically is one thing, recreating its character is an entirely different proposition. But still they go on trying. Needless to say, nobody has ever emulated the real thing. There is only one bootroom. Or at least there was.

It is not the bootroom that is important but its spirit. It was always a bootroom, even before Shankly; a simple locker room where the players' boots were stored, cleaned and repaired. But what made the Anfield bootroom different is that it was to here that Bill Shankly and his assistants retired after the day's exertions for a cup of tea and a natter. Here they would chew over the cud, analysing, putting right what might have gone wrong, assessing their team's strengths and weaknesses, debating who they might buy or sell. It was meticulous yet surprisingly democratic. The bootroom was the soul of Liverpool Football Club.

Its caretakers were, for many years, a tightly knit group of men. Shankly, Reuben Bennett, Joe Fagan, Bob Paisley, Ronnie Moran, Roy Evans, Tom Saunders and one or two others. In the true Liverpool tradition they were suspicious of outsiders, always hospitable of course, but always wary. The bootroom boys belonged to a different era. Most of them had played their football in the forties and fifties. Only Roy Evans had ever played the modern game and even he had only made a handful of appearances before being tempted by Shankly into coaching. They looked upon him as a sort of apprentice, learning the trade, a lad who might one day take over from them.

For twenty-five years the bootroom thrived. When Shankly quit, his able assistant Bob Paisley took over, reluctantly. 'I never really wanted this job,' he began his first-ever team talk as manager. Everyone believed him. When Paisley retired there were never even any questions about who would succeed him. It had to be Joe Fagan. Then, with the appointment of Kenny Dalglish as player-manager, in the wake of the Heysel disaster, came its biggest change since Shankly. Dalglish was an outsider. He might have been a player, a man they admired, but he was essentially an outsider, not quite one of them.

Players at Anfield are never invited into this inner sanctum. If they are it's usually just to get a pair of boots or some kit. They are never asked to sit down, have a drink and a chat. The bootroom is for the training staff and although there are few divisions between coaches and players, the demarcation line is firmly drawn here. This is their territory. The arrival of Dalglish, however, was to upset the balance and tradition. Not that Dalglish set out to change the bootroom, he was so superstitious he never dared to change much at all. He might have admired its history but Dalglish was his own man and was not steeped in its traditions. He had never worked within its four walls and although he might have been expected to become a part of it, instead he chose to plot his own course. His tactics were little different from what had preceded him, he simply never consulted in the democratic way that Shankly, Paisley and Fagan had before him.

Dalglish was a man of the modern era, highly paid, a TV pundit, an agent's dream. He epitomised the modern game of football. Paisley and company still lived in their unassuming semi-detached houses in Liverpool; Dalglish preferred his luxurious private home out of town. Paisley and company drove modest family cars; Dalglish swanned about in his Mercedes. Paisley and company preferred a quiet Saturday evening with the family; Dalglish could be found in an Italian restaurant. It was a difference of style, money and horizons. Paisley and company could never have been tempted away from the bootroom to the riches of Real Madrid or the like. No amount of money would have turned their heads. Anfield was their natural home, where they felt most comfortable. The bootroom was not Dalglish's natural home, he was more comfortable in the confines of the dressing room.

Dalglish took the first steps in marginalising the influence of the bootroom. It was not deliberate, nor malicious; it was just the way he was. Dalglish had his own plans and although he consulted from time to time, his ideas were usually firmly set and the influence which the backroom boys could bring to bear was minimal. Moran and Evans remained intact as his assistants; Phil Thompson joined them but, like Dalglish, he was a player of the modern era although his roots belonged on the Kop. No trusted outsiders were brought in, which perhaps in the long run was to have drastic consequences for Dalglish's health. Yet had any outsider been introduced, those inside would only have looked on them with suspicion, as indeed they would when Phil Boersma crossed its door. The black books which had for so many years detailed the daily events at Anfield with their lists of injuries, training schedules, players' fitness levels and even the weather conditions were discarded as Dalglish set up his own routines. The changes were hardly revolutionary but they were there, subtle yet significant. They were the first steps on a road to revolutionary change; the duma before the revolutionary council.

The arrival of Graeme Souness was to be even more of a challenge to the natural order. In appointing Souness the Liverpool directors felt relatively comfortable. Here was a man who wanted the job, a man of proven ability in management and a man interested in the one thing that counted – winning. What's more, his business dealings as a Rangers director spoke volumes for his entrepreneurial ability. He was a man of the eighties, like Dalglish, a product of the Thatcher years. And with his Anfield breeding he seemed the perfect man for the job. But although Souness may have played for Liverpool, the fact that he had managed elsewhere was something which no Liverpool manager had done since Shankly. In the end this was to be the key to his undoing. Souness was to arrive with his own baggage, and his own ideas, already tested in Scottish football but not necessarily applicable to Anfield.

There was something oddly democratic about the boot-room. The old miner–socialist Shankly, his sympathy firmly with those who stood on the Kop, was as much a Labour voter as he was a Liverpool supporter. It was equally hard to imagine that any of his assistants – Paisley, Reuben Bennett or Joe Fagan – were any different. They had been reared through the hard years of football, when players received a maximum wage and little thanks for their endeavours. At the end of their days they might have received a benefit game to help them through the next few mean years but they were not rich men. They may have progressed from the back-to-back terraced houses where they had been born but they were still on the fringes of their communities, neat little semi-detached houses with a small garden, just one step removed from their past but short enough to keep them in sight of their roots. Not like today's footballers, cooped up in their suburban stately homes and driving fast, elegant cars and with children at private schools. It was a million miles away from the high rise flats and council homes of so many of their fans. The football of Shankly was the football of socialism, it was the post-war Government of Attlee, it was the miners, it was about the dignity of the working man. You could hardly imagine Graeme Souness casting his vote for Labour, even for the nineties' watered-down version of social democracy. But then, football, its followers and its players have all changed.

Souness personified the modern Liverpool; commercial, spread-sheet conscious, ambitious. His were hardly the ideals of the old socialist Shankly, who would not have recognised a share certificate if he saw one. Liverpool Football Club is no longer the small corner shop it used to be with its friendly, caring image. Today it is a multi-million pound business, staffed by well-paid executives in Marks and Spencer suits, where success is imperative on and off the field. It is the football of the Premier League; sponsorship, executive boxes, agents, television and seven-figure transfer deals. Here the money is not made on the field, nor even through the turnstiles and programme sales but on the commercial sidelines. Shankly never had to worry about sponsors or hand-slapping in the executive lounges. At the end of a Saturday afternoon he retired to the bootroom for his usual cup of tea. Today's manager has a thousand executive duties in the lounges, or the press room, all playing their part in the club's PR.

Souness is ideally suited to the role. The man can be charm personified. He is articulate, good company, sharp; the perfect man for the public relations task. He is on equal terms with the men of the executive suites, as rich as they are, as commercially successful. Unlike his predecessor whose bluntness was legendary ('How did you see today's game?' asked a journalist innocently. 'From the dugout,' replied Dalglish with never a crack of a smile breaking on his poker face.) Souness will chat openly with journalists about his team, on occasion too honestly. 'He'll just come straight from the dugout and give you an interview,' says Sky director Dermott McQuarrie. 'He doesn't have to prepare and usually doesn't mince his words. Even when Rangers or Liverpool have played badly he'll be honest.'

Souness is the kind of man Thatcherism chose to espouse. Working class, ambitious, decently paid, strident, a firm believer in self-help. Many footballers are the same; high taxpayers trying to secure a future from their short-lived earnings. Souness also chose to espouse Thatcherism. She visited Rangers during his time, all organised by David Murray with his close connections to Number 10, to conduct the draw for the Scottish Cup. Souness was beaming, his players lined up behind him, all immaculately dressed.

But Liverpool Football Club is not, for many Kopites, the club it once was. The cosy corner shop where the customer came first has gone. There was always time for a smile, a chat, not like the bustling, impersonal supermarkets at Old Trafford and Highbury where money and marbled foyers ruled. People mattered at Anfield. It was a thrifty shop but never at the expense of being mean or cost-cutting. Life at Anfield was quiet. A few people would mill around during the week, maybe trying to spot a star or snatch an autograph, but it was only on matchdays that any real crowd gathered. Go to Old Trafford any day of the week and almost any time of the day and you'll see a car park jammed with BMWs and Audi 80s. There are crowds, gangs of kids and grown-ups everywhere, buying tickets, drifting around the souvenir shop, queuing for the museum or simply gawping at the stadium. Old Trafford is supermarket football.

'We'll never have executive boxes at Anfield,' the club once boasted, but by the time Souness arrived plans to install executive boxes were well under way. The corner shop was already set to become a supermarket. You can't pinpoint the precise date, occasion or event that initiated the change but it happened. And nor can you blame any single individual. It was not Dalglish's fault, nor Souness'. If anything it was the fault of ex-Kopite David Moores.

David Moores, of course, is more than an ex-Kopite; he's also a millionaire and with the kind of family background that qualifies him to know more about supermarkets than most. David Moores is the nephew of Sir John Moores, founder of the Littlewoods Pools and shopping empire and the son of Cecil Moores, Sir John's erstwhile partner.

Sir John Moores had begun his famous Littlewoods Pools by selling football coupons outside Goodison Park and Anfield in the early twenties. It was one of the most popular ideas of the age. In 1932 he diversified into mail order catalogues and four years later opened his first Littlewoods store. By 1992 his empire was reporting an incredible annual turnover of £2.5 billion and was employing more than 32,000 people up and down the country. It was also reckoned to be the largest privately owned company in the land. And with the wealth that accumulated from his successes he purchased substantial stakes in both Everton and Liverpool Football Clubs.

During the sixties he was chairman of Everton in the days when they were labelled the 'millionaires' club'. They spent big and went on to win league and FA Cup honours. They called John Moores 'Mr Everton'.

His role at Anfield, however, had always been less upfront. Football League rules restricting directors to just one club meant that he could never really take up the opportunity to be a director of Liverpool. He had made his choice and it was Everton. Even during the seventies when he was still fit enough to have played a part, and no longer on the board at Goodison, he never made any attempts to secure his rightful place on the Liverpool board. In the hothouse of Merseyside soccer it would anyhow have been looked upon as opportunist to switch allegiance suddenly from one club to the other. There can be little doubt, however, that had he wanted a seat on the board, an invitation would have been readily forthcoming. Instead he preferred to simply turn up for each home match, struggling out of his chauffeur-driven car at reception in later years, clutching his blanket, before being helped towards the doors. When Liverpool played Everton, Moores would sit in the directors' box proudly wearing his blue and white Everton scarf.

Yet despite being the largest single shareholder at Anfield, he never questioned or interfered with board decisions, nor demanded changes or attempted to influence the running of the club. He was what accountants would call the ideal 'sleeping partner'. At one time in the late fifties and sixties he did place a nominee on the board, Eric Sawyer, who was a Littlewoods executive. But as everyone, and especially Shankly, has admitted, he brought some much needed professional financial management to the club. By the eighties Sir John Moores' days as an active Evertonian were over though he remained a regular visitor and carefully placed a leading Littlewoods executive on the board at Goodison to oversee his shareholding. It was not until he was into the last few years of his life that his Saturday trips to Anfield and Goodison were curtailed. By then he had turned 90 and was failing fast.

It was the onset of old age that alerted Liverpool to the need to secure a hold on Sir John's substantial shareholding in the club. There were those on the board who realised that when he eventually died his shares could end up anywhere, which in turn might spell trouble for the club. It was not inconceivable that a majority stake might fall into unfriendly hands with the club finding itself on the wrong end of a takeover. And indeed, after his death, Everton found themselves in a quagmire of boardroom intrigue as two opposing parties battled for control of their club. It was a serious concern for Liverpool and one that had not escaped the attention of Sydney Moss, a Liverpool director of some fifteen years' standing. Moss, a genial, old-fashioned Tory who doubled as a Merseyside councillor, was also friendly with David Moores. It was Moss who suggested that Moores might have a role to play. Moores had been a lifelong Liverpool supporter, though more likely to be found on the Kop among his friends than in boardroom circles. He had time and money. When Liverpool travelled across Europe Moores would be somewhere close by. He seemed the natural heir to Sir John's football interests.

The rest of the family had concerns elsewhere. David's father Cecil had always been a keen football follower, a regular visitor at Anfield and Goodison, but John's sons Peter and John junior had never been much interested in the game even though it had initially provided the family fortune. Peter Moores with his Eton education had developed more refined tastes, more at home in the opera houses of the world as well as being a patron to the arts and a former governor of the BBC. John junior was a gentleman farmer, reckoned by some to be a 'bit of a socialist'. He was more than happy to remain anonymous and lend his name to good deeds around the Merseyside area. David was the only one who had inherited his fore-bears' love of the game.

David Moores was also rich. The Littlewoods empire was making annual profits of around £100 million a year. City analysts had calculated that if the company was to be floated on the stock exchange it could be worth as much as £2 billion. By the time of his death, however, Sir John had divested most of his shareholding and the company's shares had been spread among the thirty-two family members – sons, grandchildren and an assortment of nephews and nieces. Nobody from outside the family held any substantial shares. It meant that the total family fortune of the Moores was in excess of £2 billion. Today, David Moores owns some 16 million shares of different varieties in Littlewoods out of a total of around 282 million shares, enough to give him a five per cent stake in the company, worth upwards of £100 million. Nobody could begin to calculate what David Moores is precisely worth – much of it is potential rather than actual – but it was certainly more than the Kopites he had once stood next to week after week.

Liverpool is not a city that has wealth dripping from its buildings. There are undoubtedly some wealthy Mercedes owners cruising its streets but most scousers who do make money generally do so some distance down the M6. And once they have made it they rarely return. What's more, most of them are showbiz stars rather than indus-trialists, accruing their loot in the West End and not the Square Mile. Unlike most cities, Liverpool is noticeably short on millionaires, especially the genuine entre-preneurs. Outside of the Moores family, many of whom have loyally maintained their homes and links in the city, it is hard to name more than a handful of millionaires who still reside on Merseyside.

In 1991 Liverpool Football Club faced a problem. They needed money, not desperately, nor immediately, but certainly at some near point in the future. And although they were far from having to put out a begging bowl it was not a bad proposal to have a millionaire or two on the board. There were a number of expensive projects on the horizon. The Taylor Report, following the Hillsborough Disaster when ninety-five Liverpool fans died, had legislated that Premier League grounds had to become all-seater for the start of the 1994/95 season. It posed a problem for all clubs but in particular it presented a massive headache for the directors of Liverpool. It meant that the Spion Kop, the huge and world-famous terracing behind one of the goals that had once held as many as 27,000 swaying, singing spectators, would have to be seated. Although at the beginning of 1990 the directors had not come to any conclusion as to whether the Kop would simply have rows of seats planted on the terracing or whether an entirely new edifice would be constructed, they knew that whatever proposal they eventually plumped for, it was going to cost many millions of pounds. In the end, the cost turned out to be £7 million with agreement to demolish the Kop and construct an entirely new stand at that end of the ground.

The seating of the Kop also posed an additional problem. New safety measures, taken immediately after Hillsborough, meant that the number of spectators standing on the Kop had already fallen to a maximum of 16,000. The ground's overall capacity had dropped from its record high of almost 62,000 in 1952 to around 40,000. Although the ground had not held more than 60,000 for many years, there had been regular crowds of 50,000 and more throughout the sixties and seventies. A further reduction in the Kop's capacity when it was seated would bring it down from 16,000 to nearer 10,000. For thirty years the team had been performing in front of packed gates at Anfield. The demand for tickets was exceptional, bettered only by Manchester United. There was also a high demand for season tickets, some 30,000 each season. The inevitable reduction in capacity at Anfield would mean less revenue.

More seats were needed elsewhere in the ground to compensate for the loss of space on the Kop. To combat this, the board had already begun an extensive reconstruction of Anfield by agreeing to add an upper tier to the existing Kemlyn Road stand, now known as the Centenary Stand. This would bring the stand's capacity up from to 6,800 to 11,300. New offices, dining suites and executive boxes were also part of an ambitious plan that was costing them £8 million. In total the club was expecting to have to pay out at least £15 million to seat Anfield and to maintain its capacity at a respectable level. The intention was that once all the work had been completed Anfield would still be able to hold 40,000 spectators. But the cost was considerable. The money was not going to come through the turnstiles and nor was it going to come from the sale of players. On the contrary, not only was a massive rebuilding programme necessary for the ground but there was also the need to finance the rebuilding of an ageing side. New players would be needed and, with transfer costs escalating, a further £10 million was required to be put aside for transfer deals. Salaries were also on the increase, costing the club in May 1991 £5.4 million a year, although this sum did include the club's entire staff of 127 employees. A year later the salary bill would be topping £7 million. In the four years between 1989 and 1992 the wages bill more than doubled from £3.1 million to £7.1 million. By far the bulk of that was on players' wages.

Revenue through the turnstiles in 1991 brought in £5.7 million, a slight drop on the previous year. But by 1992 it had shot up to £9.7 million, reflecting the rise in turnstile charges. Sponsorship also brought in £2 million in 1991 and a year later was up to £3.2 million. Of course, there would be additional income from catering, the souvenir shop and programmes but all this added up to a mere £1.5 million, a pittance compared with Manchester United who raised more than half their revenue through off-the-field activities. The deal with Sky Television to screen live matches brought in extra revenue as well and there was also money from the Football Trust to help finance the cost of seating while seats themselves would also bring in extra cash as prices could be increased. The club recognised, however, that with high unemployment in the city, prices could not rise excessively. Running Liverpool Football Club was no longer a ledger and sharp pencil job. It was by 1991 an accountant's nightmare.

The Anfield board, unlike many other Premiership clubs, had never been overflowing with millionaires. There were one or two wealthy directors, but generally the board had been based on sound business principles. There was a solicitor, an accountant, someone who knew about football and one or two others who had crept on with their connections and shares. To become a director all you need are ten shares. With Sir John Smith the largest shareholder on the board with a mere 246 shares, there was no single director with a shareholding powerful enough to dictate policy. That is, until David Moores arrived on the scene.

The Liverpool shares, all 12,000 of them, were fairly evenly distributed, other than for the batch owned by Sir John Moores and the rest of his family. Sir John owned 1,849 shares with his son John junior owning a further 1,174 shares. Sir John Moores' shares were by far the largest single holding even though it was reckoned to amount to no more than a 15 per cent stake. But the total family shareholding brought the Moores' split in the club up to nearer 25 per cent. With Sir John in his nineties and ill, it was essential that his shareholding in Liverpool was kept within friendly circles. And so, in March 1990, David Moores, Kopite extraordinaire, was invited into the inner sanctum.

Moores cut an unusual figure in such refined surroundings. Not for him the pin-striped suit and short-cropped hair. Instead it was ostentation all the way; flamboyant jacket, hair down to the shoulders and heavy rock music in the background. Also in the background would be some of his pals from the Kop. You could hardly mistake him about Anfield or the city. Even his Mercedes had a showy personalised KOP 1 numberplate. The Kopites nick-named him Freddie Boswell after a character in BBC Television's *Bread*. When he was made chairman he was photographed sitting on the bonnet of his Mercedes, his feet astride his KOP 1 numberplate, scarf held, Kop style, high above his head.

Not surprisingly David Moores' entry to the boardroom was hardly greeted with universal enthusiasm. There were some directors who rolled their eyes at the prospect while those supporters long in the tooth were equally astonished. It was not the style Liverpool fans had grown used to from their directors. It might have been what you expected at some clubs, but not Liverpool Football Club. What was the world coming to. Moores may not have had the kind of image normally associated with Liverpool Football Club but there were those in high places who regarded it as a necessary and bitter pill that had to be swallowed.

It was then that the board came up with a clever scheme. In order to raise money they would follow the practice of a few other clubs and have a rights issue of shares. It was agreed to create a further 3,000 shares in the club, worth about £2.1 million, to help finance the £8 million development of the Kemlyn Road stand. The shares were offered to existing shareholders on the basis

A farewell gift for Liverpool – the European Cup, 1984. (*Colorsport*)

Graeme Souness tells an official which way Liverpool were going.
(*Bob Thomas Sports Photography*)

Yet another moment of Anfield triumph. (*Steve Hale*)

Souness of Sampdoria. (*Steve Hale*)

Real men wear vests. Souness at Sampdoria before kick-off. (*Colorsport*)

At home in Genoa. (*Bob Thomas Sports Photography*)

McCluskey carried off; Souness sent off.
Souness' first game in charge of Rangers. (*Colorsport*)

The English connection: Graham
Roberts, Chris Woods and Terry
Butcher. (*Colorsport*)

Mark Walters, Rangers' first
black player, in a not particularly
tasteful pose. (*Glasgow Herald
and Evening Times*)

The picture that would haunt Mo Johnston. A month later he signed for Rangers. (*Glasgow Herald and Evening Times*)

Mo Johnston, Rangers' first Catholic, about to sign. (*Glasgow Herald and Evening Times*)

Ibrox Park, swanky home of Glasgow Rangers.
(*Glasgow Herald and Evening Times*)

Ibrox Park, a stadium fit for a king. (*Glasgow Herald and Evening Times*)

of one share for every four shares. The cost: £700 a share. David Moores agreed to underwrite the deal, promising to buy up any shares that were not sold. In the event, barely any of them were sold, and Moores, buying up the remainder, became overnight the largest single shareholder in the club. It was the first time the Moores family had really put any money into Liverpool Football Club and at the very least it entitled David Moores to become chairman.

Within eighteen months Moores had progressed from Kopite to director and finally to chairman, taking over from the Manchester-based retired hotelier Noel White on the evening of 29 August 1991. It had to be an all-time record and he was still only 46 years old. It was always on the cards. Indeed, it was all part of the plan. Moores was no business genius masterminding a boardroom coup. He had been deliberately brought in with the intention of succeeding to the highest office. By May 1992 Moores owned 3,101 shares in the club, roughly 20 per cent of the total. Added to Sir John Moores and John Moores junior's shares, it meant that the Moores family had just over a 40 per cent holding in the club. The next highest shareholder after the Moores dynasty was the former chairman and current director Sir John Smith with his 246 shares, followed by Noel White with 208 shares. And it was as principal shareholder and key holder to the treasure trove that he was 'bestowed' with the title of chairman. Sir John Smith, chairman for 17 years in which 22 major trophies had been won, summed it up perfectly. 'The Moores family have been great benefactors to Merseyside football. David's appointment will keep the predators at bay.' At the very least, David Moores' involvement provided stability and a healthy injection of cash. In June 1994 it was announced that there would be a further rights issue, worth £10 million, and David Moores had pledged to underwrite the issue by £8 million, adding even further to his personal stake in the club. By then he had already inherited half of his late uncle's shares. In effect, he had now bought Liverpool Football Club.

Moores was still only in his mid-forties, not much older than Dalglish or Souness. He had got on well with Dalglish. He was to get on even better with Souness; they had much in common. They both enjoyed a night out, a few drinks, they could gossip, talk football and had none of the conventional restraints of the older board members. Nobody called David Moores 'Mr' Moores.

Moores is remembered as something of a playboy when he was in his twenties. Handsome, slim, plenty of money, the most eligible bachelor in town. He was the typical child of a rich family. Ironically Souness' new chairman, like his previous one, David Murray, had also been involved in a horrific car crash. Driving his Jaguar XJS home late one Saturday evening after a meal in a local restaurant, Moores crashed his car on a bend at Formby. The car overturned and ended up in a ditch. Moores himself was not too seriously injured, but his wife was thrown from the car and drowned in the ditch. A former Miss England beauty queen, she was 25 years old and they had been married just eighteen months.

Moores was delighted when Souness became manager. He had watched him as a player and had heard about the revolution he had created in Scottish football. There was every reason to believe that he could do the same for Liverpool, especially the new money-conscious Liverpool. Moores gave wholehearted support to the appointment. Over the next few years Moores would come to idolise the Scot in much the same way that David Murray had once idolised the man at Rangers. Whether his admiration was returned, however, is a different matter. Moores was a loyal supporter all along. He believed in Souness, had been captivated by his charm, and was to be instrumental in keeping him in his job on more than one occasion. At times he was almost a lone voice on the board backing Souness. Without his support Souness would undoubtedly have been out of Anfield a year earlier. When he became chairman Moores had confessed that Souness is 'a man I admire very much'. And when Souness quit the club Moores read out his statement with tears in his eyes.

CHAPTER TEN
Buy, Buy, Buy

The Souness policy of buying and selling players almost like there was no tomorrow had never been more evident than during his early years at Ibrox. In his first season at Rangers he had recruited nine players and sold fourteen in a phenomenal turnover of more than £3 million. Players were coming and going as if there was a revolving door. It was to be much the same at Anfield. And, as ever, there would be question marks over many of his purchases.

All managers like to stamp their personality on a new club. They come in, review the situation, and decide whether or not new men are needed and usually they are. Equally, old players are discarded. When Souness joined Liverpool they were second in the league, just four points adrift of Arsenal, and still in with a chance of the league title. It seemed that only the merest of tinkering was necessary. But that was not how Souness read the runes.

Derby County's Mark Wright had been linked with Liverpool all season. Desperately short of a central defender following the sudden retirement of Alan Hansen, and with their other principal man in the back four, the gangly Gary Gillespie, prone to injury, signing a top-class defender had become a priority. Wright was the obvious choice. Derby were heading for the second division and Wright was now looking for a move that would give him a more appropriate stage for his talents. It was common knowledge that Wright would quit Derby County at the end of the season and Liverpool, with their financial pull and obvious attraction, were always favourites for his signature. It seemed a sensible alliance, the England international joining an all-star line-up. Wright duly signed for Liverpool in July 1991 for a fee of £2.2 million. Everyone was delighted. Wright would plug the fragile gaps that were beginning to appear in the Liverpool defence, reckoned the football commentators. It was a good signing by Souness. Most Kopites would have agreed though in hindsight perhaps they ought to have considered why, if he was such an outstanding defender, Derby had conceded 75 goals that season. But at the same time as Derby County were unloading Wright there were hints that they might also sell their Welsh international striker, Dean Saunders. Relegation was a costly business for Derby and money had become a priority. Saunders had been attracting glowing reports all season, even though Derby had spent most of the season trapped in the bottom zone. Even at his previous club Oxford United he had spent most of his time at the wrong end of the table, and yet he still scored goals. Just think what he might do in a team that was playing well, was the thought going through most people's minds.

And yet Liverpool had seemed indifferent to the young Welshman. There was no press speculation linking him with Anfield, nor any hints that Liverpool were set to swoop. On the contrary, all the talk was of other clubs signing him, with Everton the firm favourites. Liverpool already boasted Ian Rush, John Barnes, Steve McManaman and Ronny Rosenthal for the two spots upfront. They hardly needed an additional striker. But Souness was keen, spurred on by the interest of other clubs. The Wright deal was nearing completion, as expected, when suddenly it became a double deal as Souness dramatically put in an offer of £2.9 million to bring a second Derby County player to Anfield. Derby accepted and Saunders became the most expensive player in Liverpool's history.

But the double signing of Wright and Saunders brought with it an unexpected change. One journalist who had been present for almost every major Liverpool signing in two decades remembers it well.

Whenever Liverpool signed a player, it was always done after training. Every time. We'd be called in after lunch, introduced to the new man, photos would be taken and the official signing would take place. But I remember the Wright and Saunders signing so well. Saunders had been expected to sign for Everton and I know that Howard Kendall thought he had got him. But suddenly at midnight I got this call from Anfield to come over quickly. It was a bit annoying to have to traipse over there when I was about to go to bed. I got there to discover that Saunders and Wright were about to sign. The whole place was alive, everyone was there. The receptionist was still on the door, the telephonist was still there. Souness had kept everyone up. I had never known anything like it. It was so unusual for Liverpool. It was the first change I noticed.

There is no doubt that the signing of Saunders sent a shiver of anticipation through the city. After all, Saunders had a proven track record as a prolific goalscorer. What's more, his father, Roy Saunders had once played for Liverpool and, with his Welsh international striking partner Rush set to play alongside him, it seemed that Anfield would be his natural home.

Saunders' record in the Football League was impressive

enough. He had begun his career with his father's final club Swansea, although his goalscoring ability was rarely evident in those days and in the summer of 1985 he was released by the then Swansea manager John Bond on a free transfer to Brighton. It may have been a humiliating move but it seemed to spark off his goalscoring touch. In his first season with the Seagulls he netted a useful 15 league goals and staked his claim to a place in the Welsh international squad. Two years later he was on his way again, this time to Oxford United where his talents began to fully blossom. The goals flowed, 22 in 57 league appearances, though they were not quite enough to avoid relegation. But more than enough to tempt Oxford chairman Robert Maxwell to cash in on his asset. It was a decision much against the wishes of the Oxford manager Mark Lawrenson, an ex-Liverpool favourite. Saunders was duly sold to Derby County for £1 million. The deal and the row that followed eventually cost Lawrenson his job, although the subsequent value of Saunders and the downfall of Maxwell spoke volumes for Lawrenson's integrity and ability. Oxford's loss was undoubtedly Derby's gain as Saunders shrugged off his £1 million price tag to net 42 goals in 106 games, though yet again his goals failed to halt Derby's slide out of the top division. Saunders was almost a jinx and subsequent events at Anfield did little to dispel the notion.

From the start, however, there were doubts about Saunders. He showed a quicksilver pace and had unquestionable ability, but his first touch regularly seemed to let him down and at Liverpool, with the ball often arriving unexpectedly, a sharp first touch was essential. But above all he seemed to be doing much the same as his partner Ian Rush. In the six-yard box he may have been deadly but so was Rush and there was barely room for the pair of them. He also liked to have the ball played ahead of him but this was hardly the Liverpool style where balls were usually played to feet. Could Liverpool afford the luxury of two players lying in wait in the box for loose opportunities? What Liverpool really needed upfront was someone to play off Rush. The goals duly failed to arrive. In his first season Saunders struck just 10 in 36 league appearances. In Europe he fared better with nine in five games, four of those coming against the amateurs Kuusysi Lahti of Finland. It only added to the theory that against weak defences Saunders was unbeatable but against the more thoughtful defences of the Premier League he had much to prove. There were too many missed opportunities.

The Kop gave him time. They even took him to their hearts, nicknaming him 'Deano', and although Saunders tried desperately hard, sometimes too hard, he still failed to look the part. In fairness, Saunders might have fared better with John Barnes carrying the ball to the by-line but with Barnes sidelined for most of the season there was never much opportunity for them to strike up an effective partnership. Liverpool slumped. It was hardly Saunders' fault but as the most expensive player in Britain he was obliged to shoulder some of the blame. So much had been expected of him. His confidence crumbled and he was the kind of player who needed his confidence boosted rather than destroyed. A parting of the ways was inevitable. It was best for everyone and early in the 1992/93 season Saunders was sold to Aston Villa for £2.3 million. Long before then, however, Souness was said to have offered Saunders in exchange for the Nottingham Forest midfielder, Roy Keane. Souness denied any talk of a deal but the assistant Forest manager was adamant that an offer had been made and that Forest had scathingly rejected it, claiming that 'Keane is worth two Saunders.' He was probably right.

Saunders began his Aston Villa career in fine style as if he had something to prove, even hitting a couple against

Liverpool on his home debut, but his early form soon petered out and by the following season he had gone twenty-five league games with only three goals, forcing Atkinson into the transfer market to sign another striker. Saunders' loss of goalscoring form had cost Villa dearly as they watched Manchester United snatch the title from their grasp. In the end, the failure of Saunders also cost Liverpool dearly. In the transfer market alone they had lost more than £600,000 over fifteen months and on top of that there was a hefty salary. And it was all to no avail. No manager is perfect. Even Shankly, Paisley and Fagan had made a few costly errors. One only needs to think of Tony Hateley, Frank McGarvey, Alun Evans, David Hodgson and Michael Robinson. But this was surely the biggest transfer mistake in the club's history.

At least Saunders and Wright had promised much even if neither settled to produce quite the spark that was anticipated. Wright remained at Anfield but there was always an uncertainty about his ability. He never seemed as assured a defender as Anfield had been used to in the past. Perhaps replacing Hansen and Lawrenson was simply an impossible task. Inevitably, Wright faced comparisons. When Wright and Saunders joined Liverpool there were no raised eyebrows but there was soon a warning of what was to follow. During the next year as players came and went there was little that changed the minds of most Kopites that Souness was not at his best in the transfer market.

Next to arrive at Anfield was Mark Walters. Signed from his old club Rangers for £1.25 million, it brought Souness' summer spending spree to a gigantic £6.35 million. Not only was it the biggest outlay the club had ever made, but the largest by any Football League club in so short a space of time. Mark Walters had begun his footballing career as a fourteen-year-old with Aston Villa. He progressed through the ranks adding England schoolboy, Youth and Under-21 international caps to his honours. He made his debut for Villa in April 1982 just days before turning professional and the following season established himself in the Villa line-up. He looked an exciting prospect but as team form slumped so did Walters. Villa were relegated and the young Walters found himself out of favour as Billy McNeill took charge at Villa Park. Walters, however, survived longer than McNeill but still felt uneasy under his successor Graham Taylor. And so, part way through Villa's second division promotion challenge, Walters quit the Midlands club for the good life in Scotland, registering as Graeme Souness' latest English recruit to Ibrox. The fee: £500,000. The signing of Walters by Rangers was remarkable, but for a reason that had little to do with football. He was the first black player to ever pull on the famous blue shirt of the Gers. It was a courageous decision by Souness, who must have guessed that the bigots of Ibrox would soon be showering their abuse on the pair of them. But at least Walters had one thing in his favour in that xenophobic corner of Glasgow – he was a Protestant. At Rangers Walters was an instant success. He had an open day against flat-footed Scottish defenders, winning a long-awaited first England cap and helping Rangers to the Scottish title.

It was perhaps not surprising that Souness should have turned to Walters in his hour of need at Anfield. With Barnes injured, the new manager was desperate for some additional overlapping skills down the flanks. Walters looked the part. But there were serious doubts even before he had pulled on a Liverpool shirt. Everyone knew that terrorising Scottish defences was a very different proposition from performing a similar task in the Football League. Rangers fans were hardly surprised when Walters left and seemed barely distressed that their former manager was stealing one of their men, though steal was hardly the word for it. Walters left for £1.25 million, giving Rangers a much welcomed profit of £750,000.

From the start, Walters was a disappointment at Anfield. With Barnes injured he had the unique opportunity to establish himself and win over the hearts and minds of the Kop faithful. But, on the contrary, he failed miserably. He was ineffective from the word go. He looked like a player lacking in confidence, overawed by the size and prospect of Anfield. He rarely scored goals, rarely beat a man and even more rarely seemed to cross the ball with much venom. All that he could do was to slot in a neat penalty or two and there were plenty of others around Anfield who could do that. The Kop, normally the most loyal and supportive crowd in football, were scathing, their groans echoing around the ground. In private they were even more vitriolic. Nobody could fathom the attraction of Walters. Why had Souness signed him? He was not a Liverpool player and seemed to have none of the spirit or determination that has always been such an essential element of Liverpool players. Walters had been labelled 'promising' for far too long. He was already 30 years old. And yet Souness persisted. Walters improved little and even as Souness resigned he was still there, managing the occasional game, still a 'promising' 33-year-old and still failing to show any signs of the form that had made him a Souness target. Shortly after Souness had left Walters went on loan to Stoke City, clearly no longer featuring in the new manager's plans. What was also puzzling was that while Souness was selling his older experienced players claiming that he needed younger blood, he was signing a 30-year-old from Rangers.

If Saunders had raised nagging doubts about Souness' ability in the transfer market, then Walters would only add to the doubts. Walters had been a dismal disappointment. If he had been signed to do a specific job he had failed. It should have made everyone wary of Souness' nose for a good player.

Before 1991 was out, Souness had dipped into the market yet again, this time more successfully, paying just £300,000 for Rob Jones, a callow, enthusiastic young defender with Crewe Alexandra. Jones was to prove the best buy Souness would make, and one of his cheapest. The youngster was immediately thrown into the lions' den of Old Trafford but performed heroically as Liverpool earned a draw. Before the season was over he was pulling on an England shirt and being talked of as a future England regular. The year ended with Michael Thomas, the Arsenal man who had brought such gloom and misery to the Kop one May evening, signing for Liverpool for £1.5 million. On paper Thomas appeared a good prospect. A strong and aggressive midfielder, he liked to carry the ball into the penalty area, as every Liverpool fan knew to their cost. It was just what Liverpool needed, someone like Terry McDermott. Thomas had picked up league championship honours with Arsenal, indeed, he had clinched the title for them that warm May evening at Anfield as he dashed into the penalty area, and had already pulled on an England shirt. He was only 24 years old and could only get better. In May 1992, five months after signing, he repaid some of his massive fee with an explosive volley that clinched the FA Cup for Liverpool. The Kop finally forgave him for that late Arsenal goal that had robbed Liverpool of the Double. Then injuries struck and Thomas was to spend most of the next two years recovering.

The signing of Thomas brought Souness' investment in 1991 to a staggering £8,150,000. He had only been at the club eight months. Of course, some players had also gone with some £4 million being recouped. It had been an unnerving experience for the club's directors, reaching for the cheque book time and again. Yet the board had held their nerve, showing commendable faith in their new man. Perhaps a little too much faith. In hindsight it might have been better had they pulled in the reins earlier on.

Perhaps the most puzzling signing of all was that of the Hungarian, Istvan Kozma. Kozma had left Hungary some years previously and had gone on to play with Bordeaux in France, ending up with Dunfermline in the Scottish Premier League. In many respects Kozma looked an astute buy. He was captain of his country, highly experienced and at £300,000 looked a snippet. Souness later said, 'I bought him because he had been a real thorn in our side during my time in Scotland with Rangers.' Thorn or not, Kozma's days at Anfield were to amount to very little. He joined Liverpool in January 1992 and in the following eighteen months went on to play just nine games in the Liverpool first team. And this was at a time when half their squad was laid low by injuries. But rather than play Kozma, Souness instead preferred to pick his youngsters. There was nothing wrong with that, but it did make people wonder why he had signed him in the first place if he was not going to give him his opportunity. A parting of the ways was inevitable. At least one member of the board had questioned the signing of Kozma but Souness had insisted that Kozma would be a useful asset.

And yet one still wondered why Souness had signed him in the first place. Kozma may have been a thorn in the flesh of Rangers but regular Dunfermline supporters had other memories. He had cost Dunfermline a record fee of £540,000 in September 1989 and had, not surprisingly, come under the microscope at East End Park. 'His performances against Rangers were somewhat exceptional,' remembers one Dunfermline supporter, 'but on a game-by-game basis he never really looked the part. He may have been a Hungarian international but in Scottish football he was just an ordinary player.' His transfer to Liverpool was greeted with raised eyebrows around Dunfermline. 'We asked ourselves why Liverpool, one of the greatest teams in Europe, were suddenly willing to pay us a record fee. And why should the club be so happy to

take a £200,000 loss on him after just a couple of years?'
Part of the answer was obvious. Dunfermline were glad
to cut their losses and get some of their £540,000 back.
Liverpool's motives were less easy to fathom. If Kozma
looked out of sorts in Scottish football, then in the Football League he was overwhelmed. Even in the reserves
he failed to make much of an impact. Kozma may not
have been as costly a mistake as Saunders but it was still
money wasted and again highlighted Souness' failings in
the transfer market.

Had Souness' disastrous steps into the transfer
market stopped merely with Walters, Saunders and
Kozma, it would have been bad enough but there was
also a fourth purchase that proved to be a disaster,
although the signing initially held much promise.

Paul Stewart had begun his footballing career with
Blackpool where after a quiet start he had gone on to
score 21 goals in 32 league games. It was enough to tempt
Manchester City to pay £200,000 for him. He arrived
in Manchester in March 1987 but faced a difficult spell
as the Maine Road club slid into the relegation zone and
headed for the second division. But the following season
he was a revelation, hitting the target 25 times in 40
league games. Stewart was suddenly hot property, too hot
for City to hang on to and during the summer of 1988
Tottenham Hotspur won the battle for his signature, costing them £1.7 million. For the next couple of seasons,
however, Stewart looked far from being a player worth
anything like that amount of money. He managed a mere
handful of goals, looked lethargic and awkward and might
have been on the verge of a move until Terry Venables
had the inspired notion of dropping him into the midfield.
Suddenly Stewart was a changed man, bringing back
memories of the way Bob Paisley had pulled a weary-
looking Ray Kennedy from attack into the midfield.
Stewart revelled in his new responsibility, earning a

Cup-winners' medal, even scoring in the final, and collecting three England caps.

In search of some desperately needed midfield bite after the sale of Steve McMahon, Souness pounced in the summer of 1992 and splashed out a massive £2.5 million for Stewart. Souness visualised Stewart fulfilling the same role as Ray Kennedy, neatly tucked in behind the front runners and picking up the loose chances in and around the edge of the box. But Stewart was to be a pale shadow of Kennedy. He was slow, never really certain of his role and nowhere near as powerful or inventive as Kennedy had been. He was not even a ball winner and rarely went into tackles with much determination. He scored a couple of goals but nowhere near as many as he should have converted for a former striker. Questions were soon being asked. Stewart was dropped, then injured, only to return to first team action before being dropped yet again. During the summer of 1993 Souness, desperate to raise some cash, tried to unload him to his former club Manchester City. A provisional fee of around £1.8 million was agreed between Souness and the City manager Peter Reid but the City board baulked at paying that much as the private duel between Reid and his chairman Peter Swales began to take precedence. And so as the 1993/94 season kicked off £2.5 million Paul Stewart was kicking the ball about in reserve team football, alongside a host of other expensive misfits. With nobody willing to pay much in excess of £1 million for him, Stewart eventually went on loan to Crystal Palace. At least it saved Liverpool having to pay his inflated salary.

Impetuosity seemed to be the name of the game for Souness. Spot a useful player and dive in with an offer. There was a time when the Anfield scouting system ran the rule over a player for months before making their move. Now it seemed to be one game, a good report in the papers or some player in demand and they were there with an offer. It was consumerism gone mad. Lee Jones was a typical example. In 1992 he scored a memorable goal for Wrexham in the FA Cup against West Ham United. The goal was widely shown on television and rightly earned glowing reports on the back pages. It was enough for Liverpool to pounce. Within a couple of months Jones was on his way to Anfield, signed for £300,000. And yet, two years later, Souness' reign over, Jones was still kicking the ball about in reserve team football, yet to make his first team debut. At least Jones had not cost Liverpool a seven-figure fee and with age on his side hopes remained that he might yet develop into a worthwhile player.

By the end of the 1991/92 season, Souness had shelled out £8,775,000 in building up a new side, yet although the club had won the FA Cup, in the league – the true test – they finished sixth, their worst performance since 1965. There were more purchases to come. Injuries had admittedly interrupted the building process during his early years and they would continue throughout his Anfield time, leading him to dip time and again into the transfer market. During the summer of 1992 David James, the young Watford goalkeeper was signed, appearing to signal the end of Bruce Grobbelaar's long stint as the club's number one custodian. James cost £1.3 million. In the event, Grobbelaar was still there pulling on the first team keeper's jersey when Souness left nearly two years later. Instead it was Mike Hooper, the other reserve team keeper, who had gone while James was seeing his time out in the reserves. James was given his chance immediately but in the opening games of the season the goals rattled past him. 'I didn't expect to be picking the ball out of the net much when I came here,' he explained, 'but I seem to be doing it more here than I was at Watford.' And although he was rarely to blame, it did his confidence little good. James was soon relegated to the reserves. At one point Mike Hooper even took over as first team keeper, with James and Grobbelaar battling it out for the number two spot.

It was also to be a Scandinavian season for Liverpool as they spread their scouting net far and wide. First in was Torben Piechnik from the Copenhagen club Bk 1903 for £500,000 in September 1992. It seemed a snip at the price. An experienced Danish international, Piechnik had been a member of the side that had just lifted the European Championship. The £500,000 Liverpool paid for him was tiny compared to the £2.5 million that was being asked for Craig Short, the largely inexperienced Notts County defender Liverpool were also tracking. British prices were soaring, even for second-rate players, partly thanks to the excessive spending of Souness himself and his predecessor Kenny Dalglish, who was lashing out just as much on Blackburn's behalf. The inflation was catching. As soon as Souness or Dalglish were reported to be interested, another zero was added to the fee.

Three months later Souness snapped up a second Scandinavian, this time the Norwegian Stig Bjornebye, a 22-year-old fullback from Rosenberg. Bjornebye, at £600,000, was another experienced international but, like Piechnik, he was to look equally inept and naive in the fury of the Premier League. Scandinavian imports such as Peter Schmeichel and Anders Limpar may have proved to be bargain buys for United and Arsenal, but alas, not Bjornebye and Piechnik for Liverpool. In comparison with the previous season, 1992/93 had been relatively inexpensive. Souness had paid out a mere £4.7 million while recouping £3.375 million.

The 1993/94 season kicked off with an almost injury-free squad, but after a positive start that brought three successive victories to lift everyone's hopes, Liverpool then conjured up three defeats in the next four games, including a couple at Anfield. Almost before the season had started, Liverpool's dreams of usurping Manchester United and stealing their league crown had all but evaporated. During the summer Souness had added Nigel Clough to his squad at a cost of £2,750,000. Clough, the son of Brian Clough, had all the hallmarks of a Liverpool player. Thoughtful, full of common sense and hard-working, he seemed the likeliest to introduce a dash of flair to the side. Like Dalglish, he could hold the ball, allowing players time to take up positions. A move to Liverpool was always likely but as with so many Nottingham Forest players before him, Clough seemed to stagnate away from the Trent. He began promisingly with four goals in his first four games, but other than an inspired performance against Manchester United he had little to boast for his year at Anfield. Before the season was over he had been substituted, dropped and injured. The likely lad had become the nearly lad. Before Souness resigned there was open talk of either swapping him for Derby County's Paul Kitson or selling him for what would almost certainly have been a knock-down price. Clough, like so many before him, had arrived with a sky-high reputation only to look mediocre and apathetic after pulling on a red shirt.

Nor would Clough be the last. A month later Souness snapped up Neil Ruddock, the combative Tottenham central defender for £2.5 million. Tottenham were doing very nicely out of Liverpool, raking in £5 million in twelve months through the sale of Paul Stewart and Neil Ruddock. Souness, it seemed, was going some way to ridding Alan Sugar and Spurs of their massive debt problems. Ruddock had enjoyed a mixed career. After a short spell with Millwall he had been transferred to Spurs for £50,000 without having made a single appearance. But the move had not worked out and two years and just seven appearances on he returned to the Den for £300,000. Seven months later, only 20 years of age, and still not having played a full 90 minutes for Millwall, he was on his travels again, this time to the south coast, joining Southampton for £250,000. His career finally began to take off at the Dell, though it was often marred by an alarming lack of discipline followed by frequent suspensions. At one point he was sent off twice and booked in every other game up until Christmas. But eventually he began to clean up his act and, in another bizarre twist to his career, returned to White Hart Lane in May 1992 for £750,000. Fourteen months later Graeme Souness was paying three times that amount for him. But was he worth it? By the time Souness had quit Anfield, most Kopites would have argued, no. Ruddock was tall – 6ft 2ins – and impressively strong but he was also awkward, always liable to be turned by a nippy inside forward.

If combativeness was what Souness was aspiring to, then he certainly found it in his next signing, Julian Dicks. And if ever a signing shocked Merseyside, this was it. The letters poured into the local papers. At the heart of the problem was Dicks' disciplinary record. He had been sent off on eight occasions and had collected many cautions over the years. He came with a reputation as one of the most indisciplined players in the Premier League. And yet here were Liverpool, the club that had always boasted a proud record in discipline, even though they had had their fair share of tough players, signing someone like Dicks. It seemed inconceivable. Souness argued that Dicks was the most effective left back in the division and that he would be having a special word with him about discipline. To his credit, Dicks did calm down, though the same could not be said of Ruddock who by February 1994 faced a two-match ban and had already been embroiled in an unsavoury fracas at Anfield against Blackburn Rovers.

But what was equally surprising about the Dicks deal

was that he arrived as a swap for David Burrows and Mike Marsh. Dicks had been valued at £2.5 million bringing Souness' summer spending to £7.75 million, almost as much as he had lashed out in his first season. Souness' total spending in the market at Anfield had topped £21,225,000 for 15 players. It was £6 million more than he had splashed out at Glasgow Rangers where he had at least signed 37 players for his £15,375,000 and had three championships to show for it. Of course he had also brought money into the club with a few astute sales. But his total income for the 18 players he sold was just over £12 million. It meant that there was a net loss on transfer deals of £9,150,000.

His combined deals at Ibrox and Anfield were staggering. He had frittered away a phenomenal £36.6 million at the two clubs, signing a total of 52 players. He had also sold 55 players worth £18,450,000, giving him a net loss in transfer deals at Liverpool and Glasgow Rangers of just over £18 million. It was more than any manager has spent in the history of British football. It may have brought him some domestic success at Ibrox but it brought him nothing more than an FA Cup at Anfield. In Europe the once mighty Liverpool had been made to look inconsequential while Rangers had never progressed much beyond the starting post.

Dicks was also to be the last player Souness would sign. By then the board had put a clamp on spending. Players had to be sold to pay for any new faces. The trouble was that nobody seemed interested in buying any of Souness' cast-offs. And if they did, it was for a knockdown price that made a mockery of Souness' extravagance in the first place. The talk was of Nigel Clough going for a little over £1 million and Paul Stewart being available for even less. Whatever way you looked at it, Souness' dealings had cost Liverpool a small fortune. It would probably take Liverpool years to recover.

155

CHAPTER ELEVEN
Sell, Sell, Sell

When Bill Shankly first arrived at Anfield he took one look around him and could barely believe his eyes. It was late 1959, a cold December day, enough to match his mood. Here was the famous Liverpool Football Club, the club that he had played against so often as a Preston player, the club that had won five league championships. And yet now they resembled a mediocre second division outfit. Anfield, which had regularly attracted crowds of 60,000 and more during those heady post-war days, was now less than half full. And the mighty Kop, which had frightened even that ex-Ayrshire miner, barely rumbled during a game. Elsewhere it was the same depressing picture. The offices were little better. Wallpaper curled at the edges, the paintwork had long faded and the curtains were in desperate need of a good clean. Even the training ground at Melwood looked more fitting for a non-league club than the former Football League champions. By 1960 most of the players had the aura and habits of second division players. There was no ambition, no money, no sense of urgency. Above all, there was no vision. Surveying the scene before him that first morning Shankly wondered what he had let himself in for.

'The ground was an eyesore. It needed renovating and clearing up,' he later wrote in his autobiography. 'Anfield was not good enough for the public of Liverpool and the team was not good enough for the public of Liverpool. There was only potential, little more. Melwood was just a wilderness out in the leafy suburbs of West Derby.'

But if ever a man was made for a job it was Shankly. He was the Messiah who arrived at the right moment. Others might have mucked along trying to make minor adjustments here and there, kow-towing to the directors' hesitations, but not Shankly. There was a job to be done and he set about reforming the club with a gusto that had not been seen at Anfield since the days of the great Tom Watson.

New players were needed to capture the public's imagination and to bring the crowds flocking back to Anfield. With the current squad of players there was no hope of escaping the second division. What was needed was a wholesale clearout. Anyone who looked like a second division player had to go. Shankly demanded the best and the board had to be convinced of the need to dig into its coffers. Before Shankly arrived the club had never paid more than £12,500 for a player but within six months Shankly had persuaded them to spend just over £60,000 on Ron Yeats and Ian St John. And had he had his own way, Shankly would also have signed one of his former players, Denis Law. But the board drew a line at lashing out £45,000 on a young, largely unproven, Scot.

There was much else to be done. Melwood was immediately given a new lick of paint and plans were drawn up to reform training. A new system had to be devised and new methods introduced. But the one thing Shankly did not change was his backroom staff. Reuben Bennett, Bob Paisley and Joe Fagan had been there for years. Shankly saw no reason to get rid of them and told them so. As new players joined, so Shankly swept aside the old order.

Within a month the new manager had drawn up a list containing the names of twenty-four players he thought should be sold. Within the year all twenty-four had gone, some sold, some off on free transfers, others just drifting out of the game. It was a ruthless process but one which Shankly considered crucial. 'It had to be done; there was no alternative,' he later wrote.

Within a few years Shankly had indelibly stamped his mark on Anfield. There was no denying that Liverpool was his club and that what followed owed everything to his vision. Before he died they had three times been hailed as European champions and had picked up more league championships than any other club in English football. They were respected and feared throughout the world of soccer. Shankly had turned a sleeping giant into the one of the greatest football clubs in the world.

To suggest that when Souness took over at Anfield he found a similar situation would be laughable. And yet Souness set about revolutionising Anfield with a conviction that had not been seen since those dark distant days of 1959. Souness saw himself as another Shankly, drawn to Anfield as if by fate. He was damning of what he found. He told the *Sunday Times* years later:

> The club needed major surgery when I came. Players were in disarray after Kenny Dalglish left. A lot of people had lost their desire. I had to remind them that Liverpool was *the* football club in England. I shouldn't have had to. Now players seem to use Liverpool as a stepping stone to more wealth.
>
> Every manager since Bill Shankly has inherited a stronger squad. I didn't. For the first time since the 1950s the Liverpool manager has a job on his hands.

It was an astonishing indictment of his predecessor Kenny Dalglish that went virtually unnoticed. Whether it was true or not was certainly open to debate. It was undeniably true that when Graeme Souness arrived he found an ageing side. There were many, not least in Fleet Street, who had suggested that Dalglish's resignation had more to do with his fears of how to replace his ageing stars than with any notion of pressure. It was certainly a daunting prospect but in truth it had little to do with the reasons that lay behind Dalglish's decision to walk out on Liverpool. Whatever the truth behind Dalglish's resignation, it still meant that his successor would have to face the problem of ageing stars.

Liverpool had not been enjoying the best of seasons, even though the side was four points ahead of Arsenal at the top of the table when Dalglish quit. Compared to Liverpool sides of the past they had looked mediocre, sluggish and lacking in conviction. The flowing football that personified the Anfield style was only evident on occasion. And in the weeks following Dalglish's resignation they seemed to have lost their appetite altogether. There were problems throughout the side. BBC Television pundit Jimmy Hill had infuriated many scousers with his off-the-cuff remark that 'the great stylish midfield players of Liverpool will be turning over in their graves to see the orthodox and very average way in which they are performing'. Harsh words but privately every Kopite had to acknowledge there was more than a grain of truth in his observations. There were question marks throughout the side. Top of the list of imponderables was Peter Beardsley. The England star had shown only flashes of his renowned ability throughout the season. He looked a pale shadow of the man who had drifted, almost serenely, past defences in his first year at Anfield. Beardsley was just turned 30 when Dalglish left, possibly past his best, although always a useful and cultured player to have on your side.

To Dalglish, Beardsley had been an enigma. He was a

highly talented and skilful player who thrived on confidence but whose head would drop when the going got tough. Dalglish had worked individually with Beardsley attempting to instil some grit into him, to make him a more resilient player. Subjected to ruthless punishment and intimidation, goalscorers need to be equally determined if they are to overcome the burdens of their job, to give as much as they receive. Dalglish himself had proved that skill alone was not everything. The Scottish striker may have won few fans on opposing terraces with his niggling and occasional short temper but it had been vital if you were to frustrate the intimidators before they frustrated you. Dalglish tried to teach Beardsley the same tricks but the lessons were never fully heeded. Beardsley had become a player who wasn't quite fulfilling his potential at Anfield. By 1991 even his England career looked to be over.

Liverpool had unarguably benefited from Beardsley's most productive years. Yet time and again during the 1990/91 season Dalglish had left Beardsley on the bench, even dropping him altogether on more than one occasion. At times it seemed inexplicable, given that Beardsley was also his top goalscorer. But Dalglish had persisted in making life uncomfortable for him, much to the growing annoyance of the England international. On more than one occasion Beardsley stormed into the manager's office and made his feelings known. Yet when he did return to the side he still continued to show a lack of commitment and confidence.

It might have been expected that the resignation of Dalglish would offer a new lease of life to Beardsley; on the contrary, it only added to his misery. When Dalglish resigned Beardsley discovered astonishingly that he was the focus of a bizarre newspaper story that linked him with the manager's decision to quit. Their wives were said to be at each other's throats over Dalglish's failure to select him on a regular basis. The story was nonsense but it did little to boost Beardsley's ambitions.

The problem of Beardsley needed to be resolved. The new manager soon became convinced that strong measures had to be taken. Beardsley's motivation was wearing thin and if Liverpool were to look to the future then Beardsley needed to be replaced. Perhaps it was better to take that step now, concluded Souness, rather than to wait a further year. On offer was a seemingly ready-made replacement – Dean Saunders. Although Liverpool had not shown any initial interest in Saunders, the Derby County player was clearly capable and had bagged goals at a handsome rate wherever he had played. He was more direct that Beardsley yet was not a typical out-and-out goalscorer. But herein would lie the failure of Saunders. Liverpool would eventually finish up with two direct runners and not enough creativity in the midfield to concoct chances for them. What would Rush and Saunders have given for a Beardsley behind them. Had Souness foreseen this problem he might have argued that with Barnes flinging crosses over from the flanks there would be ample openings for Saunders. And so a decision was taken. Liverpool would go for Saunders and release Beardsley if there was a reasonable offer. In July 1991 Saunders signed for £2.9 million; a month later Beardsley joined neighbours Everton for £1 million.

The sale of Beardsley sparked off a furious row among Liverpool supporters, not least because he had been sold to their Merseyside rivals. Many reckoned Liverpool might have pocketed more from the deal. Considering they had paid £1.8 million for him in the first place, £1 million seemed a knock-down price even though he was 30. But there were also plenty who could see sense in Souness' dealings. In effect Saunders, a much younger player, had finished up costing Liverpool £1.9 million. As it happened it was the selling of Beardsley rather than the buying of Saunders that proved to be the disastrous mistake, as injuries left Liverpool without any experienced schemers in the midfield. But in fairness, Souness could never have guessed at the catastrophic list of injuries that would plague the club over the next twelve months. Ironically, three years later Beardsley would be enjoying a new lease of life, back where he belonged at Newcastle, and still knocking in the goals, considerably more than Dean Saunders who by then was struggling to score. He would also have been recalled to the England side. What's more Everton had pocketed £1.5 million to give them a useful profit.

August turned out to be a wicked month for a number of Liverpool players. Once Beardsley was out of the way, the next to go was Steve Staunton, the young Irish fullback who was unloaded to Aston Villa for a handsome £1.1 million. The deal raised more than a few comments. Although Staunton was never in quite the same class as Steve Nicol, Alan Kennedy or Phil Neal, he at least had youth on his side. He had made his Liverpool debut at the age of 19 and was still only 21 when Souness became manager. Souness presumably was not impressed by him. What's more, he was Irish and Liverpool already had a surplus of foreign players. Staunton had to go. Aston Villa came in with an offer and he was gone. There was far less logic to the sale of Staunton than to most of Souness' transactions. Staunton was a useful utility player, had youth on his side and with his international appearances was developing a bed of experience that would have been beneficial for the future. Given the subsequent injuries that were to riddle the club, Staunton would have proved vital. As it was, Liverpool were repeatedly to find themselves short of defenders over the next few years and must have cursed the day they sold Staunton. Indeed, six months after Souness left, Roy Evans made a £2.5 million bid to bring back Staunton. The bid failed, but it said much about Evans' attitude to some of Souness' transfer dealings.

One defender most Kopites were not surprised, nor too upset, to see depart was Gary Gillespie. Liverpool had bought Gillespie from Coventry City in 1983 for £325,000, yet in eight years at the club he managed only 156 league appearances. Although he had an elegant touch, Gillespie suffered more than his fair share of injuries and rarely had a prolonged run in the first team. In many ways it was a disappointment, because without his injuries Gillespie could have matured into an outstanding defender. As it was he was capped just thirteen times by Scotland. Gillespie was 30 years old when Dalglish resigned and again it was hardly surprising that the new manager should look to raise some revenue by selling him. What was surprising was that Souness managed to get a £1 million fee for him from his old Scottish rivals, Celtic. It was a huge return for a player whose contributions had been so infrequent. Again, nobody could have questioned Souness' business acumen and given Gillespie's subsequent career at Celtic, Liverpool had clearly got the better of that deal.

Another player who also went without too much questioning was David Speedie. Speedie had been a surprise signing by Dalglish in the manager's final weary months, arriving from Coventry City for £750,000. Even at the time it smacked of panic buying and months later appeared even more bizarre as Speedie's early form evaporated. Speedie was not only over 30 but was Scottish as well. What Liverpool had needed most was a young English midfielder, but when Speedie scored on his debut against Manchester United at Old Trafford and then a week later netted a couple against Everton at Anfield, it seemed that Dalglish had the magician's touch. But apart from that, his impact was minimal. Dalglish was never sure where to play him. Sometimes he was upfront, but with Barnes, Beardsley and Rush also jockeying for position there, Speedie was always at the back of the queue. Dalglish tried him in the midfield but he looked a lost soul. Souness had little inkling where to play him and eventually he was cast aside as surplus. It surprised nobody when Souness sold him to Blackburn Rovers for £500,000. Again, it was a sensible slice of business.

At the same time as he signed David Speedie, Dalglish had made another foray into the transfer market bringing in the young Millwall winger Jimmy Carter. Carter was also to look hopelessly out of place, even more lost than Speedie who had at least contributed with a couple of important goals. Carter had pace but little in the way of penetration. He made just a handful of appearances and was then unloaded to Arsenal for £500,000 in October 1991. It was surprising that a club of Arsenal's calibre should have moved in for Carter and must have made a few people, Souness included, wonder if perhaps Liverpool had failed to spot something in the young man. In the event they hadn't. Three years on, Carter had hardly pulled on an Arsenal shirt.

If the sale of Beardsley had caused a stir, then the offloading of McMahon would astonish many. McMahon had joined Liverpool in September 1985 from Aston Villa for £350,000. He was to become the eventual replacement for Graeme Souness in Liverpool's engine room. Ever since Souness had left the club for Sampdoria, Liverpool had lacked a midfield general, someone who could display the same kind of authority and determination as Souness. McMahon, Dalglish's first signing, proved to be the answer to a problem that had caused considerable concern. As Dalglish packed his bags to leave, McMahon was fast approaching his thirtieth birthday. At best, Liverpool would get only a couple more years out of him. More to the point, McMahon had no wish to find himself out of favour. He survived for eight months, enough to convince him that his future lay elsewhere. It was time to move on. Fortunately a £900,000 offer came from his old Everton colleague Peter Reid at Maine Road. McMahon was off like a shot. Over the next few years Liverpool would miss his drive and determination far more than they would dare to admit. During 1991 six players had left the club, bringing in almost £5 million. On paper it looked like good business.

Gary Ablett may have had age on his side, he was only 25 years old, but his performances were well below par. He was not popular with the fans who tended to pin much of the blame for the team's defensive misdemeanours on his young shoulders. Ablett was more accustomed to playing as a fullback but injuries had often resulted in him being pushed into the centre of the defence, the kind of responsible position to which he was not suited. With a strong central defender alongside him he was capable of a competent enough performance but without that resolute support his inadequacies began to show. Hansen had been absent for much of the 1990/91 season and had retired immediately Dalglish had left. As a consequence, Ablett found himself at the centre of a makeshift defence alongside either Gary Gillespie when he was fit, Jan Molby or occasionally Steve Nicol who was more accustomed to playing at right back. The ever-changing pattern did little to boost Ablett's confidence, with the result that his performances came under even closer scrutiny. By January 1992 Liverpool had Mark Wright in the centre of defence and had recently signed the accomplished Rob Jones. There was no room for Ablett and nobody was much disheartened when he moved. What did astonish people was that it should be Everton's Howard Kendall who came in with a bid of £750,000. Surely Kendall was close enough to Anfield to know that Ablett was not the most highly rated player on Merseyside. Ablett's transfer might have been popular with the Kop but his signing hardly brought cheers from Evertonians who had seen and read all too much about Ablett. But for Souness it was shrewd business and few at Anfield would have questioned his selling the young man.

Another defender to disappear was Glenn Hysen who left shortly after Souness' arrival. The tall Swede had brought a touch of elegance to the Liverpool defence during the 1989/90 season, but was now surplus to requirements. His performances had never quite matched those of his first season and at the age of 32 it was clear that he would not figure in Souness' plans. Hysen returned to Sweden on a free transfer, glad to be out of it and somewhat shocked at what he had already witnessed in the Anfield dressing room.

But the one player whose departure would provoke disaffection was Ray Houghton. Throughout the 1990/91 season Houghton had been Liverpool's most consistent player and had enjoyed a splendidly successful career in his time at Anfield. Signed from Oxford United for £850,000 in October 1987, Houghton had been a beaver in the Liverpool midfield, supplying so many of the crosses that brought goals for the likes of Barnes, Aldridge and Beardsley. A mature, thoughtful professional, Houghton's approach and attitude were always appreciated by the Kop, although he could barely be described as a 'favourite'. That kind of honour was only bestowed on players like Dalglish, Barnes and Rush. Houghton may not have been charismatic or a crowd-puller but he served his part in the Liverpool side. It came as something of a shock when Houghton was suddenly sold to Ron Atkinson's emerging Aston Villa for £825,000. Of all the players Souness had sold so far, it was the sale of Houghton which caused most alarm. Souness insisted that Houghton had wanted to go and that any amount of persuading he had attempted had fallen on deaf ears. Houghton, it was claimed, had wanted to return to

London. In the event, he finished up in Birmingham in July 1992, linking up with his former Liverpool team-mate, Steve Staunton, and a couple of months later he would be joined by another, Dean Saunders, as Villa became serious challengers for the Premiership title. Even to this day, the sale of Houghton remains a mystery and, given the catalogue of injuries that Liverpool were to suffer in their midfield, his transfer was to have serious repercussions. It was also ironic that Houghton had been the first Catholic player Souness had tried to sign for Rangers, though Houghton had rejected his overtures.

During that summer of the long knives a fourth defender to disappear was Barry Venison. A £200,000 buy from Sunderland in 1986, Venison may not have been an international defender but was an honest professional; reliable and effective, he was always prepared to push upfield in much the same way as Phil Neal had once driven the side forward. Venison had been injured for some time during 1991 and by the time he had fully recuperated, others had taken over his spot. His transfer was probably inevitable although he was still a comparatively young man when he left. He was eventually sold to Newcastle United for £250,000 where he did fine service in helping Kevin Keegan's side into the Premier Division.

The next, and final, man to disappear that season was Dean Saunders, sold for £2.3 million to Aston Villa after a campaign that had failed to deliver the expectations that a £2.9 million fee promised. 'Dean Saunders came here and I thought he'd make a good partner for Ian Rush,' claimed Souness. 'I have to hold my hands up and say it didn't work out that way. We like to think we are more calculated and he is more direct.'

In the space of just over a year Souness had overhauled the Anfield playing staff with a vengeance. Along with the expected deadwood some of the club's most popular names had also been ousted. While some of the sales made sense, there seemed to be little logic behind others. The sale of Steve McMahon, for instance, left Liverpool desperately short of authority while the loss of Ray Houghton cut down the number of options in midfield. Admittedly, neither Souness nor anyone could have guessed at the catalogue of injuries that would so cruelly strike the club. At some point almost every first team player was struck down. There were long-term injuries to John Barnes, Ronnie Whelan, Ian Rush, all of them key players. Throughout Souness' first two full seasons in charge, he was only ever able to field the same side in two consecutive games on just a handful of occasions. It was always chop and change, forced on him by the limping wounded. Just as one player would recover so another would go down. At one point it seemed the club was jinxed. Liverpool had never been a club to use injuries as an excuse for poor performances. They had always believed that strength in depth would compensate but now they found themselves forced to use the old excuse themselves. There may, of course, have been reasons for the bad spate of injuries rather than simple bad luck but whatever the cause, it left Liverpool appallingly short. Players with years of honours and experience had been sold, with Souness forced to depend on youth and inexperience. It was little wonder that Liverpool even struggled in the relegation zone for some of the time.

Souness' final season at Anfield brought another rash of changes. First out was the Hungarian international Istvan Kozma, who left Liverpool in August 1993, but even then his departure was forced on Souness, rather than coming about by the manager realising his error. Under Home Office regulations issued in 1993, foreign players from outside the European Community had to play in 75 per cent of first team games for which they were available in order to qualify for a work permit.

Kozma had made only two appearances in the previous season and clearly did not qualify. An extension of Kozma's work permit was out of the question. Liverpool notified clubs that Kozma was available for transfer but nobody was interested and in the end he drifted back to Hungary, signing a two-year deal with Ujpesti Te. Liverpool received no money for him. There were no apologies from Souness either. 'I was hoping he would flourish in a team of better players,' was his justification. 'He was a player to enhance a team playing well, not one having to battle as we were. He's a victim of circumstances.' In effect, it was £300,000 down the drain but at least Liverpool were no longer paying out his salary. The glut of first team players on high salaries had already sent the wages bill soaring through the ceiling. Any transfers were welcomed by the board, as long as they were out and not in.

But with the season barely under way came the deal that surprised and angered fans more than any other. By now Kopites were openly questioning Souness' dealings in the transfer market. The signing of 'Razor' Ruddock had already caused a stir but when Liverpool were linked with Julian Dicks of West Ham there was disbelief. Most reckoned the newspapers were mischief-making. But it turned out that Liverpool really were interested. Not only that, but he was signed in a swap deal that took David Burrows and Mike Marsh to Upton Park. Such was the state of Liverpool's coffers that they were now obliged to swap rather than sign. But it was not just that which really shocked Liverpool fans. Rather, it was the loss of Burrows and Marsh.

Burrows, although he had never quite fulfilled his potential, had nevertheless been a committed and enthusiastic performer. He too may have been impetuous at times but he looked just as effective a player as Dicks. Marsh had stepped into the side when injuries had forced Souness to plunder the reserves. The youngster had performed splendidly, although he clearly had some way to progress before he could be considered a quality Liverpool player. But time was on his side and his ability was clear enough for everyone to appreciate. Had Marsh been slotting into a Liverpool side of the past, he would have played the occasional game until the moment arrived for him to take his place. As it was, injuries and out-of-form players forced his inclusion week after week. And when Souness was blaming the experienced players for Liverpool's poor performances it seemed strange that he should sell one of his brightest youngsters. As it was, Marsh and Burrows quickly settled into a West Ham side that was facing relegation and were soon passing the ball with an arrogance and neatness that spoke of their Anfield training.

By now Souness had sold fifteen players who were capable of forming almost a complete side. All that was lacking was a goalkeeper and a striker. By the end of September Souness had gone part way to rectifying that by selling second-string goalkeeper Mike Hooper to Newcastle United for £550,000. Admittedly, he had to sell one of his goalkeepers. All three had first team experience and it was impossible to hang on to all of them when only one place was available. At various times Grobbelaar, James and Hooper had all been linked to some possible deal. Later that season James was on the verge of joining Southampton in a transfer that would have brought Tim Flowers to Anfield, but in the end Flowers chose Blackburn Rovers instead.

Souness' final deal, just days before he quit the club, was to sell Ronny Rosenthal to Tottenham for £250,000. The robust Israeli international striker was the missing piece – the striker – in the team that Souness sold. Out there in the Premiership was a complete team of ex-Liverpool players, all sold by Souness. It wasn't a bad side either, one that would certainly have been capable of giving the current Liverpool eleven more than a game. In goal would have been Mike Hooper (Newcastle) with a back four permed from Barry Venison (Newcastle), Gary Gillespie (Celtic), David Burrows (West Ham), Steve Staunton (Aston Villa) or Gary Ablett (Everton). A midfield of Steve McMahon (Manchester City), Ray Houghton (Aston Villa), Mike Marsh (West Ham) and Peter Beardsley (Newcastle) were an attractive foursome while Dean Saunders (Aston Villa) and Ronny Rosenthal (Tottenham) upfront would have posed plenty of threats to most defences. That would still leave room on the bench for David Speedie and Jimmy Carter.

Souness had sold some eighteen first team players, not quite as many as the twenty-four Shankly had forced through the door, though Souness had certainly raised more revenue; £12,075,000 to be precise. It was useful cash for his rebuilding programme which had begun in earnest almost as soon as he arrived at the club. A couple of months after Souness had quit Liverpool, new manager Roy Evans readily confessed that 'some players were sold before their sell-by date while those coming in were not as good as those they had sold'. It was a remarkable admission.

That Liverpool needed to unload players was undeniable. There were basically two problems – age and nationality. Far too many Liverpool players were either approaching or beyond their thirtieth birthday and far too many were classed as foreign under UEFA rules. UEFA had decreed that from the beginning of the 1991/92 season Scottish, Northern Irish and Welsh players should in future be regarded as foreign players. As a consequence, British teams participating in European competition would be restricted to just three foreign players in their side, plus two 'naturalised' players. For any club, but especially for Liverpool, this posed a serious problem. Liverpool had always adopted a policy of signing players from wherever talent could be found. Their Scottish links had gone back many years. The first-ever side Liverpool fielded, in 1892, had contained ten Scotsmen and just one Englishman. It was known as the 'Team of the All Macs'. Almost a century later, in 1986, as Liverpool lifted the Double at Wembley there was not one English player in their side.

When Souness arrived at Anfield he was forced almost immediately to confront the two problems. The list of non-English players was overwhelming. Representing Scotland were Steve Nicol, David Speedie and Gary Gillespie; from Eire, Ray Houghton, Ronnie Whelan and Steve Staunton; from Wales there was Ian Rush; from Denmark Jan Molby while from Zimbabwe there was Bruce Grobbelaar; from Israel Ronny Rosenthal and from Sweden Glenn Hysen. All were regular first team players who would have been likely to have been chosen for any European matches. And yet there was room for a maximum of five of them. It was crucial that Souness brought in whatever English talent was available and so the search began. It was perhaps surprising, though, that of the many players Souness was to buy six were classed as 'foreign'. Principal among them were Dean Saunders (Welsh), Istvan Kozma (Hungarian), Torben Piechnik (Danish), Stig Bjornebye (Norwegian) and Lee Jones (Welsh). It seemed that little progress had really been made in shifting the balance of international power at Anfield.

There was newspaper talk about the number of thirty-something players at Anfield when Souness arrived. It was reckoned to be at the root of Liverpool's poor performances that season. Where were the youngsters? asked the papers. In fact, the youngsters were quietly waiting in the wings. After his departure Dalglish had come in for much criticism for not having developed a youth policy. Yet, on the contrary, almost the first action that Dalglish took on his appointment as player-manager in 1985 was to institute a youth scheme. For years the club's youngsters had been neglected. Few were ever given their chance in the first team with only the likes of Phil Thompson and Sammy Lee emerging from the lower ranks. Most of those unknown players who did make it at Anfield had been inexpensive, promising signings from the lower English divisions or from Scotland, players such as Ian Rush, Steve Nicol, Alan Hansen, Steve Heighway. Dalglish tried to add to that proven system with a youth policy but it takes time for results to show. Sadly he did not stay long enough to see his plans come to fruition. It was Souness who was to reap the benefit with Dalglish youngsters Steve McManaman, Jamie Redknapp, Mike Marsh, Don Hutchison, Dominic Matteo and Robbie Fowler all developing to challenge for places. Credit should of course be given to Souness for offering those youngsters their chances, though whether they would so readily have been given their opportunity had injuries not wrought such havoc at the club is another matter.

Principal among the thirty-something players at Anfield were Bruce Grobbelaar, David Speedie, Gary Gillespie, Glenn Hysen and Peter Beardsley. There were also those fast approaching their thirtieth birthday such as Steve McMahon, Ian Rush, Ronnie Whelan, Ray Houghton and Steve Nicol. Only four of these ten would remain at Anfield – Grobbelaar, Rush, Whelan and Nicol – though interestingly, in the week after Souness had resigned, four of the ten were still giving useful service elsewhere in the Premiership. In particular Beardsley's career had been resurrected following a move back to Newcastle with an England recall just around the corner. There was no reason whatsoever why the thirty-something players should not have continued to give valuable service for a few more years. Their experience was vital. The Liverpool ways had to be passed on to the youngsters. As it was, the youngsters were thrown in and had to fend for themselves with little support. The age crisis was always exaggerated. Perhaps Souness himself should have remembered that when he signed for Glasgow Rangers in 1986 as player-manager he himself was 33 years of age.

CHAPTER TWELVE
The Red Card Revolutionary

John Roberts writing in the *Daily Mail* once described Graeme Souness as 'Tommy Smith with a Rolls-Royce engine'. It was as delightful a description as any that have been pinned to him. But not everyone would agree. Jack Charlton reckoned he had 'a nasty streak', while Ron Atkinson, another manager not noted for his tenderness, once said 'some say he is evil'. They would be more likely to agree with another commentator who called him 'Renoir with a razor blade'.

In his autobiography *No Half Measures*, Souness devotes a chapter to defending his style of play. In the chapter, entitled 'Meanest Man in Football', Souness attempts to justify the style that made him so feared by opponents and so unpopular on terraces up and down the country. Frank Worthington had once labelled him in one of the tabloids as the 'hardest, most ruthless' player he had come across in fifteen years of top-class soccer. But far from being outraged at Worthington's remarks, most of Souness' Anfield team-mates at the time appear to have agreed and seemed more than delighted at the fact that Souness was in their side and not in someone else's. Although Souness denied the colourful tag, one suspects that he was hardly surprised at the suggestion. In a reply published a few days later in the same newspaper, the *Sun*, Souness was quick to tell his readers that he took grave offence at the suggestion that he was a hatchet man. He pointed out that the facts spoke for themselves. He had been sent off only twice in his career, first as a 16-year-old in the 1970 FA Youth Cup final following a tussle with Dennis Mortimer and then again three years later while he was at Middlesbrough after throwing a punch at Carlisle's Stan Ternent. And nor was his disciplinary record as a Liverpool player anywhere near as poor as some might imagine. He was cautioned only occasionally, four or five times a season on average. By the time he had reached Anfield the painful lessons had been heeded though he was still not averse to the occasional tackle that bordered on the insensitive.

He picked up a booking early in his Anfield career which, when added to those he had already accumulated at Middlesbrough, led to a premature period of suspension. It did not go down well with the bootroom where discipline was instilled into players from the beginning. Liverpool needed their men on the field, not twiddling their thumbs in the stands and the club's disciplinary record was for many years second to none. In a period of ten years only a handful of players had been sent off. Souness took the lesson on board and in his entire Anfield career was never sent off.

At Middlesbrough he had been encouraged to do just the opposite. Jack Charlton, as tough a centre half as any, was the instigator who gave him the authority to take matters into his own hands. Charlton was even reputed to have a little black book with names in it 'He would pick out players competing in my territory and, if it could influence the direction of the game, get me to sort them out,' wrote Souness in his book. 'He believed the odd kick or two was quite legitimate within the framework of football.' Souness had run-ins with Charlton's old team-mates Terry Yorath and Billy Bremner and Middlesbrough soon attracted a reputation as the toughest side in the division. But who was going to complain? Certainly not Middlesbrough, its fans or directors, especially when they were heading for the second division championship.

Anfield had been given an early indication of what to expect from him when Middlesbrough, along with Souness, were the visitors that next season. Liverpool's midfield sergeant major, Jimmy Case, soon found himself scrapping for the ball with Souness. Case ended up on the ground with Souness bending over him, his fist held threateningly in his face. It was an astonishing sight. Nobody had ever done that to Jimmy Case before. The Charlton lesson stuck. But what Anfield taught him was that he should learn to be more subtle. 'By all means be hard but don't get yourself sent off,' they told him. Joe Fagan advised him to stay on his feet and not to go lunging into the fray. That way he wouldn't get booked. But as he admits, on the odd occasion, he was not averse to taking revenge on behalf of some of his team-mates. There were plenty who carried the scars: Siggi Johnsson of Iceland; Peter Nicholas of Wales; Tony Galvin of Spurs; George McCluskey of Hibs; Iosif Rotariu of Steaua Bucharest; and Lica Movila of Dinamo Bucharest whose jaw was smashed in two places. Ray Wilkins can also testify to the quality of some of his tackles. 'I've been on the wrong end of every part of his anatomy – almost every part anyway. We've had a few tussles but it's all forgotten,' he says, adding graciously that 'it's just the winner in him coming out.' Others might not be so generous.

There is a myth that the sixties introduced a new breed of player that epitomised the doctrines of managers like Don Revie. But hard players have always existed. Admittedly in the sixties the iron man in the heart of the defence became the norm as defenders like Dave Mackay, Billy Bremner and Tommy Smith emerged to become the game's heroes. But it remains a fact that over the years all the finest sides have employed at least one defender capable of terrifying a few forwards. Graeme Souness was a neat progression of this trend. He was, as John Roberts suggests, a hard player, as tough as Tommy Smith, but with an elegance that Smith never possessed and a passing ability not usually associated with intimidating men. There is no doubt that Souness ranked among the hardest players in the league but he was not alone. The Leeds contingent of Yorath, Giles, Bremner and Hunter could have matched him tackle for tackle while at Nottingham Forest Kenny Burns had a frightening reputation as did Graham Roberts at Tottenham and Remi Moses at Manchester United. All were as tough, maybe even a shade more resilient than Souness. But for some reason Souness was tagged and it remained with him. Perhaps it was his arrogance, perhaps it was the fact that Liverpool came under the media spotlight more often than their opponents. Whatever it was, it hardly endeared Souness to the average, fair-minded supporter.

It wasn't just on the pitch that Souness was likely to flare up. He also had his share of dressing room rows. The former Liverpool captain Phil Neal remembers how fiercely even five-a-side games were conducted at Melwood. With so many Scots around Anfield, it was usually a case of England v. Scotland. Souness, he says, 'treated practice games almost as seriously as full-blown internationals and on the odd occasion things got out of hand with players picking up needless injuries'. On more than one occasion players squared up to him in the heat of the moment. 'One morning he was in a particularly bad mood,' recalls Neal, 'and seemed hell bent on needling me. He was pushing and shoving, tapping my ankles and generally making a nuisance of himself until finally I snapped. The next thing I knew we were shaping up to each other and Ronnie Moran and a couple of the other lads had to pull us apart.' But it was all over in a flash and Neal admits that there were no hard feelings.

Mark Lawrenson also remembers the Souness flash of temper that once had him diving down the gangway of the team coach after someone had thrown a brick at it. 'It didn't smash the window but, quick as a flash, Graeme was down the aisle telling the driver to stop while he went looking for the hooligans. That was his style, he hates cowardice of any form.' Lawrenson also remembers that the first time he met Souness he was sporting a black eye, apparently brought about after he had been cornered in a toilet by four or five men. But if Souness' playing career branded him as a tough man, his managerial career was to be even worse. Mellowness seemed to have passed him by. He became a born-again disciplinarian, losing all sense of perspective. What's more, his very first game as a manager set the trend. There was no looking back after that.

Souness made his eagerly awaited debut in Scottish football on 9 August 1986 against Hibernian at Easter Road. It was his own backyard, a ground just a stone's throw away from Albert Street where he had spent his formative years. His entire family were in attendance, Dad, brothers, relatives, all among a capacity crowd, the best Hibs had seen for many a day. The press were out in force as well, binoculars pinned on the moustached man in blue, and then right in front of them all Souness lunged in on George McCluskey of Hibs. Down went McCluskey. Five minutes later the agonised Hibs man was being carried off, in need of nine stitches in a knee wound. Seconds later he was followed by Souness.

'I've never been more depressed,' admitted Souness later. 'I remember seeing the red card and looking up, there was 30,000 people jeering and I could see my Dad in the front row of the directors' box. I can still feel the shame now. I know it sounds like Hollywood but I've never felt so alone. I'd let my Dad down, humiliated him in his own street. That was my lowest moment in football.'

Once he was back in Scotland, Souness was arguably a marked man, both by players, and, some would suggest, by referees as well, who perhaps tend to be more strict north of the border. Souness was not the most popular of men and, especially as manager of Rangers, he had become the number one target. What wouldn't most players do to have a few kicks at the Rangers manager? At Anfield he had learnt to walk away from trouble but in Scotland trouble came at him from every conceivable angle.

It may have been his lowest moment, the new player-manager of Rangers making the long lonely trek to the tunnel, but there would be a few more shameful moments to follow before he walked out on Rangers and Scottish football. For his sins Souness was given an immediate one-match suspension with an additional fixed three-match ban later imposed by the Scottish FA. Humbled by the experience Souness did his utmost to keep out of trouble. There were the occasional bookings, mostly for incidental fouls that went almost unnoticed by the press and players. But then, in the Old Firm clash with Celtic at Ibrox on New Year's Day 1987, he encountered trouble again as he was shown a yellow card for ungentlemanly conduct. The booking took him through the points threshold and brought with it an automatic one-match suspension. It was his second suspension in Scottish football.

The appointment of Souness as the Rangers player-manager had added to the intensity of Old Firm clashes. Always fiery, they were now highly inflammable. The signing of so many English internationals was also to give those derby matches an additional spark. Celtic fans joked that not only could they now beat Rangers but they could beat England as well. In his second Rangers/Celtic derby in charge, the Skol Cup final in October 1986, there had been a touchline punch-up between Celtic's Mo Johnston and Stuart Munro of Rangers. Both players were booked, but as it was Johnston's second offence he was shown a red card. Souness did not play that day. It was just as well. Nine other players were booked and the game was described by the *Daily Telegraph* as 'unsavoury'. It was to set the tone for the next few years.

In February 1987 Souness was again shown a yellow card for ungentlemanly conduct as Rangers beat Hearts 5–2. Given the rising temperature in the Old Firm games, another yellow card was almost inevitable. It came in early April as Rangers went to Parkhead. They lost 1–3 that day. The season ended with Souness sent off for the second time, as they drew 1–1 with Aberdeen at Pittodrie. It was his second bookable offence in the game. The Scottish FA gave him an immediate one-match ban followed by a two-match fixed ban. It was his third suspension in what was his first season in Scottish football. But worse was to follow. Barely into the new campaign, 1987/88, Rangers went to Parkhead for their first league encounter of the season. Shortly after the interval, Souness, who had already been booked for abusive language, launched a tackle on Celtic's Billy Stark who at the time had just lost a boot. It was a reckless challenge and the referee had no alternative but to send him off. But instead of taking his punishment with good grace Souness persisted in arguing with the referee. At the end of the game the arguing erupted yet again and Souness was once more reprimanded by the referee. In the end it transpired that the referee had given him three red cards for his misconduct. It was almost unprecedented. Souness was immediately banned for two games and then given a three-match fixed suspension by the Scottish FA.

He had been playing in Scottish football for only twelve

months and already he had been sent off three times, shown a total of five red cards and six yellow cards and had faced the Scottish FA on four occasions, receiving four separate suspensions. He was hardly setting much of an example to his players. At the end of 1987 Souness was shown yet another yellow card. Sandwiched in between these yellow cards, in October 1987, had been another disgraceful scene in an Old Firm game, although it did not personally involve Souness. Seventeen minutes into the game at Ibrox, the Rangers goalkeeper Chris Woods and the Celtic striker Frank McAvennie squared up to each other. A moment later Terry Butcher joined in, followed by Graham Roberts who promptly punched McAvennie on the side of the head. By now all hell was let loose as players threatened one another, with the crowd, the most sectarian in football, baying for blood. The referee eventually restored order and promptly sent Woods and McAvennie off. That was shameful enough as it was, but then in the second half Terry Butcher was judged by the referee to have deliberately struck the Celtic goalkeeper Allen McKnight. A third sending off followed. Three experienced, and highly expensive, internationals had all disgraced themselves. It was one of the most shameful Old Firm games since the war.

Following the match, four players – Butcher, Woods and Roberts of Rangers and McAvennie of Celtic – were summoned to appear at Govan police station where they were charged with 'conduct likely to provoke a breach of peace amongst spectators'. It was a serious charge. Graham Roberts was also said to have been provocatively 'conducting' his own supporters in a sectarian song. Eventually there was a more general charge that they did 'conduct themselves in a disorderly manner and commit a breach of the peace'. In the heated nature of Glasgow's sectarianism, there were accusations about the religious affiliations of those conducting the legal case. It was pitiful. In the event, Chris Woods and Terry Butcher were found guilty of a breach of the peace. Both players were fined. The other two players were acquitted.

Fortunately, Graeme Souness had not played that day and while he obviously cannot be blamed for what happened on the field, as manager he was obliged to take some responsibility. The events of the day had not got off to an exemplary start with Rangers even refusing to take the field alongside Celtic. There can be little doubt that Souness would have had a say in that decision. It was a decision that hardly set the seal for friendly relations.

In January 1988 Souness was shown another yellow card, this time for ungentlemanly conduct. By now his appearances in the Rangers blue were becoming less frequent. He was again booked in September 1988 for dissent and then finally in March 1989, again for dissent.

But all those incidents concerned Souness the player. Souness the manager had just as many problems with the Scottish FA. Even off the field his self-control left something to be desired. In March 1989 he received his first rebuke as a manager for using foul language to a linesman as Rangers played Dundee United at Tannadice. He was subsequently fined £100 and banned from the dugout until the end of that season. The ban had little effect. Weeks later he was spotted at St Johnstone entering the dugout on at least two occasions during the game. The Scottish FA were furious and for a second time inside a month hauled the Rangers manager before their disciplinary committee at Park Gardens. This time Souness was fined £2,000 and banned from the touchline until the end of the following season. In effect it was a year's ban.

Souness spent much of the 1989/90 season watching from the stands but he could not resist occasionally slipping down to the touchline. Against Hearts at Ibrox the Scottish Television cameras caught him red-handed. He was spotted standing in the tunnel urging his team on, with the shot included in the edited highlights of the game broadcast the following day. It was an incident that went almost unnoticed until the *Daily Record* brought it to everyone's attention. Souness was summoned to the Scottish Football Association. This time the fine was even heavier – £5,000 – and the ban was extended until the end of the following season, 1990/91. Souness was furious, convinced that he had been set up by Scottish Television but just as angry at the attitude of the SFA. In effect it meant that the Scottish FA had banned him from the touchline from March 1989 until May 1991. By then Souness was walking a tightrope. 'He was testing our system,' says one SFA member. The word inside the SFA was that one more conviction would present them with a very difficult problem. Just how far would they be prepared to go next time in their punishment?

And nor had his players helped to make the record any better. When he arrived at Ibrox he inherited a club with an appalling disciplinary record. In Jock Wallace's final season, there had been seven sendings off and 134 cautions throughout the club. This included both first team and reserve team players. They were the worst behaved club in the Scottish League. In Souness' first season discipline barely improved. There were seven red cards again and 98 cautions throughout the club while their first team was the worst behaved in Scotland. In the 1987/88 season, 10 players were sent off with 91 cautions. In the Scottish Premier League they were only ranked as the fifth worst, but a separate table drawing on the three seasons 85/86, 86/87 and 87/88 found Rangers the second most badly behaved club in Scottish football.

After the disgraceful scenes that marred the Rangers/ Celtic game in October 1987, when three players were dismissed and a court action followed, strenuous efforts were made at the club to improve discipline. And to

Souness' credit it showed. During the following season, 1988/89, there were only five red cards and 109 yellow cards and although the club ranked as the second worst in Scottish football, the first team came out as the second best in the Premier League. The following season Rangers maintained their improvement with five sendings off and 75 cautions placing them in the middle of the behaviour table. But a year later, Souness' final season at Ibrox, it had deteriorated again. This time there were 18 dismissals and 103 cautions, making Rangers the worst behaved club in the Scottish League. And on top of that, there were players sent off in European competition. In Souness' first European campaign Stuart Munro and Davie Cooper both received their marching orders against Borussia Moenchengladbach. Then in the 1988/89 campaign Ally McCoist was ordered off against Cologne.

It is, of course, possible to prove anything with statistics and it would be unfair to draw too many conclusions from these figures. But it would not be unfair to suggest that the club's record during Souness' period was not as exemplary as it should have been. The record for the club as a whole was among the worst in Scottish football. But perhaps Souness' record is best seen in context, particularly when compared with his successor, Walter Smith. Since Souness left Glasgow there has been a marked improvement in the club's disciplinary record. During the 1991/92 season the Rangers first team was the second best behaved in the Premier League and the following season, 1992/93, the first team topped the behaviour league with only one sending off. The Rangers first team is currently regarded as the best behaved in the Premier League.

Even in his final month at Ibrox there was trouble. Terry Hurlock, Mark Walters and Mark Hateley were all sent off in the Scottish Cup defeat by Celtic. At Dunfermline Ian Ferguson received his marching orders while

Brian Reid, his £300,000 buy from Morton, went off against Hibs.

From day one until his final day at Ibrox, Souness was in trouble with the Scottish footballing authorities. There was little love lost between them. They probably resented Souness, the flash, self-made millionaire who was a law unto himself. He in turn no doubt despised them for their bureaucratic, narrow-minded ideas steeped in the forties. There are some who reckon it was the Scottish FA who really drove Souness out of Scotland, that he grew weary of their bans. But Souness, for all his faults, would never be one to allow himself to be driven out of a job by people he did not respect. The Kop may have helped drive him out of Anfield but there is no doubting that Souness had far more respect for the Kop than he ever had for the Scottish FA. What finally drove Souness out of Scotland were attitudes in general, from the terraces to Park Gardens.

Footballing attitudes south of the border might not have been quite so blinkered or bigoted but they were still enough to land Souness in more trouble. The warnings were there for all to see and should unquestionably have been heeded by those at Anfield. It wasn't long before Souness was at loggerheads with the authorities again. Liverpool has always been a club that has assiduously avoided discipline problems on the field. Even off-the-field problems were kept private but that was something else that would slip by the wayside during Graeme Souness' brief reign at Anfield. Bookings, suspensions, sendings off, all were rare events at Liverpool but were to reappear at an alarming rate during the Souness years. Liverpool players openly argued with referees, crowded around officials and in one appalling fracas during the 1993/94 season against Blackburn Rovers, the likes of which Anfield had not seen in decades, players threw punches and jostled with opponents. It was an ugly incident that did not go down well with supporters used to more exemplary behaviour from their heroes.

It was also almost unknown for a Liverpool manager to be in trouble with the Football Association, but again that was to change. Souness had been in the job a year before he encountered his first spot of bother with the footballing authorities. That was in March 1992 when he launched a verbal assault on referee Stephen Lodge of Barnsley following a goalless draw with Southampton. No action was taken on that occasion, but six months later in October 1992, UEFA imposed a five-match touchline ban on him after he had rowed with a referee on the pitch in Moscow as Liverpool tackled Moscow Spartak in the European Cup-Winners' Cup. Tough disciplinarians, UEFA took a grim view of his behaviour pointing out that 'Mr Souness' words were very bad and insulting'. A UEFA spokesman even refused to elaborate on what the words were because they were 'so bad and went on for so long'. Souness was also banned from the dressing room area. Liverpool, still mindful of the appalling tragedy at Heysel and their delicate relationship with UEFA, sensibly felt obliged to apologise to UEFA. Board members were not too pleased. In the event, the ban had little impact as Liverpool crashed out of Europe.

Before the year was out, Souness was again being reported to the Football Association after he criticised referee Brian Hill following a 1–1 Coca-Cola Cup draw with Crystal Palace in which David Burrows was injured. Souness was incensed but again no action was taken by the FA. But in April 1993 the FA's patience finally snapped after referee Roger Dilkes had ordered him off the touchline in another game against Crystal Palace. Souness had continued an angry debate with the Palace bench before directing his protests towards the linesman. The linesman, Mike Bullivant, summoned the referee, who promptly ordered Souness out of the dugout. After

189

the game Mr Dilkes reported that 'my senior linesman reported to me that Mr Souness had persisted in using abusive language to him'. Souness was later found guilty of 'ungentlemanly, insulting or improper behaviour' by the FA and fined £500. It didn't seem to have a great deal of effect. On a number of occasions at Anfield he was to be seen leaping out of the dugout, remonstrating with linesmen and referees. He was usually fortunate. A stern lecture from the referee or a sensible restraining hand from Ronnie Moran would calm him down.

Discipline among players also reached a low point. During the 1992/93 season three Liverpool first teamers were sent off with 47 cautions credited to the first team alone. Such indiscipline was almost unheard of at Anfield. In that same season 105 players received cautions in all club games – first team, reserve and A team football included – with a total of six players sent off. By comparison, in Dalglish's final full season at Anfield, 1989/90, there had been only two red cards throughout the club, a figure which again included all first and second team games as well as the A team players while there had actually been only 46 cautions. In other words the club's disciplinary record was twice as bad under Souness as it had been under Dalglish.

The decline was depressing, getting worse with each year. Souness was impetuous, abrasive and far too emotionally involved. It was a style more suited to Spain or Italy, but among the controlling elite of English and Scottish football it was severely frowned upon. Even when his side was winning, as it had been at Ibrox, he still could not resist a few exchanges with those in authority. As a player he had succeeded in controlling his ill-humour but as a manager he was to be all the more involved, taking it as a personal affront when a decision went against the team. Souness might have been a winner, a man unusually determined, but his lack of discipline did not win him many friends at the Scottish FA, nor with the English FA, nor in boardrooms up and down the country. He was fast becoming his own worst enemy.

CHAPTER THIRTEEN
Suness

Even the most charitable of football managers can be capable of a sharp word or an insult flung in the general direction of the press. It's an odd relationship, a business where the two co-exist somewhere between harmony and hatred. Football reporters are often privy to private goings-on as well as off-the-record thoughts. The relationship, much like the parliamentary lobby, generally works smoothly, until the papers publish something disapproving. It may be a criticism of team selection or, even more more dangerous, revelations about late-night drinking. Most football journalists, especially the local ones, instinctively know the parameters of their etiquette. They understand just when to turn a blind eye or how far they can venture in their criticism and they rarely step beyond those bounds. To trespass over them is to invite the wrath of the manager and the club.

The club always holds the upper hand. Journalists want information; they need to fill the back pages each day and rely on the club's goodwill to supply that information. Likewise football clubs, although they will never formally acknowledge it, also need the publicity. It should be a two-way relationship, but football clubs have only ever regarded it as a one-way ticket with themselves as the principal benefactors. The clubs have the ultimate sanction; they can withdraw their co-operation. Journalists can be refused entry to the press box, banned from the team coach or the training ground. Interviews with players can be refused and more than one reporter has been physically threatened. Even at the supposedly more enlightened clubs such episodes are sadly all too common. It is rarely mentioned or even questioned by many in the footballing fraternity; it's accepted as part of the game where football managers need to exercise their authority. Where being macho and being seen to be macho is an essential element.

Scottish Television holds the ITV franchise for that region that spreads across the lowlands of Scotland taking in Glasgow and Edinburgh. For a number of years STV had a contract with the Scottish Football Association to televise edited highlights of Scottish soccer. The agreement was jointly held with BBC Television Scotland and between them they would take it in turns to show edited highlights the following day. One Sunday in February 1990 it was the turn of STV to televise a match. They had chosen the top of the table clash between Rangers and Hearts. Over the years STV had developed a close relationship with Scotland's premier club. STV director Dermot McQuarrie and presenters Jim White and Gerry McNee had known and dealt with Souness over the years. They all liked him, finding him friendly and helpful. Players and the manager would gladly give pre-match and post-match interviews. There was accord. But it was not to last.

Graeme Souness' ban from the touchline was still in force but during the second half of the match an STV cameraman on the gantry at Ibrox spotted Souness lurking in the players' tunnel urging his team on and offered his director a shot. It was a powerful image which the director liked and, as any TV director would, he took the shot. Over the shot the commentator could be heard saying '. . . and Graeme Souness obviously unhappy with his team'. The director thought no more about it. That evening the match was edited back at Scottish Television's Glasgow headquarters. During the course of the editing none of the sports staff noticed anything untoward about the shot. The following day the edited highlights were transmitted but still nobody paid much attention to it or realised the importance. Within 48 hours, however, all that was about to change. What brought about the change was a sharp-eyed journalist on the *Daily Record* who had been sitting at home watching the game on television when suddenly he spotted the shot of Souness standing in the players' tunnel. It struck him straight away. What was Souness doing there when he was supposedly banned from the touchline? It had the makings of a good story. He immediately got in touch with his sports editor who agreed that they had a good tale on their hands which STV had astonishingly missed and between them they conjured up their story. But what they needed most of all was evidence, a photograph to prove that Souness was standing where he should not have been. They began rummaging through their own shots of the game in the hope that Souness might be spotted lurking in the background. But they could find nothing. Then someone had a brainwave. Why not take the shot from the TV footage? They doubted that STV would voluntarily allow this so they decided simply to lift a still frame from the video recording. It was possible although the quality was always questionable. But it was, they all agreed, worth the risk. And so on the Tuesday the story was splashed across the back page of the *Daily Record*.

Prior to the publication of the article on the Tuesday, Scottish Television had not received one complaint or query from Graeme Souness or any member of the public. The *Daily Record* article, however, quickly alerted Souness and placed a new complexion on the issue. Souness was in trouble again, standing on the touchline in violation of his SFA ban. The consequences were considerable; Souness knew it and flew into a rage, immediately blaming STV.

A few days later Jim White of STV's sports staff called Ibrox to ask Souness for an interview in preparation for the following weekend's game. Souness' response took him by surprise. 'I'm not having anything to do with you lot. I shall be in trouble now and it's all because of you,' he yelled, adding 'You better get your bosses up here quick.' The programme's producer, Denis Mooney, who had never actually met Souness, immediately made an appointment to see the Rangers manager and, along with the programme's director Dermot McQuarrie, rushed straight to Ibrox to find out why he seemed to be blaming STV. Souness kept them waiting. When they were eventually called into his office, Souness demanded to know 'What are you going to do?' Mooney, not one to be bullied by anyone, especially footballers, was taken aback by his aggressive attitude.

'It's not the first time I've had to complain about Scottish Television,' he insisted. 'I had to complain about you before because your people weren't asking my permission before interviewing my players.' Mooney said that they had accepted that and it had been dealt with. But Souness saw it all as part of a wider plot. 'Someone at STV is out to get me,' he kept telling them. Mooney assured him that this was not the case. It had not even occurred to them that there was a problem until the *Daily Record* had noticed it. He also explained that it would have been technically difficult anyway to have cut that particular shot out of the edited highlights. The shot came in the middle of an exciting and important part of the game. It had to stay in. And anyhow it was not their problem if Graeme Souness chose to stand in the players' tunnel when he should not have been there. Mooney tried to reason with him, but Souness was not prepared to accept their explanation. 'No malice was meant,' insisted Mooney. 'We received no phone calls, nobody even noticed it until we saw the piece in the *Daily Record*.'

'If you and I had met in different circumstances we could have been friends,' was Souness' only response as they stood up to leave. Souness did, however, promise to think about it and gave Mooney his car phone number. 'Call me tomorrow,' he said as they left.

Sitting in his cramped office the next day, Mooney decided he had better give Souness a call. Souness was surprisingly chatty. 'I've thought about it,' he said, 'but I've decided I can't change my mind. It would be seen as a climbdown.' He added that neither he nor any of his players would in future co-operate with Scottish Television. From now on there would be no interviews either with himself or any of his players, he insisted. What's more, he promised to maintain the ban for as long as he was banned by the Scottish FA.

Mooney reckoned that Souness fully understood and accepted their explanation but for some reason, best known to himself, he would not back down. Souness had made his stand and even though he was half prepared to accept that he had been wrong, his own vanity would not allow a public climbdown of any sorts. It was Souness at his most vindictive and stubborn. The truth was that it was not the first time Souness had stood in the tunnel, out of sight of the officials, urging his team on. He had been chancing his arm for months. He had been finally caught out.

Souness, however, could not ban the cameras from Ibrox altogether. STV had an agreement with the Scottish FA and there was nothing he could do about that. Games still had to be televised. But Souness was successful in stopping all pre-match and post-match interviews in front of the cameras. But he had little success in stopping his players talking to STV off camera and even to this day he probably does not know just how much the players continued to co-operate with STV.

STV took a policy decision to cut down on the number of games they showed from Ibrox. As the top club in Scotland, Rangers would normally have expected a significant amount of coverage on television and sold much of their perimeter advertising on the basis of their games being televised. When that did not happen, the advertisers began to complain. In truth STV were not all that bothered by the ban and rather than takes games from Ibrox they concentrated on showing Rangers away from home. They regarded it as petty and inconvenient rather than as a major problem. But the ban persisted until Souness left. What's more, Souness went to enormous lengths to stop anyone within his persuasion from co-operating with STV. When interviews were given with other ITV companies, particularly in later years with Granada, he would insist that the pictures were not given to STV.

From his very first day at Anfield, Souness laid down the policy. On the day he joined as manager he appeared live in the Granada Television studios in Liverpool to give an interview. Talking to Souness after the interview, Jeff Anderson, the show's producer, casually mentioned that STV were hoping to show the interview. Souness' response took Anderson by surprise. 'I'll be very annoyed if that happens,' insisted Souness, explaining that he did not give interviews with STV. 'Can you call them up and see what's happened? See if you can get it stopped.' A nonplussed Anderson promptly called STV only to discover that in fact they had not been able to use the interview. Anderson was much relieved. But it would not

David Murray, millionaire and Conservative, the new boss of Ibrox. (*Glasgow Herald and Evening Times*)

David Murray and Graeme Souness take over at Ibrox. (*Glasgow Herald and Evening Times*)

Souness and assistant Walter
Smith. Scottish league champions,
1987. (*Bob Thomas Sports
Photography*)

If you want to know the time, ask
a policeman. (*Glasgow Herald and
Evening Times*)

Graeme Souness and Ally McCoist. There were times when they did have fun together. (*Glasgow Herald and Evening Times*)

Souness after another disciplinary hearing at the Scottish FA. (*Glasgow Herald and Evening Times*)

Graeme Souness joins Liverpool, April 1991.
A pensive Ronnie Moran looks on. (*Steve Hale*)

Souness' first game in charge at Anfield. Those were the days. (*Colorsport*)

Souness with new
signings Mark Wright and
Dean Saunders, his first
buy at Liverpool. (*Steve
Hale*)

'I did it my way.'
(*Colorsport*)

Souness and Phil Boersma wait for the final whistle at Wembley.
(*Bob Thomas Sports Photography*)

The FA Cup 1992 – Souness' only trophy as manager of Liverpool.
(*Bob Thomas Sports Photography*)

Souness, post-triple heart bypass operation, leaves Wembley accompanied
by his doctors after the 2–0 victory over Sunderland. (*Steve Hale*)

The end is nigh. Liverpool v Bristol City, January 1994. (*Colorsport*)

be the only time when Granada were warned by Souness not to give any footage to Scottish Television.

The only time when the ban did cause a problem was during the Italia 90 World Cup finals. ITV, like most other media organisations, had made a payment into the Scottish players' pool for access during the World Cup. The access guaranteed the ITV companies on-camera interviews as well as off-the-record chats. However, when they got to Italy, the ITV team discovered, much to their amazement, that Souness had warned the Rangers players that they must not talk to ITV as the material might be shown on Scottish Television. They were to adopt the same policy with Scottish Television in Italy as they had throughout the season. With so many Rangers players in the squad, there was a potential problem for ITV. In fact, they took the ban so seriously that they even made representations to the club. David Murray himself was asked to intervene but he declined with nobody feeling that they could either usurp their manager, or even challenge him. It posed a dilemma for the television companies.

In the end, ITV backed away from a confrontation, deciding to take the wise course of letting the situation ride. Instead, they simply did not bother interviewing any Rangers players throughout the tournament. The Scottish FA was powerless and kept well out of such politicking. Players' pools, agents and dealing with the press were not a part of their hallowed world. ITV probably had the muscle to have forced the situation but chose instead to avoid upsetting Souness. At least Scottish Television had had the courage to challenge the might of Rangers and its manager over the season by cutting down on the number of games it screened from Ibrox and by refusing to issue any formal apology or back away from its initial position.

ITV even made an offer to Souness to come and be part

of their team in Italy. Souness was offered £15,000 but declined saying that he wanted £40,000. That kind of money was out of the question and nobody really took it seriously, least of all Souness, who had claimed all along that he wanted to spend the summer break with his family.

Although Scottish Television later had their problems with Souness, their reporter Jim White remembers a very different Souness. White recalls:

> We were in Italy making a film about him, before he ever came to Rangers. When we arrived, Sampdoria had just been beaten. Souness had set up everything with the club but suddenly the mood at the club had changed; Sampdoria were not welcoming press coverage. I was alarmed and could see all our film arrangements being washed away. I had this crew with me and just a few days to make our film. I was about to panic but then Graeme appeared, waved his magic wand and simply said, 'Don't worry, I'll sort everything.' And he did. It was such a relief. He immediately made me feel more relaxed.

While Souness could on occasion be hot-tempered with journalists, there are many others who will testify to a more genuine warmth. Freelance Liverpool photographer Steve Hale also remembers visiting him in Italy to do a photo session at Sampdoria. 'He could hardly have been more hospitable,' says Hale. 'He invited me into his home and insisted that I stay with him. He was so co-operative, friendly and helpful. In all the time that I knew him, and that was over many years, he was brilliant with me and I never had any problems with him.'

Souness' confrontation with Scottish Television was never likely to cause any waves within Ibrox itself, but the same could not be said of another press flare-up, this time when he was at Liverpool. It was to be a flare-up that almost cost Souness his job. But ironically, this time it would be because of his all too cosy relationship with the press.

It is almost impossible to put into words the sheer naked hatred felt towards the *Sun* newspaper on Merseyside. Liverpudlians have long memories. They can parcel and carry a vendetta as long as anyone. Perhaps it's the Irish blood, perhaps it's the notorious chip on the shoulder. Whatever it is, they never forget a miscarriage of justice.

Saturday 15 April 1989 is a day no Liverpool fan, and for that matter barely anyone else in the country, will ever forget. It was the day ninety-five Liverpool fans met their death at the Leppings Lane End of Hillsborough. It was an appalling moment, the worst sporting tragedy in British history and one that can readily bring tears to the eyes of most people in the city. There was not one Liverpool fan who did not know someone who died that day, so tightly knit is this community.

Few disasters have been so comprehensively covered by the press as Hillsborough, though ironically, four years previously, in the full glare of the TV cameras, Liverpool had been involved in another tragedy. At the Heysel stadium in Brussels, immediately prior to Liverpool's European Cup final with the Italian side Juventus, thirty-nine fans had died as Liverpool fans rioted. They were mainly Italian fans, supporters of Juventus, along with a handful of Belgians, who were killed. Most had died as they retreated from the marauding English hordes heading towards a wall which was to collapse causing mayhem. Millions throughout the world had watched on television as shame came to British football and in particular to Liverpool Football Club and its supporters. It was a disaster that had been in the making for years.

Liverpool fans were rightly blamed for the tragedy

although there were other contributory factors, such as the delapidated state of the Heysel stadium and the total inadequacies of the Belgian police. But at the end of the day the blame had to rest with those who attacked the flimsy fencing on that terracing in the first place. Over the next few weeks Liverpool fans faced hostile criticism, a criticism which all were forced to bear no matter what their involvement. For those who had supported the club over the years, and had helped foster the image of fun-loving, friendly fans, it was a bitter pill to swallow. Everyone was now tarnished with the same brush. Many ended their association with the club at that moment, too ashamed and maybe even too afraid ever to venture on to the terraces again.

The subsequent tragedy at Hillsborough had to be viewed against this shameful background. As the crowd spilled on to the pitch at Hillsborough that spring afternoon and the referee called a halt to the proceedings it was inevitable that commentators would talk glibly about yet more crowd trouble. But even though the full horrors of the disaster quickly became apparent there was still a knee-jerk reaction from the press aimed at blaming hooligans for the disaster. One policeman had even talked of how the fans had stormed a gate, forcing it to be opened. It was some days, if not weeks, before the full truth would be revealed.

Over at the *Sun* newspaper, some eighteen journalists and photographers were thrown on to the story. The first sign of brazened reporting came on the Tuesday morning when they ran a leader under the headline 'SCAPEGOATS' and asked 'Is it fair to make the police the scapegoats for the Hillsborough disaster? It happened because thousands of fans, many without tickets, tried to get into the ground just before the kick off – either by forcing their way in or blackmailing the police into opening the gates.' And so on.

The following day their coverage adopted an even more sinister approach. Kelvin MacKenzie, the *Sun*'s notorious, ebullient editor, had helped pull together a story that threw an altogether different light on Liverpool fans to the one being portrayed by some newspapers. MacKenzie, sitting in his Wapping office, sketched out a front page under the headline 'YOU SCUM'. In the event that headline was dropped and another replaced it which was to prove just as damaging. Under the headline 'THE TRUTH' the *Sun* revealed a side of the disaster hitherto unreported. It had three subheadings.

> Some fans picked pockets of victims.
> Some fans urinated on the brave cops.
> Some fans beat up PC giving kiss of life.

The story began:

> Drunken Liverpool fans viciously attacked rescue workers as they tried to revive victims of the Hillsborough soccer disaster, it was revealed last night.
> Police officers, firemen and ambulance crew were punched, kicked and urinated upon by a hooligan element in the crowd.
> Some thugs rifled the pockets of injured fans as they were stretchered out unconscious on the pitch.
> Sheffield MP Irvine Patnik revealed in one shameful episode a gang of Liverpool fans noticed that the blouse of a girl trampled to death had risen above her breasts.
> As a policeman struggled in vain to revive her, the mob jeered: 'Throw her up here and we will . . . her.'

And so the story continued. But the *Sun* was not the only newspaper to jump on this contemptuous bandwagon.

The *Sheffield Star* had already voiced some of these allegations while *The Times* and *Today*, both part of the Murdoch empire at News International, were also splashing similar allegations on their front pages. The *Star* also went in hard but qualified its headline 'Dead Fans Robbed By Drunk Thugs' with the sub-headline 'What Cops Say About Hillsboro'. The *Sun*'s story was based on non-attributable quotes. It was either an unnamed policeman who was being quoted or the MP Irvine Patnik who was quoting stories told to him by others. There was no hard evidence. The story was a classic smear.

When the *Sun* thudded onto doormats throughout Liverpool the following morning there was outrage. The switchboard at Radio Merseyside was jammed with complaints. There had already been an outpouring of emotion to Radio Merseyside following the *Daily Mirror*'s gratuitous front page colour photographs. But now a much more bitter contempt for the press was being voiced. Radio Merseyside telephoned the *Sun* asking for a comment. The *Sun* ignored their call. All it would say was 'no comment'. It was to be some time before the *Sun* issued a formal apology. The *Sun* had totally miscalculated the depth of feeling after the disaster. Elsewhere in Liverpool, people began to burn the paper. A TV news crew filmed the ceremonious bonfire while the *Liverpool Echo* challenged the *Sun* and other newspapers to produce its evidence. If you didn't know about the *Sun* story that morning everyone on Merseyside certainly did by late evening. Meanwhile, one radio DJ suggested *Sun* readers might like to vote with their feet by boycotting the newspaper. His suggestion was taken up with a vengeance.

Before the disaster sales of the *Sun* on wider Merseyside had topped 524,000 copies a day. Within days of their story it was down to 320,000. Heaps of unsold bundles lay on newsagents' counters. Some shops even refused to display the paper, hiding it shamefully under the counter or leaving the bundles, still wrapped, on the floor. And nor was it to turn out to be an idle, one-off gesture. Months later sales were still nowhere near what they had been prior to the disaster. It was costing the *Sun* around £10 million a year in lost sales. Liverpudlians had marked the *Sun* and they would not forget.

At the time of the Hillsborough tragedy, Graeme Souness was managing Glasgow Rangers, 200 miles away, and no doubt somewhat sanitised from the outpourings of emotion that swept over Merseyside. But this was scant excuse for what was to happen. You hardly needed to be sensitive to realise the depth of feeling on Merseyside and the attitude towards the *Sun*. And yet from his hospital bed where he was recovering from a triple heart bypass operation, Graeme Souness delivered an insult to Liverpool fans that was to tarnish his reputation for ever and lay the seeds of his own destruction.

Souness had always had close links with the *Sun* newspaper. Ken Gallacher, chief Scottish sports writer of the *Sun* had helped co-author one of Souness' books. And it was the *Sun* who had exclusively revealed that Mo Johnston was set to become a Rangers player.

It was a front page *Sun* exclusive on Monday 6 April 1992 that broke the news of Souness' need for a triple heart bypass. Then on 14 April there was a sixteen-page souvenir pull-out in the *Sun* called 'Souness King of the Kop'. The following day the *Sun* carried another Souness exclusive. This time it was Souness' own story of his triple heart bypass operation. The story caused a sensation. Not because it revealed anything unusual or unexpected. It was simply that it was the *Sun*, the most despised newspaper on Merseyside. On the front page, beneath the headline 'LOVERPOOL', there was Souness, passionately kissing his girlfriend Karen Levy by his hospital bed. Liverpool had just beaten Portsmouth in a penalty shoot-out in the FA Cup semi-final and Souness and Karen were celebrating in suitable style. Inside the paper was Souness' own story of his operation and illness. But it was also a double disaster for Souness. Not only had he chosen the wrong newspaper but, even worse, the story appeared on the very day of the Hillsborough anniversary. It was exactly three years to the day. It was an appalling misjudgement.

Ever since the Hillsborough disaster the *Sun* had been scorned and despised on Merseyside. Its misreporting and its sickening criticism of Liverpool supporters had caused outrage. Even hardened journalists had cringed at its reporting. That Souness should have sold his story to the *Sun*, of all newspapers, caused even further offence. Souness had totally misjudged the city's mood. Not unexpectedly, there was outrage. Letters poured into the city's two newspapers, the *Liverpool Daily Post* and the *Liverpool Echo*, while others rang the local radio stations, Radio City and Radio Merseyside. The front page headline in the *Daily Mirror* the following day was 'The Shame Of Souness'. Barry Devonside, who had lost his 18-year-old son at Hillsborough was quoted as saying 'Graeme Souness has sunk to the lowest form of life.' It was a sentiment to be repeated by many relatives of Hillsborough victims in the press that morning. Everyone was bitter about Souness' lack of sensitivity. Why the *Sun* of all papers, they asked, and why on this day of all days?

Within twenty-four hours Souness was being raced back into intensive care, postponing any apology. But a couple of days later he was fit enough to issue a statement. He apologised unreservedly and said that he had 'reluctantly' agreed to talk to the *Sun* about the operation in return for a donation to a children's hospital in Liverpool. 'I received payment from the newspaper after giving them the exclusive story ... the lion's share of the agreed payment will go the children's hospital at Alder Hey. They

will benefit more than Graeme Souness.' But it did little
to calm the storm. The hospital received £25,000, a figure
which they say was secured some ten days before the
article appeared. The cheque from the *Sun* arrived on
22 April.

Souness had never been popular with some Liverpool
supporters. His brash style, his multi-millionaire ways
and his 'Champagne Charlie' image were a million miles
from the average beer and a pie unemployed Kopite. The
Liverpool fanzines had a field day. They had never really
liked him. One dubbed him 'Suness', another 'Sourness'.
There was no doubting their opinions. The anger grew
worse and within days fans all over the city were demanding the resignation of their manager.

Typical was a letter to one of the fanzines. It read:

On the 15th April 1992, that bond between club and
supporters was cut in one fell swoop by Graeme Souness. Since that day I have not attended a single
Liverpool match and will not until the first match
following Souness' departure, which cannot come
soon enough for me. As a Reds fanatic this was not
an easy thing to do, but I immediately returned my
season ticket and gave up my Cup final ticket. To
have done otherwise would, I feel, have been an
insult to the supporters I saw perish in the Leppings
Lane End in 1989.

Had the Cup final and a Liverpool victory not intervened,
then Souness might well have been packing his bags. The
board was already fidgety. At least three directors had
privately decided that the time had come to call it a day.
Everyone on the board was deeply embarrassed by the
incident. But it was not just the fact that it was a story
sold to the *Sun* that concerned them. There was more to
it than that. For a start, the club had not been informed

of Souness' heart condition and need for an operation as early as they would have liked. There had been a delay. The board felt that Souness might have been holding back, doing a deal with the *Sun* for an exclusive. They did not like that.

Even the Cup final had brought its problems. The question everyone wanted to know was whether Souness would be there, leading the team out at Wembley. The club was deeply concerned and did not want the day spoiled by an unnecessary focus on Souness and his medical condition. There was already intense press speculation. They also felt that it was in his interest to remain in hospital or at least to keep away from the limelight and pressure of a Wembley trip. Watching your team in a Wembley Cup final is hardly the best form of recuperation after triple heart bypass surgery. Indeed, it would be difficult to imagine anything worse.

The board met and decided to send a deputation to tell Souness of their concerns and to ask him not to go to Wembley. Chairman David Moores and vice-chairman Sydney Moss were the two men given the task of making the trip down the M56 to the Cheshire hospital where Souness was recovering. Both men were fond of Souness and it was thought that hearing the news from them might lessen the blow, that they could make him see sense. Moss tried to convince Souness that it would not be wise to appear at Wembley.

'It won't help your recovery,' Moss argued.

'Are you ordering me?' asked Souness.

'Well, let's put it this way,' answered Moss. 'The board really would prefer it if you stayed away.'

Moss and Moores left the hospital certain that they had conveyed the board's views to him but unsure of what his final response would be.

Up until the last few days, nobody was quite sure whether Souness would appear or not. He probably was not sure himself. Then, 48 hours before the final, he announced that he would be there. The board were furious. In the event he arrived, hollow-faced, unsteady, clearly shaken and showing all the anxieties of the preceding weeks. He was accompanied by the club's doctor who sat behind him, a restraining arm for the more excitable moments.

It had not been a good first season. Just over twelve months in the job and already Souness had lashed out nearly £9 million. Eight players had been signed, seven had been sold; it had been the biggest turnover in the club's history. There was dressing room discontent, poor results, and team performances that looked a million miles from the traditional Liverpool style. Everyone inside the club was tense. And now this. A serious operation that brought into question whether the manager would be able to carry out his job in the future to the best of his ability and a story sold to the *Sun*. For some it seemed as good an excuse as any to get rid of the manager. But then Liverpool had just gone and won the FA Cup.

On Wednesday 13 May, just three days after winning the FA Cup, an emergency board meeting began at Anfield at 9 a.m. It was to last for five hours. Rumour and speculation were rife. Thirty minutes into the meeting, Souness arrived, driven by his girlfriend, Karen Levy, and went in to face the eight-man board. He left the meeting for a short period but then returned before finally speeding out of Anfield shortly after 1 p.m. looking grim-faced.

Inside the boardroom at Anfield the arguments raged. At least one director insisted that Souness had to be fired. Now was the time to get rid of him. If he was sacked now, everyone would understand. Souness' future hung on a knife edge and even to this day he probably does not know just how close he came to being fired. Director Tony

Ensor told the board that he had enough. What was going on at Anfield was appalling, he argued. Souness had to be sacked. Money was being wasted, their authority was being usurped. The club was drifting out of control. Ensor eventually offered his resignation but was then talked out of it by his fellow directors. This would not be the right time to resign, they told him. It will only detract from what we decide today. He agreed but insisted that as soon as the time was right he was going, probably at the Annual General Meeting. David Moores argued that Souness should be given the benefit of the doubt. There had been so many injuries, and while it had been a difficult year they had just won the FA Cup. Reluctantly the board agreed that Souness should be given a further chance.

Eventually the club issued a statement. It was read out by club secretary Peter Robinson. It said:

> The board ... have held a lengthy meeting with the manager, Mr Graeme Souness, to discuss the circumstances surrounding his recent illness and his entering into an exclusive agreement with the *Sun* newspaper.
>
> The board expressed their disapproval at what has happened, but accepted that at the time of entering the agreement in question Mr Souness was under considerable medical and emotional pressure.
>
> Mr Souness has already expressed his sincere regret for what has happened. He has repeated this and now given clear assurances that there will be no recurrences of any such incident.
>
> He has accepted the board's recommendation that it is inappropriate for the manager of Liverpool Football Club to enter into an exclusive agreement with any section of the media. The board and Mr Souness now regard this whole unfortunate matter as closed,

and we will not be making any further comment on it.

But they did; Robinson later confirmed that the club had delivered a public rebuke to Souness.

Souness has always been repentant about the incident. 'I alienated a lot of supporters,' he admits, 'but I held up my hands and apologised.' It may have been foolish to have given the story to the *Sun* in the first place but you could hardly blame him for the timing. That was sheer bad luck. The embrace was captured on the Monday evening after the replay against Portsmouth and should have gone in the Tuesday paper but because the game finished so late, it missed the deadline and had to be held over until the Wednesday. Unfortunately that was the anniversary of Hillsborough.

And that was it. Everyone disappeared, off for their summer break; Souness to get some sun and rest, the players to bask in the glory of their FA Cup triumph, the board to reflect on the last few months. But the bad taste lingered. Even those normally loyal journalists had to admit that something had disappeared that week. The *Daily Mail*'s Colin Wood, a reporter closer than almost any other journalist to Anfield, reckoned 'the family spirit has gone. The family used to include the fans and it doesn't any more.'

But there was a footnote. In June 1994, six months after his resignation from Liverpool, Graeme Souness remarried. The ceremony took place in Las Vegas and the story was broken as a 'Match of the Day' exclusive in, of all papers, the *Sun*, with pictures of Souness and Karen Levy.

CHAPTER FOURTEEN
Heartache

Graeme Souness may have won league championships and European Cups; he may even have engineered a revolution in Scottish football and he may have faced a mammoth task on his return to Anfield. But in April 1992 he faced the biggest match of his life. He had just learned that he needed immediate heart bypass surgery and, unknown to him, had probably suffered a heart attack already. For a man like Souness it was a devastating blow.

The announcement that Souness was about to enter hospital came a day after Liverpool had drawn with Portsmouth in the FA Cup semi-final. Souness had been hoping that the tie would have been settled and that he could enter hospital without any additional worries. But nothing was going to plan for Graeme Souness. There would have to be a replay and he could be under the anaesthetic by then. The operation could not be delayed. It was only a week earlier that he had learned the news. It came as the biggest shock of his life. It also came as a shock to millions of others. Nobody expected a fit, healthy looking man of 38 to be facing a crossroads like this. Souness took his confidant Phil Boersma aside and told him almost immediately. Boersma thought he was going into hospital for another nose job. 'No it's not cosmetic this time,' explained Souness, 'it's far worse.' Boersma was staggered and sworn to secrecy. Only a few others at Anfield were told.

Doctors offer a variety of reasons for heart disease. The most common is smoking, the biggest single killer of all. Too much alcohol, especially spirits, can also lead to a clogging of the arteries. A bad diet with too many fatty foods is another factor, while anyone with a high cholesterol level can also face dangers. Poor fitness, lack of exercise and overweight are also contributing factors. Then there is stress. It was not difficult to know which category was at work here. Souness didn't smoke, he wasn't a heavy drinker, he wasn't overweight, he was supremely fit and a man careful with his diet. But in the pressure-cooker world of football management, it's a wonder that more managers do not suffer heart problems. Twelve months earlier his predecessor had slumped out of Anfield almost a broken man, beaten by the gnawing daily pressures of football management. In Dalglish's case the pressures had sent his head spinning. Souness thought he could cope with those pressures. He seemed to thrive on them but all the time they were taking their toll. His own father had undergone heart surgery as well as an uncle which suggested an inherited problem as well. The warning should have been there. The combination of family heart problems and stress can be fatal.

Doctors had discovered blocked arteries during a routine examination and were convinced that he had already suffered a heart attack without even knowing it. One artery was reported to be 90 per cent clogged while the other was 70 per cent blocked. Without immediate surgery, he could have a fatal heart attack at any time. The arteries supply the heart with essential oxygen and nutrients. The heart cannot function properly if part of a coronary artery becomes blocked or diseased. The solution is to build a new route for the blood supply by putting a bridge across the blockage in the artery. Souness needed three such bridges.

On the morning of Monday 6 April Souness drove his black J-reg Mercedes into the grounds of the Alexandra Hospital in leafy Cheadle, a suburb of Stockport, not far from the Cheshire stockbroker belt where Souness lived. Patients peered out of their windows, attracted by the noise, as the gathering journalists outside surrounded his car.

'I can't say I'm looking forward to it,' he told them as he opened the boot of his car to take out his overnight bags, 'but it is essential, so it has to be done.' He admitted that he had heaped it on himself because of 'the way I live and the way I treat football. I am passionate about it.' And with that he was into the hospital to face the loneliest few weeks of his life.

During those first weeks following the operation he admits that he wondered if it was worth carrying on at Anfield. 'I couldn't walk along the hospital corridor,' he says. 'I used to stop by the window to take in some fresh air. I really wondered if I should carry on with the job.' But he wasn't, as it was reported, averse to telephoning John Major to congratulate him on his general election victory that week. That was something else that hardly endeared him to the unemployed of the Kop.

Some papers had already written him off; one was running a bookies' list on who the front runners might be to take over. John Toshack was the favourite, Peter Reid another fancy and even the name of one of his own assistants, Phil Thompson, was being mentioned. Most wondered if it was really possible to make a full recovery and return to the appalling grind and pressure of football management. Others just wondered if it was sensible. David Moores promised the full support of the board. But if Souness really had any doubts, they did not linger too long. Being single-minded can have its disadvantages, but it can also have its benefits. It was only his single-mindedness and determination which pulled him through so quickly. Most would have taken months off work; Souness was back, at Wembley, within the month, determined to see his side lift the FA Cup. It may have been foolhardy and much against medical advice, let alone the advice of the Liverpool directors, but it was typical Souness. He may have been his own worst enemy but it was the stuff that drove him to a full recovery. Only those closest to him can know the trauma he suffered in those weeks and the psychological effects it has had on him.

As if the trauma of a triple heart bypass operation was not enough there was to be an added problem. Liverpool fans awoke on the morning of 15 April 1992 to see a *Sun* exclusive – Souness' own story of his triple heart bypass operation.

Nobody, other than Souness' wife, probably cared too much about his passionate embrace with Karen Levy, but what they really did care about was that not only had he given his own story to the *Sun* but it had appeared on the anniversary of the Hillsborough disaster.

Karen Levy was a model who had appeared in the James Bond movie *A View to a Kill* and had been a TV hostess on Anglia Television's *Sale of the Century*. Levy lived close to Souness in the Cheshire stockbroker belt and they had struck up what seemed to be a steady relationship. After nine years of marriage, Souness and his wife Danielle had split up three years earlier while he was still in Scotland. Judging by what she was later to recount, there was considerable acrimony and when Souness entered hospital there was much speculation in the tabloids about whether she and the children would be visiting him.

Danielle, some years later, revealed in the *Daily*

Express that on the Saturday before entering hospital, Souness had called her to tell her about his operation. At the same time he also asked her to do an interview with the *Sun*. It was all part of the package. She was shocked, not only to discover that her estranged husband was about to have a serious heart operation, but that the *Sun* had been informed before her and his children.

A few days later she was to get another surprise. A *Sun* reporter turned up on her doorstep to do the interview. At the end of the interview he asked her what she thought of Karen Levy. 'Karen who?' she asked. Danielle knew nothing of her husband's new girlfriend. She called Souness who then told her about Levy. She then inquired if she could bring the children to the hospital to see him. 'All I can say,' replied Souness, 'is that your paths will cross.' Danielle was furious, and refused to visit him. She was to be even more angry when the interview appeared with the photograph of her husband kissing Levy and with speculation in other papers that they were to wed.

The *Sun* exclusive appeared to the accompaniment of a barrage of criticism. What sympathy Souness might have garnered over his operation was now lost. It was to be a major turning point in his relations with Liverpool fans. Twenty-four hours after the *Sun*'s exclusive, and while everyone was in the midst of venting their anger, Souness was rushed back into the intensive care unit at Alexandra Hospital. He was in for only half an hour but it was thirty minutes that caused more than a few flutters among the hospital staff. Souness had suffered a relapse with a blood clot on the lung. It was soon dealt with, but he was forced to spend the remainder of the day in the progressive care unit. Whether or not the *Sun* affair had anything to do with it will always be conjecture. But once he was fit enough Souness issued an immediate apology. He held up his hands, admitting that he had been wrong to sell his story to the *Sun*.

Souness was discharged from hospital a month after

the operation, just two days before his side were due to
face Sunderland in the FA Cup final. He had lost weight,
his face looked gaunt but he was in good spirits. Considering he had just gone through major surgery and had
experienced a relapse he was in remarkable shape. He
smiled at the waiting press corps as Karen helped him
into his car. But what everybody wanted to know was
whether he was going to Wembley. He was noncommittal.
Souness and his girlfriend drove straight to Anfield where
they met David Moores and Peter Robinson, then went
on to Melwood where Souness spent a little time with
the players as they prepared for Wembley. Souness took
Moran to one side and told him that he would not be
leading the team out.

'I don't think I could walk that distance unaided,' he
confessed. 'I'll be there, though, but you lead the team
out,' he told his assistant.

CHAPTER FIFTEEN
Poacher Turned Gamekeeper

The two overwhelming footballing influences in Souness' soccer career were undoubtedly Jack Charlton and Bob Paisley. He had brief spells under other managers like Bill Nicholson, Harold Shepherdson, Stan Anderson, John Neal and Joe Fagan. But none had anything like the influence of Charlton or Paisley. Charlton made it clear from day one that Souness could either knuckle under and work or waste himself away. Souness was to be ever grateful to the big man. In his autobiography he wrote: 'He was a man to whom I could respond. He recognised my problems from the moment he took over and not only improved my whole attitude but also pulled me off the scrap heap and turned me into a professional. I have a lot of time for him and his methods.'

Charlton, the lanky, chain-smoking, World Cup-winner who took over at Ayresome Park in May 1973, was a no-nonsense manager. Players quaked in his presence. It was partly his size, partly his roar, partly his reputation. As a player he had been feared by team-mates as well as opponents. At Leeds they called him 'Big Jack' and it wasn't just because of his 6ft 2ins frame. He was beholden to no one whether they were chairmen, FA officials or temperamental strikers. He might call the chairman 'Mister' but it was out of politeness rather than respect or deference. If he wanted a day off fishing, he went; if he didn't like a player, he told him. That was the Charlton style. It was uncompromising but it was a style that soaked into the Souness mentality.

Souness did not pick up all his habits. It has never been Souness' style to take a day off or be able to flick a switch and cut himself off from the job. Souness was to be the very opposite of Big Jack, far too involved for his own good, unable to escape the demands and pressures of the job. But what he did cream off from Charlton was that you had to be the boss and lay down the law. If you were going to bark you also had to bite. On more than one occasion, according to Souness, Charlton hurled a crate of lemonade across the dressing room at Ayresome Park in order to reinforce his point. Souness, like everyone else at Ayresome Park, was intimidated by the big man.

Although Charlton could get angry, it was mostly show, contrived to put fear into his players, and to remind them of who was in charge. The anger never seeped into his bloodstream. An hour later he could be calmly casting a fly in some quiet trout stream or shooting on the North Yorkshire moors. He seemed almost schizophrenic. That was his secret, his ability to be able to escape, flick a switch somewhere in his body mechanism and forget all about football. With Souness the anger and the angst were too connected ever to be separated. They were too much a part and parcel of him. But there was one vital lesson he picked up which in time would become a hall-mark of the Souness style. 'Only one thing mattered to Jack in football,' he wrote in one of his books, 'and that was winning. He was one of the school who knew that there were no prizes for coming second.' Souness' ex-wife recognised more than anyone how the lesson had been learned. 'He had to win and had to have good results. The stress was enormous. He was so serious and dedicated.'

Souness learned similar lessons from Bob Paisley, his manager at Liverpool. Paisley may have seemed like everyone's favourite uncle as he ambled around Anfield in his slippers and cardigan, a friendly nod and smile here and there. But beneath this genial grin he ruled with a rod of iron. Nobody dared to step out of line and as Souness himself testifies when Paisley was around the atmosphere changed dramatically. Paisley was Mr Authority with a friendly face. 'If you have all had enough of winning,' he was fond of telling them, 'then come and see me and I'll sell the lot of you.' And he meant it. But Paisley had a canniness that Charlton lacked.

Paisley was the undisputed master, the most successful manager in the history of the Football League, a genius at spotting quality players, a cunning old fox when it came to substitutions and a master of psychology. When Liverpool and Spurs were drawing 1–1 after 90 minutes of their 1982 League Cup final he strode over to his players as they collapsed around the centre circle awaiting extra time. 'Get up,' he yelled at them. 'Don't let Spurs think you're knackered.' It worked, Liverpool went on to win 3–1. He knew when to coax or cajole, yet rarely flew into a rage. He left that to his trusty lieutenants. Anyhow, there was little need to in those days at Anfield; players were fighting for their places. And when he did let rip, you knew about it. Generally, if there was a problem, Paisley and his men would retire to the bootroom, brew a pot of tea, and work the problem out between them.

Souness was always generous to his managers. It was Souness who pushed Bob Paisley up the steps at Wembley after Liverpool had won the League Cup, making him the first manager ever to receive a trophy at Wembley. He also organised a whip-round among the players to buy Paisley a retirement present. With the money he bought a clock and had it engraved 'To Bob from all the lads'.

Mark Lawrenson also recalls Liverpool's Joe Fagan being on the end of a similar Souness gesture.

They had enormous respect for each other. Joe rarely raised his voice in the dressing room and that appealed to Graeme. Joe was never impressed by anyone with a big mouth, and Graeme admired Joe because he could always find time for a laugh which is not always the case at a football club. When he signed for Sampdoria he went to the famous boot-room at Anfield with two bottles of champagne to say his farewell in typical fashion. He knew what to expect and he got it. 'Thanks for coming, now clear off because we have a job to do here,' was Joe's parting shot and Graeme wouldn't have expected anything more.

When Souness arrived at Anfield he was still a rough diamond. Charlton may have discovered him buried in some dark corner of the dressing room but it was Paisley who would cut him down to size and smooth the rough edges. Paisley's stroke of genius was undoubtedly his decision to appoint Souness club captain. It was a decision that would later cause more than a few ripples within the club as his predecessor Phil Thompson took unkindly to being stripped of the honour. And in this would also germinate a future row. But for Souness it was to be the coming of age. The captaincy mattered to him, an acknowledgement of his pedigree and authority. It was another masterstroke by the canny old Paisley, based on the well-proven hypothesis that if you want to get the best out of a troublemaker then make him the boss. Many a trade union militant has been appeased by a management job. Souness was no exception. He thrived on his new responsibilities and from that moment on he was poacher turned gamekeeper.

Paisley demanded a code of conduct and Souness gave it him. The man who enjoyed a late night out was suddenly setting a fresh example and expected the same of others. And as a manager he was to take that attitude to even further excesses demanding the utmost professionalism from his charges. He even banned his players from their regular round of golf, both at Rangers and Liverpool. It led to a few words between the golf-loving Bruce Grobbelaar and his manager.

Souness would forget what it was to be young, fancy-free and living in a big city with a pocketful of cash. The temptations for footballers can be all too overwhelming and in his youth Souness had tasted the good life as much as anyone, even, on his own admission, to excess at times. Paisley always adopted the attitude that what he didn't see, he was never going to grieve over. As long as a player performed on the park on a Saturday afternoon, then he could have his fun on a Saturday night. Souness, however, was to be even more demanding than those who had tutored him. Mark Lawrenson recalls how surprised he was to learn from Terry Butcher and Chris Woods that Souness had become such a strict disciplinarian. 'He certainly did not learn that at Anfield,' says Lawrenson.

Souness' managerial career was to be peppered with a series of dressing room rows, some public, some not so open. The most public row he was to have during his spell at Ibrox was with the former Spurs defender, Graham Roberts. Souness had signed Roberts in December 1986 after Roberts had been controversially shifted into the Spurs midfield, a position he loathed. It was not long before Roberts was itching for a move. He came to Ibrox for £450,000 and soon settled into the heart of the Rangers defence. Roberts was even made captain during the enforced absence of Terry Butcher and although his Ibrox career began positively it was to end in acrimony and one of the fiercest dressing room rows Ibrox had seen in years. The 1987/88 season had not gone well for Rangers and one player was blaming another for the various catastrophes. The forwards reckoned it was the defence's fault, the defence blamed the midfield, and so on. Souness had always encouraged open discussion in the dressing room, letting his players have their say. That was fine when Rangers were winning trophies but as soon as they fell on hard times, it became a catalyst for problems. There were a number of strong personalities in the Ibrox dressing room who inevitably were laying the blame for Rangers' demise with anyone but themselves. In these situations it's always the youngsters and the quiet ones who have to be protected.

When Rangers lost their final game of the season, 1–0 at home to Aberdeen, it was to be the spark that finally ignited the gunpowder. Rangers had gone down to a senseless goal when their defence had pushed out to play Aberdeen offside. Unfortunately Graham Roberts failed to read the runes and was left behind, playing Aberdeen onside. They scored and in the dressing room after the game the accusations were being hurled around. Most were directed at Roberts who refused to accept that the goal was his fault. Richard Gough and Roberts were at each other's throats, pushing and shoving, eyeball to eyeball. Insults were bouncing off the wall.

Outside the dressing room Souness could hear the row. He was seething, the argument pumping up his own blood pressure. He could contain himself no longer and stormed into the dressing room and immediately pointed at Roberts. 'It was your fault,' he told him. 'I blame you.' Roberts defended himself, still refusing to acknowledge that it was his fault. The row became even more heated with Souness now the principal sparring partner. He yelled at Roberts, telling him in no uncertain terms that he was simply a Tottenham player who had got lucky and won a few medals and that he was little more than that. The inference was clear; Roberts was not a Rangers man.

When Souness had finished hurling insults, Roberts turned to him. 'If that's how you feel about it then why don't you sell me?' he argued. It was the worst thing he could have suggested and not the kind of challenge to offer Souness. As calmly as he could Souness looked him in the eye. 'When you are going through the door,' he replied, 'take your boots with you, son, and don't bother coming back.' And that was the end of Graham Roberts' Ibrox career. Some time later he was sold to Chelsea.

Ally McCoist called it 'a nasty, unsavoury episode that left a sour taste in the mouth'. He clearly reckoned Souness was out of order. 'I don't think you treat people like that,' he says, adding, 'I know managers have to be tough, but this was unnecessarily severe. He had been publicly challenged and had to be seen to win.'

Souness might have encouraged democracy and discussion in the dressing room, but at the end of the day he was the boss and in 99 per cent of cases he was right. And woe betide anyone who dared to challenge his authority. However, there were others who dared to argue with him as well. Like Roberts they did not last too long. Former Rangers captain Richard Gough insists that Souness demanded the highest commitment from his squad. 'In the dressing room there were players who had problems with the way Graeme approached the job. They found him difficult and they found him demanding. If a player was not ready to conform to the code of conduct which Graeme had at Ibrox then he was on his bike.' And quickly. Similarly if anyone ever questioned his tactics or even his approach to management then that player was on borrowed time from that moment. More than one player has testified that there was only one boss at Ibrox, and his name was Graeme Souness.

The Danish player Jan Bartram was one who questioned the manager's style. Perhaps it was his cultural background or maybe in Denmark players were used to quieter dressing rooms. Whatever the reason, Bartram simply could not understand why it was necessary to fly into a rage and throw objects around the dressing room when the side had lost. Bartram would watch agog as Souness ranted and raved. He was not used to such antics and on more than one occasion leapt to the defence of a colleague or questioned the manager's interpretation of events. A parting of the ways was inevitable. It came just seven months after he had been bought. Signed in January 1988 for £180,000 he was sold to Brondby of Denmark for £315,000 in July 1988.

Even his most respected players had their argumentative moments. Chief among them was the Rangers favourite Ally McCoist. McCoist was a pre-Souness signing, bought by John Greig from Sunderland in 1983. McCoist has always claimed that the fact that Souness never actually bought him was held against him. But whether Souness liked McCoist or not, the Ibrox crowd certainly loved him. And there is little doubt that Souness was a secret admirer.

McCoist was an entertainer; intelligent, impish and with a wicked sense of humour that would frequently land him in trouble. Typical was the occasion when Souness was laying down the law about being careful about the kind of medicines they took. McCoist had already arrived late for the talk-in. Souness then went on to tell the players about how some Italians had 'spiked' Trevor Francis' food in Italy.

'Can you imagine that?' asked Souness. 'They spiked Trevor's chicken.'

In the background McCoist piped up. 'Well boss, the Italians are famous for that.'

'Famous for what?' snapped Souness.

'Fowl play,' replied McCoist, a grin spreading across his face. The dressing room erupted into laughter, except for one man. Souness did not see the funny side of it.

'I could see him glaring at me,' says McCoist, 'obviously annoyed that I had ended the discussion on a flippant note. I'm sure he wanted to join in the laughter but felt he couldn't – that his authority had been challenged.'

Souness did not like his authority being challenged – by anybody. McCoist reckons he even disliked the Rangers fans siding with him. Despite everything, the fans still chanted McCoist's name. 'They might have done me a disservice as far as the manager was concerned,' says McCoist. 'He was a man who didn't like being told what to do. And there were 30,000 voices giving him their advice. No way was he going to be told by them.'

Their biggest flare-up came after McCoist had nipped down to Cheltenham for the races. The team had been given time off by Souness before a cup tie with Celtic. Souness told them to relax for a couple of days. So McCoist went off to the races. When they re-gathered at Ibrox two days before the big game, Souness asked McCoist if he had enjoyed Cheltenham. McCoist nodded and thought no more of it but then discovered that he had been dropped from the Celtic clash. McCoist was furious and almost walked out on the club. Rangers lost 0–2. Two days later Souness ordered McCoist to apologise to the fans through the press for his behaviour by going to the races. 'Souness had wanted me to admit to an indiscipline, and say I was wrong.' McCoist's apology made headlines the next day. McCoist was humiliated but had no doubt what lay behind it. 'The idea was to make me the scapegoat for what had gone wrong at Parkhead. He decided to drop me for Parkhead, then tried to make me carry the can when it went wrong.' McCoist was not impressed by Souness' behaviour.

McCoist was the one always getting in trouble. At the centre of their long-running dispute was Souness' less than enthusiastic support for his striker. McCoist was in and out of the team, Souness never quite convinced of his ability. He spent so much time on the bench, they called him the 'judge'. And when yet another striker, Mark Hateley, arrived it made selection all the more difficult. The relationship between Souness and McCoist was not helped either by a court case in March 1987 when McCoist was found guilty of assault and fined £150 after a night out with Ian Durrant and Ted McMinn. The headlines did little to embellish the name of Rangers or the temper of the manager. 'The club, quite rightly, were furious,' admits McCoist. 'Graeme Souness went bananas at us. We were all being sold, cut price if necessary – he just wanted us out of the door.' Of course it never came to that and after a while everyone calmed down and got on with their jobs. But McCoist is big enough to hold up his hands and admit that at times he could be very foolish, a little too quick to speak when silence might have been more beneficial. 'I had this ability to annoy him when he didn't want to be annoyed,' he claims.

Following a defeat by Celtic on New Year's Day 1988 McCoist once more felt the sharp end of Souness' tongue.

'You were the worst man out there,' yelled the manager back in the dressing room, jabbing a finger at McCoist.

'No, I wasn't,' snapped McCoist. 'You were.'

Souness flew into a rage. Nobody had ever seen him so angry. The minute he said it, McCoist knew he had overstepped the boundary between player and manager.

'I should never have said that,' admits McCoist. 'I was so sick at the way the game had gone that I just couldn't bite my tongue. Across the dressing room I could see Ian Durrant shaking his head in disbelief as if to say "What have you done, Coisty?" But by then it was too late. The manager tore my game to shreds.'

McCoist admits, though, that when it came to playing there was nobody who could beat Souness. 'He was an absolute dream to play with. He had great vision and brought a new dimension to our play as a team and my own as an individual. You'll never hear a bad word from me about Graeme Souness the player.' Even Tommy Smith would agree with that.

Mo Johnston may well have been the most publicised signing in the history of Scottish football but even that was hardly enough to protect him from the mighty man's wrath. A year after the headlines heralding Rangers' first Catholic, all the back page talk was that Johnston would never play for Rangers again. After being sent home from a close season training session in the hills of Tuscany, Johnston looked to be on the brink of leaving the club. Everyone maintained that it was all a misunderstanding. Whatever it was, it did little to cement relations between Johnston and his manager.

The dispute had begun with a discussion about the role of Ally McCoist following the signing of Mark Hateley. Johnston, loyal to his striking partner McCoist, got into a heated debate with Souness about the sense of signing Hateley and what it would mean for his partnership with McCoist. It was no holds barred as the decibel level hit new heights. Yet it all might have ended sensibly had Johnston and McCoist not then gone off on a prank later that evening, charging into Scott Nisbet's room. A tired and emotional Johnston hurled himself onto Nisbet's bed only to discover that Nisbet had put his mattress on the floor. Johnston hit the springs with a thud causing considerable bruising about the face. Souness was livid and told Johnston to sort himself out or go home. Johnston, clearly misinterpreting this message, promptly packed his bags and caught the next plane home.

When he arrived unexpectedly back in Glasgow sporting bumps and bruises about the face journalists wanted to know why he had come home. 'Ask the manager,' replied Johnston. The press put two and two together and made five. 'SHAME FACED MO!' was the headline stamped across the front page of the *Daily Record*. Heated debate with Souness there may have been, but punches there were not. But it was all good copy for the Scottish papers. Explanations were made and after a public statement of good intent Souness and Johnston kissed and made up.

Richard Gough, his £1.1 million signing from Spurs, almost became a Souness victim as well and was on the verge of leaving the club just months after he had joined. Gough readily admits: 'Yes, I had a couple of barneys with him. We didn't see eye to eye on everything.' Their biggest flare-up came as Gough was experiencing problems with a mysterious foot injury. The injury would often crop up part way into a game with Gough having to limp off or play on not knowing whether or not he was exacerbating the injury. Despite medical advice nobody seemed to be able to diagnose the problem. Souness was never one to make allowances for injury, especially if they were mysterious. When Gough hobbled off one night in a friendly against Arsenal, the manager strode over to him while he was lying on the treatment table. 'I think you're at it,' he said. Gough resented the accusation of cheating and stormed out of the room, convinced that his career at Ibrox might be over.

'I knew that if I had a confrontation with Graeme over this then I'd be off. That was guaranteed. One major row with Graeme and the player involved was very quickly off the premises. He made no secret of that and, to be honest, he couldn't because we had seen it happen so often in the past. It had to be Graeme's way and he would not brook interference from any of his players.'

Gough gritted his teeth expecting the worst the next day. But oddly it never happened. At the club's annual Burns' Supper the following evening, Souness rose and made an astonishing public apology. 'I have got to apologise to a certain player because of some very unfair remarks I made to him last night,' he told his audience.

Nobody except Gough and Souness knew what he was talking about. 'He didn't name me,' says Gough, 'because he would never want to look as if he was losing face or backing down to one of his players. I knew straight away that this was the biggest peace offering I would ever get. For Graeme to apologise was unusual – for him to apologise in public was unique.' But apologise he did.

Gough reckons that Souness relished confrontation. Comparing Souness and his successor Walter Smith, he says of Smith that he 'is much more of a diplomat than Graeme could ever be. He does not go out of his way to seek confrontation with people. Graeme relished a bit of that. Things were black and white with him. You were either with him or against him. There was no halfway house.'

Gough may have managed to avoid the ultimate confrontation; Terry Butcher didn't. The man he had bought from Ipswich for £725,000 and called the 'finest defender in the world', the man who was the cornerstone of Souness' Ibrox revolution, eventually came off second best against his manager. Butcher's problem with Souness came shortly after the 1990 World Cup finals. Butcher had decided to join his England colleagues in Italy despite a knee problem. He had not been 100 per cent fit for some time. The Ibrox medical staff reckoned he would be better resting at home. But Butcher, wanting to be loyal to his former Ipswich boss Bobby Robson, then manager of England, decided to go. When he returned, his knee was even worse. Souness was not happy, especially with the new season set to kick off. Butcher played but was clearly labouring with the injury and his lack of fitness showed. He had not been doing any training so as not to further damage the injury but when he scored a spectacular own goal against Dundee United at Tannadice, the manager's patience was severely tested. A Skol Cup semi-final was looming against Aberdeen and in one of the most controversial selections he was ever to make at Ibrox, Souness decided to drop his captain. The news was splashed across the front pages of every Glasgow paper. Everyone was amazed, even the players. Butcher was furious, his pride deeply wounded.

McCoist remembers spotting Butcher moments after Souness had told him. 'The big man was in tears,' he says. 'It was a slap in the face to see that colossus crying. It could have been done in a different way to save the big man's dignity. He was due that.'

That was the beginning of the end for Butcher. Rangers won but then lost to Red Star Belgrade in the European Cup, again without Butcher. Souness called Butcher into his office the week of the Skol Cup final. What happened next remains shrouded in mystery. One suggestion is that Souness asked Butcher to prove his match fitness in a reserve game, another is that Souness simply told him that he would not be playing in the final. Whatever it was is irrelevant, but what ensued was important – a furious row. A few weeks later Butcher was gone, sold to Coventry for £500,000.

There are rows in every dressing room. Not all players like each other, they have their moods as well as managers, and where players spend so much time together there will inevitably be conflicts. Anfield is no exception. One player will tell you that under Souness the rows were no worse, others argue the opposite. Whatever the truth, they certainly went on behind the firmly locked dressing room doors of Anfield and Melwood. There were shouting matches, threats and, above all, silences. Souness would cold-shoulder those he disliked, refusing even to acknowledge their presence. And it wasn't just the few fringe players who suffered this indignity. Many of the club's top stars were ignored by the manager. 'He hasn't said good morning to me for months,' complained John Barnes at one point.

Paul Stewart was another who felt the icy stare of Souness. Stewart, a £2.5 million flop at Anfield was dropped at the end of November 1993 as Liverpool faced Aston Villa at Anfield. Stewart had just had a ten-game run and clearly felt that he was being made the scapegoat. He complained to the manager. But it did little good. If anything, it made matters worse. From then on there was a silence between them. Two months later, in mid-January 1994, Stewart was offered a loan spell with either Crystal Palace or Tranmere Rovers. Souness was forced to talk with him. As the deal went through taking Stewart to Crystal Palace, he told told Radio City that it was 'the first time Souness has spoken to me since the Aston Villa game'.

Glenn Hysen, the Swedish defender brought from Fiorentina by Kenny Dalglish, was another who had difficulties with Souness almost from day one. 'I am not a happy man,' he told one director within weeks of Souness' appointment. And nor was he. In December 1991 he told a Swedish paper that 'nobody is happy here but nobody is talking about it. In the corridors, offices and changing rooms the climate is bad.' Hysen was the first Liverpool player to go public and he was soon transferred back to Sweden.

It was all so unlike Liverpool. In the rumour circles of the city, tales were soon being eagerly told and passed on. And once players had departed the club for some more friendly dressing room they were suddenly splashed across the back pages as Fleet Street pounced for their behind-the-scenes stories of Anfield. One by one they trotted out their tales of despair. David Burrows was typical.

Within days of signing for West Ham United in a swap deal that took Julian Dicks to Anfield, he had sold his story to the *Daily Mirror*. Burrows was bitter at being blamed for Liverpool's demise and admitted that it had been so bad that he had been considering quitting the club anyhow. Souness showed no interest in him, he raged. 'In the last five years I have watched the club decline steadily with all the buying and selling of players, the way the team was picked and the way the whole routine was changed.'

It was a damning indictment. 'Graeme has his own thoughts on the way the club should be run,' he continued. 'He doesn't mix with the players as much as they would like, although he has tried to change his attitude towards them this season.' Burrows argued that Souness showed no interest in him as a player. 'He's virtually got rid of all the players who were there when he came to the club and made me a scapegoat for things that went wrong,' he added. 'I felt uncomfortable when he was there.'

It was the veterans who felt it most. Souness had swept in, threatening to uproot all before him. Experienced players such as Beardsley, Houghton and McMahon had been cast aside in the Souness revolution. Ian Rush, Ronnie Whelan and Bruce Grobbelaar, the club's most experienced players, looked on in bewilderment. But even they were to experience their problems with the new manager. Grobbelaar, more than anyone, was under pressure. Mike Hooper and new £1.3 million signing David James were both after his jersey. Grobbelaar, however, was not prepared to stand idly by and be pushed around by anyone, even if it was the manager doing the pushing. At one point Grobbelaar and Souness were not on speaking terms. Grobbelaar had been sent off in the European Cup-Winners' Cup tie against Moscow Spartak at the end of October 1992 and had conceded a penalty. Souness was furious. Says Grobbelaar, 'I watched the penalty, went back to the dressing room, showered, changed and didn't speak to the manager again until he wished me a Happy New Year.'

But it didn't end there. In January 1993 Grobbelaar was selected to play in two World Cup qualifying games for Zimbabwe. It meant a ten-day trip to Africa with the prospect of missing a Premier League game and an FA Cup replay but Grobbelaar promised to return to Anfield if he was needed. At the time Grobbelaar was acting number two and, at times, even number three goalkeeper. Souness, however, took him aside and told him that he would be needed. Grobbelaar consequently agreed to fly home in between World Cup games. Unfortunately, when he did arrive home from war-torn Angola, expecting to play against Bolton Wanderers in the FA Cup, he was told that he would not be wanted; Hooper was playing instead. Grobbelaar was furious.

'After eleven years at Liverpool, the way I am being treated is disgraceful,' he raged to the papers. 'I wouldn't wish this on my worst enemy. What are they trying to do? Destroy me? Humiliate me? He knew I was away for ten days ... and I willingly agreed to return when he talked about a goalkeeping crisis at the club. What is the point of going back for a couple of training sessions when I cannot even sit on the bench in an FA Cup tie?'

Grobbelaar is a maverick, both in his playing style and his attitude to life. Of all the players at Anfield, he was the one who would stand up to Souness. He had nothing to lose. If Souness wanted to sell him, then fine, he'd go. There was at least one memorable row when the two men stood eyeball to eyeball threatening blows.

Ian Rush also had his moments with Souness. 'Behind the scenes the atmosphere was so tense,' he confessed just as the manager fended off a sacking in May 1993. 'I had begun to prepare myself for a move. It reached the stage where we hardly said a word to each other for a month.' Rush, Grobbelaar, Barnes; was Souness talking to anyone?

He certainly had not been talking to John Barnes. 'Souness and I have had our problems and up until recently we weren't talking to each other,' admitted John Barnes, shortly before the manager resigned. In fact, it was well known in Liverpool circles that the two had not been talking to each other for months, though a truce had just been called between the two.

Even the final player to be sold by Souness – Ronny Rosenthal – burst into print with his complaints. He groaned:

I never had a fair chance under him. I felt I was banging my head against a brick wall. I remember playing in one game which we lost but I scored and put up a good performance. At the team meeting on the following Monday he mentioned that I was one of the few who was trying to create things. But the following Saturday I wasn't in the team. I went to see him and asked him why, but he then said he didn't think I had played well.

At the root of the problem was Souness' tendency to blame the experienced players. Barnes stated:

He wants to be a winner, but when things don't go well he blames the experienced players in order to protect the youngsters. I can understand that to an extent. I don't want the burden of the past to rest on our promising young players. It could destroy them. But the whole team hasn't functioned, not just the experienced players. We've had such terrible injury problems that on occasions he has criticised the experienced players after a game, and I've sat down with the only other experienced man in the side and said: 'He must mean you and me!' It's that ludicrous. It would be different if there were seven experienced players in the side who could all get together in a game and try to work it out.

It was rule by intimidation. The seasoned professionals

were not used to it and didn't like it. They expected to be treated with some respect as they had been under previous Liverpool managers, while the youngsters were either terrified or bemused. There was more grudge than goals.

One photographer remembers the dressing room rows.

They always put a tea trolley just outside the home dressing room at Anfield for us at half time on match day. Now normally I never bothered going for a cup of tea but the word got round that it was an event not to be missed. So every week we'd all race there, particularly if Liverpool had been playing badly. I remember one week Souness slamming the door with such force that it almost came off its hinges. Week after week there would be the most awful shouting going on as Souness laid into them. We'd all be standing there supping our tea, in total silence, ears pinned to the door, listening to Souness raging. I'd never heard anything like it. During Shankly's days you'd hear some shouting but he'd be laying into the opposition, not his own players. And with Paisley, Fagan and Dalglish you never heard a thing. But it was very different with Souness.

Most Liverpool players will tell you, however, that Shankly and Paisley could speak their mind when necessary. Confrontation is inevitable in dressing rooms whether between players themselves or between players and the coaching staff.

But it wasn't just the experienced players who felt the sharp end of Souness' temper. Even the backroom staff were to find him a prickly character to work with. In all the years that the bootroom had been in operation there had rarely been rows or splits. Indeed, during the reigns of Shankly, Paisley and Fagan nobody could ever recall much of a row, whether public or private. It had changed, however, under Dalglish. Chris Lawler, reserve team coach had been sensationally sacked to be replaced with former captain Phil Thompson and chief scout Geoff Twentyman had also been shown the door. Twentyman had been replaced by another Anfield favourite, Ron Yeats. Their sackings had proved acrimonious with bitter follow-ups in the tabloids that had done much to tarnish the good name of Liverpool Football Club. But at least Dalglish had continued winning honours and as long as the cups came pouring in, nobody was going to disagree too much with his methods. Souness did not have the luxury of trophies. There was little he could point to. He had won the FA Cup in 1992 but, that apart, there was nothing much to boast about.

It was ironic that the bootroom's biggest row under Souness should concern Phil Thompson whose appointment had caused Dalglish more than a headache or two. Thompson had been carefully guiding the reserves with more than a fair degree of success. Youngsters were coming through and, in spite of the appalling level of injuries, Thompson was turning out players capable of holding their own in the Premier League. It was a difficult time for Thompson who rarely had a settled reserve side because of the heavy call-up of reserve players for the first team games. Most of the time he was having to rely on youngsters from the A team or first team players struggling back to fitness. Back in the days of Shankly, Paisley and Fagan the reserves had always been an academy where new players would serve their apprenticeship, learning the ways of Anfield, before finally breaking through into the first team. Even expensive stars like Ray Kennedy were forced to spend months playing in front of empty echoing stadiums before they were deemed to have made the grade, ready for the big time. It was the job of the reserve team coach to nurture and develop the talents of the future, to teach them the Liverpool style. There is little doubt that Thompson had struggled along purposefully given all the difficulties. But then, shortly after Liverpool had won the FA Cup he was sacked by Souness.

There had never been much love lost between the two men. Phil Thompson was a scouser, born in Kirkby, one of those run-down areas that throws up footballers like the Rhondda Valley used to throw up rugby players. Thompson had supported Liverpool from the day his mother took him to see the Shankly side of St John and Yeats tear the heart out of Inter Milan in the European Cup semi-final. He had sat with his mother that night, a ten-year-old, in the Kemlyn Road stand marvelling at the sight of the Kop swaying and roaring in all its majesty. From that moment he was converted and wanted to be part of it. Thompson was to be one of those rare breeds who not only spent his childhood watching his favourites from the Kop but then went on to join the club, playing at every level before finally becoming captain of the side and of his country. Thompson was a Liverpool man through and through. Cut his leg off and like a stick of rock you'd find the words LIVERPOOL in red letters inside it. His legs weren't much fatter either. To be made captain of Liverpool was his greatest honour and to lose it was to be one of his deepest disappointments. And the man who took the captaincy off him was none other than Graeme Souness.

Not that you could blame Souness for any part in the decision. The decision was wholly that of Bob Paisley. Paisley had simply decided that Thompson's days were numbered. He saw Souness as a man of authority and ambition and the man to lead Liverpool through the next few years. It was as simple as that. Souness' role in the affair was totally innocent. Thompson, however, saw it differently. He was deeply hurt by Paisley's decision but rather than vent all his anger towards the manager, some was directed towards Souness. It was a typical and understandable reaction and his relations with Souness were never quite the same from that day onwards.

It all came to a head in the summer of 1992. While he was in hospital recovering from his heart bypass operation Souness heard whispers that Thompson was ambitious for his job. There had been speculation in the press, as well as among those associated with the club, concerning Souness' future. If Souness did not return to Anfield, the club could be searching for a new manager. It is not unreasonable to assume that Thompson, as reserve team coach, would have been a contender. Whether Souness had read the stories in the press or whether he had other reasons, within weeks of Souness leaving hospital Thompson learnt that his contract was not to be renewed. In effect, he had been sacked. It was a grave embarrassment for the club to see one of their former and most popular old boys sacked by the manager. But there was little they could do about it. The Thompson sacking inevitably hit the back pages, adding further scandal.

Thompson was furious. He had devoted twenty years to Liverpool Football Club and cared deeply about it. To find himself suddenly shown the door was not only a humiliation but, as far as he was concerned, totally unjustified. Thompson decided to take the club to an Industrial Tribunal claiming unfair dismissal, threatening to tell all. At first nobody took the threat seriously. Everyone just assumed that it would be quietly forgotten. But Thompson persisted and dates for a hearing were even discussed. It could have made a fascinating case, but then just as everyone was beginning to book their ringside seat the club came to the rescue, agreeing a deal with Thompson. Thompson accepted an out of court settlement of £28,000. In return he promised to withdraw his claim for unfair dismissal and not to discuss the matter with the press for two years. No public explanation was ever given for the sacking.

But Souness' rows with his coaching staff did not stop there. In November 1993 there was a further damaging split. This time it concerned another ex-player, now a member of the backroom staff, Steve Heighway. Heighway had been one of the most exciting wingers ever to play for Liverpool. A product of the Shankly years, he had joined the club from Skelmersdale United after studying for a degree at Warwick University, and soon went on to bring a new dash and width to the Liverpool side of that era. In his time he won league, FA Cup, UEFA Cup and European Cup honours as well as a bagful of international caps for the Republic of Ireland. When he ended his playing days with Liverpool he made for America to play with the Minnesota Kicks but he returned in the late eighties and was snapped up by Kenny Dalglish and given the job of Youth Development Officer. It was his responsibility to find and develop the next breed of Liverpool stars. And there was little doubt that he was highly successful, bringing on youngsters like Robbie Fowler, Don Hutchison, Mike Marsh, Dominic Matteo and Steve McManaman. But, in an astonishing incident, Heighway was to be humiliated by his boss Souness.

Heighway had been booked by Sky Television to appear in a discussion for their Sky Footballers Football Show. He was to appear on a panel alongside FA Director of Coaching Charles Hughes, the England assistant manager, Don Howe, and Dutch coach Bert van Lingen to discuss grass-roots football in England and how it might be developed over the next few years. But an hour before the show was due to start recording, as they sat chatting, Heighway received a phone call at the studios. It was Graeme Souness. He had just learned of Heighway's involvement. He tore into Heighway in earshot of everyone, berating him for not asking his permission and

241

ordered him to return home immediately to Liverpool.
Heighway was furious and was forced to find the programme's producer to tell him the embarrassing news
that he would not be able to appear. The producer was
astonished, especially given that they were about to go
on air. They would now have to find a replacement. Heighway meanwhile slipped on his coat and went in search of
a cab and the next train back to Lime Street. For a man
of Heighway's ability, track record and intellect, it was a
humiliating experience and one that he would not forget
easily. But such were the rules governing footballers and
staff. There was a general rule at Anfield that any player
wanting to talk with the press had to seek the manager's
permission first. Irrespective of whether Heighway had
in fact sought such permission, it might be considered
that he was mature and intelligent enough to conduct
himself with some dignity and sense. But a rule is a rule
and if players are expected to abide by the rules then so
the staff need to set an example.

The programme's director, Dermot McQuarrie, an old
Glasgow friend of Souness rang him immediately. Souness eventually came on the phone. 'I'm sorry,' he
explained. 'It's not you or the programme. But how would
you react if one of your employees was going on television
to talk about your organisation without having first asked
permission, and especially when you have a rule that you
have to get permission first?'

'I had to admit that I had some sympathy with Souness,' says McQuarrie. 'Heighway had been brought onto
the programme because he was Steve Heighway, coach at
Liverpool, and not just because he was Steve Heighway.
Souness was right, in any other organisation you would
have to get permission before talking to the press as a
company representative.'

It was a fair point. But it did make life difficult for
reporters. Before you could talk to anyone you had to get

the manager's permission. That meant you had to track down the manager, ask his permission, then go back and ask the player. It was so difficult and painstakingly tedious that most just gave up.

There were plenty of other stories as well, especially in Scotland, concerning broken doors and other incidents. Most of them were wild and totally untrue. But of all the rows Graeme Souness was to encounter, none surpass the day Souness came face to face with Aggie Moffat. Souness may have impressed multi-millionaire David Murray and mega-rich Paolo Mantavani, the owner of Sampdoria, but he did not impress a working-class, middle-aged woman from Perth. His smart suits and dashing good looks cut no ice with Aggie Moffat. Aggie was the tea lady at St Johnstone Football Club, the woman who looked after the players and she was not to be trifled with. Alas, Graeme Souness did not know this. The incident was to go down in Scottish folklore, though the full story has never been revealed. Although 'Wee Aggie' was to hit the headlines the incident was considerably worse than was ever reported.

It occurred after a miserable mid-week draw between Rangers and St Johnstone at Perth. After the game Souness was well into his usual dressing-down of his squad. Twenty minutes after the game had finished he was still ranting and raving. Most of his players were showered and dressed when in walked Aggie. Aggie was outraged at what she saw. Someone had smashed a large water jug against the wall, shattering it. Glass was strewn all over the floor of the dressing room. Aggie was appalled as she picked her way through the broken glass and told Souness that this was no way for anyone to behave. Souness immediately flew into a further rage. A distressed Aggie stormed out of the dressing room, off to see the club manager, only to be followed by the Rangers boss. Souness chased her up the stairs still screaming and shouting. Amidst all the commotion outside the board-room, Geoff Brown, the chairman of St Johnstone appeared and tried to calm things down. One onlooker remembers it well, 'As the chairman was trying to quieten things Souness looked him in the eye and yelled, "I don't like you, let's go outside." ' Eventually peace was restored and Souness and his team skulked off back to Glasgow.

Souness was already in serious trouble with the Scottish FA. If an incident like this was to be reported, then he could find himself banned from Scottish football alto-gether. Not only was he the manager of Rangers but he was a director of the club as well. It was hardly polite to be seen inviting the chairman of another club outside. It was that serious. St Johnstone, realising this and not wanting to further damage the reputation of Scottish football, as well as their relations with the biggest club in Scotland, decided to take the matter no further, despite the pleas from two executives of the Scottish FA to report the matter. That night, Geoff Brown told a Rangers director that they would not be taking any action. The following day David Murray called St Johnstone, 'Thanks,' he said, 'I owe you one.'

The man who had humbled Graham Roberts and Terry Butcher had finally met his match with 'Wee Aggie'. To this day, Aggie is still awaiting an apology from Graeme Souness.

CHAPTER SIXTEEN
The Anfield Revolution

In his influential book *Foundations of Corporate Success*, management guru Professor John Kay suggests Liverpool Football Club as an example for all businesses to follow. 'There are organisational routines – complex manoeuvres, perfected through repeated trial, in which each player fulfils his role without needing, or necessarily having, a picture of the whole,' he writes.

Liverpool Football Club was even being held up by the corporate strategists as a model of professionalism. It may have only been a football club but there was still plenty to illustrate that in organisational terms it was streets ahead of everyone else in the Football League and offered a splendid example of how a business should be run. What's more, Liverpool Football Club also proved that you did not have to throw money at a product to make it better.

Money may have been important to Liverpool but it was never the crucial element. Any analysis of their spending on transfer fees and wages shows that it was at least roughly equal to its closest rivals, Manchester United, Arsenal, Spurs and Everton, before 1991. And yet Liverpool's playing performances had been considerably better, though why this should be is the question that has puzzled football pundits, managers and players for more than two decades. It even raised the interest of the business analysts.

Stefan Szymanski, of the School of Management at Imperial College, London, is another who has looked closely at the club and suggests that it is something to do with Liverpool's method of organisation. 'What appears to have happened at Liverpool is that the structure of the club has raised the performance of individuals to levels they could not achieve elsewhere,' he has said. 'They all point clearly to a strategy that was laid down more than thirty years ago. It was a system of playing and of club organisation that would continue regardless of the board of directors or manager.' Graeme Souness was to disprove that theory.

For thirty years Liverpool Football Club ran as effortlessly and as elegantly as a Rolls-Royce. Shankly had been its designer, engineer and chief driver. Over the years the driver might have changed from time to time but the engine still functioned as smoothly as the day it was built. It needed just the occasional spot of oil and every few years the slightest of tinkering, but never anything more. Envious rivals would come and peer under its bonnet, impressed by its elegance, confounded by its power, anxious to discover its secret. Nobody ever dared to take the engine apart. 'If it ain't broke, don't mend it,' was the Anfield maxim. But then along came Graeme Souness, wanting to turn the Rolls-Royce into a supercharged Ferrari.

Over the years Shankly had instilled in his players a sense of loyalty and pride. Pulling on the red shirt for the first time was akin to a Welsh rugby union international stepping out to make his debut at Cardiff Arms Park. It was an honour that did not fall to many. A Liverpool player making his debut was an occasion. There was a time when it was even a ritual. Someone from the Kop would race out on to the pitch as the teams had their pre-match kick-in, give the new player the traditional peck on the cheek and then return triumphantly to be swallowed back into the crowded Kop, usually chased by a policeman. It didn't happen very often but when it did it was a moment to savour. Kevin Keegan remembers that it was like joining a new social club, 'an honour was being bestowed upon you'.

For years the Rolls-Royce ran smoothly. Liverpool won championships, FA Cups, League Cups, UEFA Cups and topped all that with four European Cups. There was no team in British history to match them. They were a phenomenon. The Shankly legacy was passed on to Bob Paisley and then to Joe Fagan. And still the trophies rolled in. Then in an unprecedented move, Kenny Dalglish was handed the field marshal's baton. He was the first player-manager in the club's history. The bootroom legacy had come to an abrupt end. Ronnie Moran, Chris Lawler or Roy Evans might have been expected to be tapped on the shoulder but instead the club looked to its most professional and distinguished player. Yet it seemed to make little difference. The trophies still poured in, two in his first season and three more before he shocked the soccer world with his resignation.

Dalglish made one or two changes and often puzzled the fans, maybe even the players, with some of his selections. Everyone could sense that things were not quite the same but you could hardly carp when they were picking up trophies. There was a triumvirate – the manager, the players, the fans. It was just like any other business; the company, its workers and its customers. Each acknowledged the importance of the others. Each knew that without the others they would collapse. And in the case of Liverpool never was that more poignantly illustrated than with the Hillsborough disaster. Dalglish may have been wealthy, a representative of football's modern era, but the Kop warmed to him and at Hillsborough he had more than shown them a caring, sensitive side.

And yet a myth would soon take root that it was all Dalglish's fault. That Dalglish had allowed the club to sink into bad habits, that he had failed to sign young players and that all Souness' problems could be traced back to Dalglish's poor management. When Souness first arrived at Anfield he talked of a massive job. 'The club needed major surgery when I came,' he later said.

But there was little evidence to support the theory. It was arguable that Dalglish had constructed a new style of management. Dalglish was the first bootroom outsider and as such did not have quite the same rapport or dependence on his lieutenants as most of his predecessors. Dalglish was his own man. He did not consult as others may have wished or as others did in the past. He was essentially a one-man operation. Yet his results justified his style. Dalglish's ability in the transfer market also was impressive. Among his more important signings were Steve McMahon, John Barnes, Peter Beardsley, John Aldridge, Ray Houghton, Barry Venison and David Burrows. Of course there were less successful acquisitions with the likes of Nigel Spackman, Mike Hooper, Jimmy Carter and David Speedie. On top of that there were the inexpensive youngsters, full of potential but little more, such as Jamie Redknapp, Steve Staunton, Don Hutchison, Steve McManaman, Nicky Tanner and Steve Harkness, most of whom were to mature under Graeme Souness.

No matter how you analyse Dalglish's dealings, it has to be admitted that the club emerged in credit. In his five years in charge Liverpool captured three championships and never finished out of the top two. They also won the FA Cup twice and were runners-up once as well as being runners up in the League Cup. They had picked up the Double in 1986 and had missed two others by a whisker.

Even if Dalglish had steered a slightly different course from the fixed line of Shankly, Paisley and Fagan, he had still brought enormous success to the club. He may have tinkered with the engine more than his predecessors but he had never dared to take it apart.

It was Graeme Souness who was to take the engine apart and who would try to put it back together again. He bought and sold more players than any manager since Shankly. But whereas Shankly was inclined to scour the minor divisions for budding talent, Souness dipped into the expensive end of the market, paying outrageous fees for half-proven quality. When Shankly arrived at Liverpool they were a second division club; when Souness came they were second in the league.

Liverpool Football Club is about evolutionary change. They don't like to make too many reforms at Anfield. It's part of the Liverpool character; take things steadily, don't take drastic action. When things went wrong for Shankly he simply stuck with it. If the team wasn't playing well he rarely substituted players. Even more rarely did he drop a player. 'We never drop players,' he told everyone, 'we just shuffle things around a bit.' If a player was playing badly he'd still be there the next week, and the next week. Eventually things would get better.

Souness was about revolution. At Ibrox his revolutionary zeal was famous. He had swept aside the old order and replaced the insularity and sectarianism with a new attitude. He had his problems, especially with the authorities – what revolutionary doesn't? – but he widened the horizons of Glasgow Rangers, bringing fresh ideas and vision to the club. Souness once told the *Sunday Times* that the world had moved on since Shankly. He insisted that there was no point in thinking back to those days or trying to recapture them. Liverpool had to adapt to the times. At Anfield Souness tried to create another revolution. But he was to misjudge the mood and the conditions to such an extent that his revolution would destroy those cherished traditions that had made the club such a fine example to management strategists and football followers alike. It was a legacy from which the club might never recover. Liverpool Football Club would never be the same again.

There were so many other areas where Souness instituted changes. His influence was Sampdoria and Italian football. The super-rich clubs with their stylish stadiums, film star players, and high profile business activities were in a different hemisphere to the dreary Scottish League and Football League. He believed we had so much to learn from them, and indeed we did. But what Souness forgot was that Liverpool had more than proved themselves. They were four times winners of the European Cup, twice winners of the UEFA Cup and had a total of eight European finals behind them. Liverpool were already on a par, in playing terms, with their greatest continental counterparts.

On the training field, Souness began to try new techniques, schedules that had been practised in Genoa, tested and proven at Ibrox. They might have worked in Scotland, and even Italy, but nobody could see the sense of changing things at Anfield when the old methods had been so successful over the years. One seasoned observer who had watched training at Anfield for more than twenty years remembers how astonished he was when he suddenly spotted the changes. He recalls:

The players used to come out of the changing rooms at Melwood, and then do a series of laps around the perimeter of the pitch. They would begin by walking and would then do a jogging lap. This would be followed by a sprint, then a few more sprint laps, all the time getting harder before they started winding down until they ended with another lap walking around the pitch. After that they would do some stretching exercises of one kind or another. Finally they might do a bit of heading practice or something else but often they would go straight into their five-a-side games. These games were terribly important. They would last for at least an hour. They were hard and fast but were clearly popular with the players. It was usually the first team lads against the others. It did vary a little, building up to a peak on a Wednesday but, all in all, the training was not quite as you might expect from such a top club but they all seemed to enjoy it.

But then suddenly it all changed after Souness arrived. They would come out of the changing rooms and immediately start doing their stretches. But most unusually they also started doing set pieces. Souness would have them practising for ages, corners, free kicks. As you know, Liverpool have never been very good at set pieces, probably because they never practised them. But all of a sudden there they were, practising them. Once that was finished they would play their five-a-side game but it was never for as long as they used to. There was a lot of standing around while they did the set pieces and I know that a lot of the players got bored. The other thing which they began to do more of was weight training and gym work.

Phil Neal has testified in the past to the simple training routine at Anfield. 'At Anfield we do not do anything in excess. We are not over-coached with emphasis on set moves. Individuals are trusted to react to opportunities,' he wrote in his book *Attack From The Back*.

Melwood became an important factor in the Souness revolution. He had seen the set-ups in Italian soccer, especially at Sampdoria where everything revolved around the training camp, and demanded a similar arrangement at Anfield. It was Souness who suggested that the club transfer all its training and medical facilities from Anfield to the training ground. A new gym was built, equipped with all the latest weight-training paraphernalia as well as a modern treatment room. The weights room became a focus for achieving a superior fitness level. The emphasis was no longer simply on stamina and ball control but on strength as well.

'The standard of fitness wasn't great,' Souness said at the time. 'Something had to be done. I told the players the price on the ticket was to look after themselves twenty-four hours a day. Binges the night before a game are long gone. Football is for athletes.'

Melwood had now become the centre of the club and was given a £300,000 facelift. Souness insisted that nothing had really changed. But there was no doubt that things had altered. The move to Melwood had a knock-on effect and had meant an important break with tradition. For a start it mean re-arranging the daily schedule. It had long been the custom for players to make their way to Anfield in the morning where they would change before boarding the club coach for the three-mile trip to their training ground at Melwood in West Derby. After their morning's session they would then board the bus again and return to Anfield where they would shower, change and enjoy a communal lunch. It was a tradition that had gone on for years. Former players testify that this itinerary, simple though it may seem, fostered a close harmony between the players. One, who experienced the routine over the years, remembers how they would lark about on the bus and then all enjoy a good lunch together before disappearing in the afternoon. 'It was fun, we got to know each other, took the piss.' But once Melwood became the focus of all activities, the players simply drove to Melwood in their own cars, did their training, changed, had lunch and then drove home. It was all impersonal with little chance for players to talk and have fun together. Souness' secretary was also uprooted, moving office from Anfield to Melwood. Everything moved to Melwood. Eventually there was no need for the players to go to Anfield at all, other than on match days, or to see the club's chief executive.

Bob Paisley, in his autobiography, emphasises the sense in the daily routine of going back to Anfield for the post-training bath. 'It's what I called the warming-down period,' he wrote, 'and it is as important as warming up at the start of the training session. That is when players come off the training field, sit down while they have a cup of tea, and then relax on the bus back to Anfield before having their bath and changing.'

When the new Main Stand was being built at Anfield in the early seventies, Paisley and Shankly had been forced to drop the tradition of returning to Anfield for their bath. The result, as Paisley points out, was that Liverpool had their worst ever season for injuries. And Paisley had no doubts as to why, for he had been a qualified physiotherapist, reckoned by many to be the best in the business.

It is impossible to say whether the changes in training were the principal cause of so many injuries but it does seem a remarkable coincidence that so many players should go down with such serious injuries. Almost every player was under treatment for a long-term injury at some point during Souness' reign. Ronnie Whelan missed an entire season. John Barnes had two serious lay-offs, the second as a result of sustaining an injury while with the England squad. Steve McManaman, Michael Thomas, Jan Molby, Rob Jones and Paul Stewart all spent months on the sidelines, unable to play or even train. It was even more frustrating that so many new signings should find themselves hobbling about Anfield after only a few weeks.

The injuries began almost as soon as Souness arrived

and gradually mounted until they reached a peak in 1993. Nobody could ever recall so many injuries at the club. It was ironic that the old treatment table had been replaced early in Souness' reign by a smart new medical room decked out with all the latest new-fangled equipment – and they would need it. A few former Liverpool players joked that the old slab had been enough to put anyone off getting injured. Tommy Smith would also recall how Shankly would ignore you if you were injured. 'He'd just walk past you as if you weren't there, cold shoulder you. He seemed to think players should never get injured. He took it personally.'

Liverpool players also had a dread of injury and would fret about ever getting back in the side. 'So many good players found themselves permanently sidelined after injury simply because some youngster got his chance and took it,' says Tommy Smith. 'Neither Shankly nor Paisley was inclined to change a winning side. In those days when you got your chance at Anfield you had to take it otherwise you might be hanging around for years waiting for another opportunity.' Often it never came.

The reality was that over the years Liverpool had rarely used more than 20 players a season. Indeed, in the 30 years between 1960 and 1990 they had used in excess of 20 players a season on only a handful of occasions and in 1965/66 had played just 14 men in the entire season. Yet, after just a dozen games of the 1993/94 season, they had already used 21 players. It was all down to the glut of injuries. It was impossible to pick the same 11 men for more than one match and in the whole of Souness' period at Anfield on only a few occasions was he able to pick the same team in consecutive weeks. The chopping and changing was bound to have an effect. There were already enough new faces at the club as it was, without players finding yet another stranger playing alongside them. It was little wonder that defenders looked confused or that midfielders were getting in one another's way. The Liverpool style of accurate passing and intelligent running off the ball was impossible when no rapport or style had been engendered.

It had never been Liverpool's policy to blame poor results on injuries, yet even Souness was forced to concede that the spate of injuries was dictating his season almost from day one. Young players had to be blooded far sooner than was ideal and were forced to continue turning out week after week when really they should have been given the occasional rest. It is interesting to compare the way Manchester United's Ryan Giggs was introduced to the game with the way Steve McManaman was blooded. Both burst on to the scene at much the same time but Giggs was allowed to develop slowly, a few games in the first eleven and then a few weeks off, so that his strength and experience could gradually develop. For many weeks he sat on the subs' bench, appearing for the final twenty minutes or so. Giggs was rarely thrown into a difficult situation or tense match. McManaman, on the other hand, was forced to pull on a red shirt week after week as injuries demanded his presence. You could hardly blame Souness for playing him; he had little option but it was far from ideal and in the end it showed. Not only was McManaman another to suffer a long-term injury but his form deteriorated and after three years he was looking a shadow of the player who had begun the 1991/92 season as such an exciting prospect. Giggs, on the other hand, had matured into a world-class striker.

Injuries also forced Souness into the transfer market all too readily in search of replacements and quick solutions. It only added to the confusion. By the 1993/94 season Liverpool boasted 24 first team players on their books, 14 of whom were internationals while the non-internationals included regulars like David Burrows, Steve McManaman, Jamie Redknapp, Michael Thomas and Neil Ruddock. Although Liverpool had always believed in a strong squad of players, two dozen was, to say the least, excessive. And no doubt all 24 would have been on first team wages. The cost of simply maintaining the squad was topping £5 million a year.

Within days of his arrival at Anfield, Souness had introduced a major change, and one that was to have long-term effects. No other Liverpool manager had ever brought his own assistant with him. When Shankly came to the club he met with the bootroom staff and told them that their jobs were safe. Over the years new faces were introduced as old hands retired but the changes were always evolutionary and never disruptive. Shankly brought Roy Evans into the bootroom; Dalglish introduced Phil Thompson and Steve Heighway to his set-up, but did so only gently and never gave them any authority over first team matters. What's more, both had years of experience of Anfield behind them. But Souness' first decision was to introduce Phil Boersma into his set-up.

Boersma had been a Liverpool player between 1965 and 1975. Born in Kirkby, a run-down, lively community that excelled in producing footballers, he had begun his playing career at Anfield, making his debut in September 1968. But he made little impact and with John Toshack the natural choice to lead the Liverpool attack, Boersma's opportunities were always few and far between. But he had his moments. He began the 1974/75 season in rip-roaring form, slamming in six goals in Liverpool's opening eight matches, including a first half hat trick against Tottenham at Anfield. People talked about him as the heir to Toshack's throne but then the goals, just as suddenly, dried up. He failed to find the net in the next ten games and was inevitably dropped. In all he made 98 appearances for the club, scoring 29 goals. Then in December 1975 new manager Bob Paisley sold him to Middlesbrough for £72,000. And it was at Middlesbrough

that he first encountered the man who was to have such
an influence on his later life, Graeme Souness. They soon
became pals, roomed together for away matches, enjoyed
a good evening out. Boersma remained at Ayresome Park
for just eighteen months before joining Luton for £35,000.
He later teamed up with some of his other former Liverpool colleagues at Swansea and retired from football in
April 1981. He trained as a physiotherapist and then
found himself invited to join his old pal Graeme Souness
at Ibrox. Souness trusted him. They were loyal to each
other. Get on the wrong side of one and you would have
the other to contend with.

It was to be the same at Liverpool. Boersma came to
Anfield as part of the Souness package. When Souness
met the press for the first time, Boersma sat alongside
him. And there they were in the public photographs, Souness and Boersma smiling to each other with a con-
templative Moran sandwiched in between. There was
little doubting where Boersma stood in the pecking order.
He may not have been a true outsider in that he was a
Liverpool player of the past, and may have known the
Liverpool ways, but he came with a position that put into
question the role of Moran, Evans and Thompson. The
pecking order became confused. On match days the
dugout at Anfield was so crowded with the manager and
his assistants that there was barely room for the substitutes. And when Souness went, so too did Boersma. No
more room for him at Anfield.

But not all Souness' changes caused confusion. Some
made sense, particularly his influence over players' diets.
Footballers, never the most healthy of eaters, were introduced to more sensible eating patterns. Junk food, lager
and chocolate were discouraged in favour of high energy
foods such as pasta. It wasn't always popular with the
players, particularly the elder statesmen of the club who
felt that their diets had brought enough honours in the

past not to warrant changes. It was also noticeable that the new diets did little to improve the waistlines of one or two portly stars.

Many of the Anfield youngsters would be sad to see Souness go as he had given them their chance. Jamie Redknapp comments: 'There were a number of players here who were unhappy while Graeme was in charge and were quite pleased when he went, but there were also a number of us younger players who were disappointed. I haven't got a word to say against him because he always encouraged me and played me on a regular basis.'

By the time Souness joined Liverpool in April 1991, they had fallen away in the championship race and were trailing Arsenal by five points. There were only five games left. Time and fixtures were running out. But Souness, with typical Liverpool determination, was not about to give up. 'Our immediate aim is to win the league championship,' he told supporters, 'and whilst matters are not entirely in our own hands, in my book there is no such thing as a lost cause.'

Souness took up residence in the dugout for his first game as Liverpool faced Norwich. The Kop gave him a rapturous welcome, his side won 3–0 and nobody was giving up on the title. It all looked so promising. Of the thirteen players named that day, only four would survive the next three years. They were Bruce Grobbelaar, Steve Nicol, Ian Rush and John Barnes. The remainder, the heart of a side that was challenging for league honours, would be sold. A few days later Liverpool beat Crystal Palace 3–0 at Anfield but then crashed 2–4 at Stamford Bridge and all hope of the championship had vanished. The league title was no longer within their grasp and they wound up the season as runners-up, seven points clear of third-placed Crystal Palace but seven points behind champions Arsenal.

But the omens still looked favourable. As the 1991/92

season kicked off, the pundits, to a man, predicted success for Souness. With new signings Dean Saunders upfront to give them added variety and Mark Wright at the back to strengthen their one weak area, Liverpool began the season as favourites to capture Arsenal's crown. They made a promising start, even though they lost their second fixture; after half a dozen games they were in second place. But by then the injuries were beginning to mount. The first to limp off was John Barnes in the second game, followed almost immediately by Mark Wright. A few games later Ronnie Whelan joined them. By the end of September they had lost a second game and had slipped into mid-table as Manchester United and Leeds began to open up a gap at the top. Two months later, Liverpool's position had barely improved. They had won a mere five of their fifteen leagues games, drawn seven and lost three. The pattern had been set. Autumn was barely over and Liverpool were already fourteen points off the top and well out of contention.

But at least they were back in Europe. But even there they had hardly looked impressive. They began with a 6–1 home win over the part-time Finns, Kuusysi Lahti, though it was not until the last fifteen minutes that the Finns fell apart. Liverpool had huffed and puffed, a mere shadow of the side that had once swept so majestically across Europe. Saunders, who had looked out of place and had managed only two goals so far that season, hit four against the Finns and eased a few anxious minds on the Kop. In the second leg Liverpool lost 0–1, an embarrassment even if it hardly mattered. In the next round, they faced the French side Auxerre and again went down in the away tie, this time 0–2. It looked to be all over for Liverpool but in front of a flag-waving, noisy Kop that reminded Anfield of the old days, they pulled off a remarkable 3–0 win. Liverpool's season looked to be on course again. That was until Liverpool went to third division Peterborough United for a Rumbelows Cup game and were humiliated, losing 1–0. By then Mark Wright had returned to action; Barnes would return only briefly before injury again struck and Whelan would be sidelined for the rest of the campaign. Rush was also injured and missed more than twenty games after a cartilage operation, while Jan Molby was out for ten weeks following a similar operation. By the end of the season Liverpool had used twenty-six players in league matches. What's more, their European campaign also came to an abrupt end as they crashed 0–2 in Italy to Genoa. Back home there were hopes of another fightback, but instead quality showed as the Italians had the audacity to win 2–1; it was only the fourth time Liverpool had lost a European tie at Anfield in twenty-five years of European football.

But if the league had slipped from Liverpool's grasp – they would eventually wind up in sixth place – there was hope elsewhere. Luck seemed to have deserted Liverpool for much of the season but in the FA Cup the luck of the draw found them facing lower division opponents. Crewe Alexandra, Bristol Rovers and Ipswich were all dealt with before they eventually faced a first division outfit, and then they were drawn at Anfield. Aston Villa were their opponents but a 1–0 victory was enough to set up a semi-final against second division Portsmouth. They drew the first game 1–1 at Highbury, with Liverpool riding their luck. In the replay, they again pushed their luck and, after a goalless draw following extra time, won the penalty shoot-out 3–1.

In the final, Liverpool were pitted against yet another second division side, Sunderland. They had met four lower division sides en route to Wembley, with their fifth, Sunderland, surprisingly offering the least resistance. Sunderland might have edged the first half against a docile Liverpool midfield but in a crafty half-time move Souness switched Steve McManaman to the right wing.

He was a revelation. The pencil-thin winger ran riot, carving holes in the Sunderland defence. Liverpool won 2–0 with goals from new signing Michael Thomas and old boy Ian Rush. It had taken Liverpool eight games to win the Cup and it would be the only trophy Souness would win in his three years at Anfield.

Just as the 1991/92 season had opened with a rush of optimism, so too did the following season. 'Liverpool's unexpected FA Cup triumph will be the starting point for a new swelling of pride and achievement,' predicted one pundit. Goalkeeper David James of Watford and mid-fielder Paul Stewart from Spurs had been added to the squad, although there had been a surprise exit for Cup-winner Ray Houghton as well as Barry Venison. Stewart was expected to provide some much-needed muscle in the centre of the field, something that had been lacking since the transfer of Steve McMahon. But it was not to be. After six games Liverpool had only one win to their credit. They had drawn three and lost two. After ten games they had lost five and drawn three and had managed only one more win. David James, who had arrived at Anfield expecting little to do, found himself picking the ball out of the net every game. It was an appalling start; their league campaign was over virtually before it had begun. Souness quoted the old Shankly maxim that the league was a marathon and not a sprint. 'A lot can happen between now and the end of the season,' he told the papers, but nobody really believed him. It was true that in the past Liverpool had recovered from appalling starts. But anyone watching Liverpool in the autumn of 1992 knew that this was not the same Liverpool. No way was this team suddenly going to surge up the table. In fact, Liverpool were in serious trouble, hovering just above the relegation zone and would barely improve until later in the season.

During the autumn Souness, now searching frantically

for some defensive cover, had ventured abroad first to sign the Dane Torben Piechnik and then the Norwegian Stig Bjornebye. Neither was to prove impressive. To finance these deals, as well as the overpriced Paul Stewart, Dean Saunders had been sold to Aston Villa. Saunders, a £2.9 million misfit, had gone off to join his former Liverpool colleagues Steve Staunton and Ray Houghton at Villa Park. There were murmurings of discontent as much in the boardroom as on the Kop. Why had he signed Saunders in the first place? Why were Liverpool taking a £600,000 loss on the deal? Had Saunders really been given a chance?

And, of course, there were further injuries. John Barnes had damaged his Achilles tendon, this time while on international duty during the summer and did not put in an appearance until the end of November. Rob Jones was absent with a shin splint injury and would also be out until shortly before Christmas. Ronnie Whelan had reappeared briefly at the beginning of the season, only to be injured yet again. Michael Thomas would also miss large chunks of the season as would Mark Wright, Jan Molby, David Burrows and new boy Paul Stewart. It was left to a crop of emerging youngsters, most of whom were Dalglish's protégés, to hold the team together. In all, twenty-five players would be used in the league that season.

But if the league was looking a lost cause, there was still Europe to play for. Liverpool began with an effortless 6–1 win at Anfield over Apollon Limassol followed by a 2–1 win in Cyprus. In the next leg they faced Spartak Moscow and suffered one of the most depressing defeats in the club's European campaigns. Spartak won 4–2 in Moscow after Bruce Grobbelaar had been shown a red card and Graeme Souness had also voiced his disapproval to the referee. Back at Anfield, Souness was cranking the Kop into action, hoping for a repeat of the Auxerre result, and urging them to get behind the team. Liverpool began promisingly but soon faded when the early goal failed to materialise. In the end, Spartak won 2–0 and it was back to the domestic cups as the only hope of salvation.

In December 1992 there was also to be a personal tragedy for Souness when his father, Jimmy, died suddenly in an Edinburgh hospital. He was only in his early seventies, but had undergone heart bypass surgery two years earlier. It would be a stark reminder to Souness of his own condition and mortality.

By Christmas they were out of the Coca-Cola Cup, beaten by Crystal Palace and by mid-January they were also out of the FA Cup, humbled 0–2 at Anfield by Bolton Wanderers in one of the biggest cup shocks in years. Liverpool had a habit of drawing against lowly opposition in the FA Cup but always snatching victory at Anfield. This time it would be different. Bolton outclassed them both at Burnden Park, where Liverpool were lucky to force a draw, and at Anfield where the Wanderers thoroughly deserved their victory. Liverpool's season was effectively over. In the end they dragged themselves away from the relegation battle to finish in a respectable sixth place.

There is an old saying at Anfield: 'First is first, second is nowhere.' In May 1993 the knives were out for Souness. It wasn't just that Liverpool had ended the season without a trophy or that they had not qualified for Europe for the first time in thirty years. It was the way they were playing. Souness was as baffled as anyone.

But there was worse happening off the field. The club were desperately in need of a new press room at Anfield. The old press room was little bigger than a broom cupboard where there was not even space for managers and journalists to sit. The traditional post-match interview with the manager had become a cramped affair as a dozen or more journalists battled for the manager's ear. It was an embarrassment. A club of Liverpool's standing rightly needed to present a better image. There should have been other options, but instead the club's directors decided to knock down the old bootroom and turn it into the new press centre. You couldn't blame Souness, but you could wonder what Shankly's reaction would have been to such a suggestion. Even as it happened he was probably turning in his grave. The very soul of Liverpool Football Club had been ripped apart. Admittedly, they created a new bootroom, further down the corridor, but it would never be the same. The magic was gone.

If the bootroom was the soul of Liverpool Football Club, then its heart was the Kop. The Taylor Report had ruled that Premiership clubs would have to become all-seater stadiums for the start of the 1994/95 season. It was inevitable after the deaths at Hillsborough. The club might not have liked the idea but they could hardly argue against it when so many of their fans had died. It was incumbent on Liverpool to set an example, to give a positive lead. And so, plans were drawn up to build a new all-seater Kop. The old Kop would be bulldozed in May 1994. That giant terracing, probably the most famous in world football would be torn down. Fans campaigned against the decision, knowing all along that they were fighting a losing battle. Like the bootroom, Shankly would have voiced disapproval at his beloved Kop being ripped down. But even Shankly, in the end, would not have been able to do much about it. Souness said little. He could do nothing either. Pulling down the Kop was totally out of his sphere of influence but it was another vital tradition that was disappearing. Training schedules, transfer traditions, injuries, executive boxes, the bootroom, and now the Kop. It was all change at Anfield. The old spirit was disappearing. The Rolls-Royce had failed its MOT.

CHAPTER SEVENTEEN
On The Ropes

It was the nightmare scenario. Manchester United racing away with the championship while Liverpool sickeningly trailed them, by more than twenty points, in sixth place. United had last picked up the title in 1967, a year after Liverpool had claimed their second post-war championship. Since then the Merseysiders had won umpteen titles and trophies. For most of the past twenty years Liverpool supporters had been crowing from their perches on the Kop. They liked nothing more than to sing 'Are you watching Manchester'. They hated the 'Mancs'. Manchester was a wealthier city, always had been, while Liverpool had declined into a city that would not have looked out of place in the Third World. There were jobs in Manchester, leafy suburbs, a stockbroker belt and ambitions to host the Olympics that made it unarguably the north west's number one city. But, at the same time, Mancs were faceless and nondescript, not like scousers. They may have been poor and unemployed, but Liverpudlians had spirit, humour and irony. In particular they loathed Manchester United and their supporters. One of the Liverpool fanzines even carried a column titled 'Manc Watch' which recorded Fleet Street's love affair with Old Trafford.

For years there had been an unhealthy rivalry between the two sets of fans which had less to do with football than was generally imagined. In fact it had far more to do with the respective ambitions and status of the two cities. But, thanks to their outstanding successes, Liverpool Football Club had always held the upper hand over United, especially when it came to polishing the silverware. And in the end most Liverpool supporters knew that was what really mattered.

Yet, since the Munich Disaster when Matt Busby's brave young side had been all but wiped out, the nation had developed an affection for the Old Trafford club. They were the nation's side. Liverpool may have won countless trophies in the intervening years but they had never quite captured the hearts and minds of either Fleet Street or the people. Best, Law and Charlton had played with elegance; Souness, Dalglish and Hansen with gusto and a methodical consistency that some reckoned bordered on the boring. United were the glamour club with a huge following throughout the country. Even when they had crashed into the second division in 1974 it was with 40,000-plus crowds. No matter what position United held or how poorly they might play, the crowds still flocked to see them. United's appeal was even reflected on the streets; schoolkids bought Manchester United kits rather than Liverpool shirts, while on the continent it was the name of Manchester United that was mentioned before that of Liverpool.

It irked Liverpool fans that they had won six European trophies and yet United still captured the headlines. But Liverpool supporters could at least gloat over the fact that Old Trafford's trophy room was bare. There was even a T-shirt on sale outside Anfield emblazoned with the message 'Lord Lucan Found – Hiding in Manchester United's Trophy Room'. United might have won some trophies in those years but they had never held aloft the one that really mattered – the league championship. Liverpool–Manchester United fixtures have long carried the reputation of being the fiercest contest in the entire Football League. Even Liverpool supporters would agree that while beating neighbours Everton gives them that extra boost, there is nothing quite like dishing out the punishment to Manchester United.

Managers had come and gone at Old Trafford but none had ever been able to recapture the romance and success of Matt Busby. Millions had been spent in the transfer market yet despite the outlay few players had ever displayed the flair of a Best, Law or Charlton. What's more, the youth scheme that had thrown up so many of the famous Busby Babes in the fifties and then the likes of Best, Stiles and Aston in later years had produced only a handful of protégés in the seventies and eighties. But under their latest manager, Alex Ferguson, United had created a system and an attitude throughout the club that not only rivalled Liverpool but was now overtaking it in terms of quality and trophies. In a highly successful three-year spell, United had lifted the FA Cup, the European Cup-Winners' Cup and the League Cup, and in 1993 they stood poised to capture that elusive league championship.

While Liverpool fans looked on United with a mixture of envy and disdain, there were United fans who could remind them that Ferguson himself had not been without his critics during his years at Old Trafford. Ferguson had come to United from Aberdeen in November 1986. In his first season the club had finished in only eleventh place. The following season results improved but United could still do no better than end up in second place behind Liverpool. The 1989/90 campaign was even worse as they slumped back into mid-table anonymity once more. There was speculation that Ferguson's days were numbered but the board persevered and at the end of that season

Ferguson was able to afford a smile as United lifted the FA Cup, even though the opposition throughout had not always been testing.

Success in the FA Cup, however, was not followed by any improvement in United's league position, the real litmus test for Ferguson. In September 1990, Old Trafford had emptied ten minutes before the final whistle as United trailed Nottingham Forest by a single goal. In a dire performance that was greeted with a chorus of whistles and the sound of upending seats, it must have crossed Ferguson's mind that his days at Old Trafford might be numbered. It was their third defeat already that season which had also included a 4–0 drubbing at Anfield; Ferguson's brief reign at Old Trafford looked to be all but over.

The more astute observer, however, pointed not at their current results but at what was happening elsewhere in the club. Ferguson had arrived at Old Trafford to discover that the club's famed youth policy had fallen by the way-side. In an area rich in young footballing talent it was their rivals Manchester City who were successfully unearthing the talent ahead of United. Given United's history and attraction for so many youngsters, it was an astonishing state of affairs that they were unable to spot and attract the region's best players. Ferguson's first task had been to repair the damage and to create a nursery system that would once more make United the pick of the region's and the nation's teenagers. It was a slow process but one which in a few years would produce talent in rich abundance, led by Ryan Giggs. Giggs, in fact, had originally been at City's school of excellence.

Ferguson's dealings in the transfer market had also at times puzzled many a United supporter. Sometimes justifiably. They had not always proved to be successful. Principal among his expensive failures was Neil Webb. The gifted Nottingham Forest midfielder had cost United

£1.5 million but after just a handful of games he damaged an Achilles tendon while on duty with England. It took Webb six months to recover and, although he returned to play more than a hundred games for the club, he was never quite the same player again. He seemed to have lost a yard in pace and, following a row with Ferguson, was eventually transferred back to Nottingham Forest for a knockdown fee. Other less than successful signings included Ralph Milne, Danny Wallace, Viv Anderson and goalkeeper Jim Leighton. For a time, large question marks also hung over a number of other signings, including Gary Pallister who cost a record-breaking fee of £2.3 million when Ferguson signed him from Middlesbrough in 1989. He was reckoned by many to be grossly over-priced. A few years earlier Liverpool had put in a bid for Pallister but refused to pay more than £1 million for the young man, arguing that he was not worth any more. It was a big gamble on Ferguson's part and it would be some years before Pallister settled and began to look anything like a £2.3 million player. Another who took time to emerge was Paul Ince who, for more than a season, could never be certain of his place and who often bore the brunt of Old Trafford criticism. Michael Phelan also failed to make an immediate impact. Ferguson's signings seemed workmanlike rather than inspired.

But Ferguson's biggest problem when he arrived at Old Trafford was to rid the club of some of its most famous names. It took courage, the same sort of courage that Souness had needed in ridding the club of its old guard. Similar moves by Ferguson proved equally unpopular. Norman Whiteside was sold to Everton, Paul McGrath went to Aston Villa, Gordon Strachan was offloaded to Leeds United while Remi Moses, Peter Davenport, Mike Duxbury, Jesper Olsen and others would all make way for new players and youngsters. The selling of so many star names proved unpopular on the terraces, particularly when long-time favourite Norman Whiteside was shown the door. But Ferguson saw the clear-out as essential. He had kept his patience with the squad when he arrived but had soon decided that changes were inevitable. Although some of the players still had something to offer they were not, for one reason or another, good enough for the club.

Ferguson's clear-out eventually began to pay dividends. In 1990 they won the FA Cup. Then a year later they lifted the European Cup-Winners' Cup, beating Barcelona in the final to give English soccer a much-welcomed boost in European eyes. Earlier they had lost 1–0 to Sheffield Wednesday in the League Cup final at Wembley and although they ended the season with just one trophy they had at least been in contention for silverware on three fronts. The following year they reached the League Cup final again, this time successfully lifting the one domestic trophy that had eluded them. Ferguson had now won a trophy in three successive seasons. But the league championship continued to elude them with Leeds pipping them to the post, thanks mainly to a 2–0 defeat of Manchester United at Anfield in the penultimate game of the season. United were playing with confidence but still lacked the flair and drive of their famous predecessors. The drive would finally come as their confidence increased, while the flair would arrive in the shape of Eric Cantona's Gallic skills and Ryan Giggs with his youthful energy and audacity.

It had taken Alex Ferguson five and a half years to produce a championship side. It had cost millions of pounds, at least £15 million in new signings, and with not a great deal recouped from outgoing transfers. It had been a difficult and often fraught journey but Ferguson had always stuck with his beliefs. He knew what he wanted and was determined to succeed. All that he had asked for was time and a little luck. The Old Trafford board had kept faith with him, graciously giving him the time when many were calling for his head. The luck had undoubtedly arrived with the emergence of Ryan Giggs and a chance telephone conversation with Howard Wilkinson, manager of Leeds United, that resulted in the transfer of Eric Cantona. The result of Ferguson's endeavours was a United side that resembled the Liverpool of old in so many ways. You could always bet on them to win. They had acquired patience; they rarely panicked, even when a goal or two adrift. They simply kept working at their game and inevitably would be rewarded. And, like Liverpool, so many of those equalisers and winners arrived in the final moments. The set-up throughout the club was impressive, from the first team down to the reserves and the youth sides. All of them were winning trophies in their respective leagues. Ferguson had bought well, making mistakes early in his career, but he had learned from his mistakes and after 1990 most of his expensive signings were to become established players.

As the 1992/93 season wound to its conclusion over a Bank Holiday weekend, United were the acknowledged champions of the Premiership. Liverpool were left languishing hopelessly in their trail. Even the watery evening sun was still dazzling on Old Trafford as United took the field to face Kenny Dalglish's Blackburn Rovers knowing that they were already champions. And in the evening warmth United supporters partied with a revelry usually associated with Kopites. Liverpool supporters could not even claim to be football's most vocal fans any longer. It seemed that, for the moment, at least, the gods were against Liverpool. Back on Merseyside the Kopites switched off their radios and TVs and even refused a cursory glance at the back pages of their tabloids the next morning. Everywhere it was Manchester United this and Manchester United that. Nobody ever went quite this ecstatic when Liverpool won the title. It was the climax to the season all Liverpool fans had dreaded. At least they had not been relegated and nor had United clinched the title at Anfield as seemed possible at one stage. But all that was only scant compensation. United were champions, England's number one team and with players who looked like they might be able to carry on pulling in the trophies for a few more seasons.

United manager Alex Ferguson had dealt a masterstroke in signing Eric Cantona, the enigmatic but highly effective French striker. He had brought a sense of the dramatic back to Old Trafford, lacking since the days of Best, Law and Charlton. All Liverpool had was Torben Piechnik. The papers made gloomy reading. United, they reckoned, were set to become the new Liverpool. There seemed no reason why they could not go on and dominate English football in the way that Liverpool had for twenty years, they argued. Behind their public picture of championship-winning stars was a crop of highly talented youngsters itching to make the break into the first team. Success seemed guaranteed for years. Over at Anfield it was another indication of just how far Liverpool had sunk since Graeme Souness took over. Souness' job was on the line.

All season the fans had been muttering about him. The letters had poured into Anfield, filling chairman David Moores' in-tray. And you only had to look at the *Liverpool Football Echo*'s letters page to see what Liverpool fans thought of their manager. Former Liverpool iron man Tommy Smith was the most damning of all Souness' critics, slamming him week after week in his column in the paper. Smith could make no sense of Souness' transfer dealings. A scouser to the core, he still had strong links with the club and cringed at the sad deterioration at Anfield. It didn't make him too welcome over the doorstep. Even the letters page of the *Independent* was carrying a regular spray of letters from disgruntled Liverpool supporters. And on Radio Five's Saturday evening phone-in there was usually a queue of callers from Liverpool, all expressing their frustration. Never in all the years of Shankly, Paisley, Fagan and Dalglish had a word against the manager been voiced publicly. There may have been the occasional groans, and they were only occasional, when a manager's decision was questioned but the criticism was rare. Some of Dalglish's ideas may have seemed eccentric, but at the end of the day it was the results which counted and anyhow, most criticism of Dalglish came from the press. The Kop would never have dared voice any public criticism of their man.

But it was very different with Souness. As a player he had never been overly popular with the Kopites. His extravagant lifestyle was an anathema to their own experiences of life. The Kop may have appreciated his footballing skills but they never warmed to him in the way that they had to Dalglish, Phil Thompson, Bruce Grobbelaar and one or two others. Poverty, unemployment and poor housing were generally the lot of the Kopites. A bathroom with gold bathtaps, a pretty girl on the arm and a champagne lifestyle were far removed from their version of everyday life in Kirkby, Walton or Bootle.

Dalglish and other Anfield stars might have been just as wealthy but at least they weren't flash with it and had succeeded in bringing continued glory to Anfield. Their extravagant lifestyles could be forgiven. Had Souness succeeded in the way that his predecessors had, he too would no doubt have been forgiven his misdemeanours. But his failings only highlighted his private life.

His extravagant signings had proved unimpressive. Only Rob Jones, one of his least expensive purchases at £300,000 from Crewe Alexandra, had looked the part. Dean Saunders, Mark Wright, Mark Walters, Istvan Kozma, Paul Stewart, Torben Piechnik, Stig Bjornebye – not one of them looked like a genuine Liverpool player.

And not one of them would ever have been chosen to line up alongside Souness and company in that famous Liverpool side of the eighties. The only players who did look useful were the youngsters – Steve McManaman, Don Hutchison and Jamie Redknapp – and ironically they were all Dalglish signings. Back at Christmas Souness had been telling the papers Liverpool 'were two players short of being a top side'. Liverpool always seemed to be a couple of players short of a decent side.

A showdown was inevitable. Throughout the season more than one member of the board had been questioning Souness' future. As the season reached its climax, more directors joined the chorus. By April those on the board baying for Souness' blood had reached a majority. Two weeks before the end of the season, in April 1993, the board met and decided that enough was enough. It had not worked out. At the end of the season Souness' contract would be ripped up. He was to be sacked. They agreed to open negotiations with Souness in order to resolve the problem with as little fuss as possible. Souness had three years of a £250,000 a year contract left to run. He would have to be paid off and Liverpool hoped that they might be able to reach a compromise. At the time nobody foresaw this as a major stumbling block. But a decision had been made: Souness was going. There were just a couple more games left.

A further meeting was held on Sunday 2 May to formalise Souness' departure. Souness was not told about the meeting, but the news was to leak out. Who leaked it is something a number of people wanted to know, not least David Moores who promised that 'their feet would not touch the ground'. The following day the back pages were filled with 'Souness Sacking?' stories. It was an appalling embarrassment for the club. Souness had not yet been informed and here were the papers announcing his departure. In many ways it played into Souness' hands. Forewarned is to be forearmed. Souness had not known about the board meeting and demanded to talk with them to put his case. He needed to know whether he had their support or not. It was not the Liverpool style to wash its dirty linen in public. When things happened they normally happened quickly without the kind of speculation that was splashed across the tabloids.

The board met again on the Monday. By now Souness and his advisers were girding their legal loins, heavily into talk of money and the terms of departure. The future of Phil Boersma was said to be on the agenda as well. Board meetings were convened every day that week as new problems appeared while other difficulties remained unresolved. On the Wednesday evening Souness took Liverpool to Oldham where they crashed 2–3. Even worse, Don Hutchison was sent off, the third first team Liverpool player to be dismissed that season and the sixth in the club. Souness left Boundary Park via a side door after failing to turn up for the post-match press conference.

The following day further discussions took place. By now the press were camped outside Anfield attempting to interpret every move, departure and smile. It was all cloak-and-dagger stuff. By Friday all the newspapers were confidently reporting that Graeme Souness' reign as manager at Anfield was over. They had even begun to speculate about his successor, with the name of Dalglish being heavily touted on some back pages.

'All I want to do is see out my three years at Liverpool,' Souness was telling people. 'Anyone who knows me will tell you that I've never run away from anything. I'm being portrayed as a mercenary, someone who is holding the club to ransom. That's not true.'

But behind locked doors the arguing continued. At the root of the problem was the pay-off to Souness. At the very least it appeared that it would cost Liverpool a minimum of £1 million. Souness wanted to be well compensated for what he called his 'humiliation'. The board met again on the Friday. It was Graeme Souness' fortieth birthday and, by way of a birthday present, a number of directors were visibly shifting ground. David Moores was now arguing strongly in Souness' favour. A further problem, it was pointed out, was who to appoint as his successor. Dalglish probably would not be interested and nor would Kevin Keegan. Alan Hansen was another they might have fancied but he too had ruled himself out. It might well be that they already had the best man available. As a way out of the chaos a new plan had been floated. By now it was clear that a negotiated settlement was becoming more and more unlikely. The board, desperate to find a solution, had fixed their sights on an agreement with Souness that would allow him to remain as manager but would place a straitjacket on him, appeasing some of the concerns of board members. The idea was to appoint Roy Evans as assistant manager. That might temper some of Souness' extravagances in the transfer market and help keep some of the more experienced players content. Souness had been insistent that he was only two or three players short of an outstanding side. Why not give him a chance, argued David Moores. A further consideration was that Souness should perhaps spend his Saturdays in the directors' box rather than on the touchline. That way he might keep out of mischief and not be tempted to argue the toss with referees and linesmen, bringing the club into disrepute again.

The Liverpool board, usually so stable and sure, was suddenly drifting. It was all so unlike Liverpool. There was a feeling that it would never have happened in the days when Sir John Smith was chairman. Then they prided themselves on acting first and telling the world later. How had it all come to this? It was surely a case of bad and inflexible management.

Director Tony Ensor, who was also the club solicitor,

was losing patience. He had already threatened to resign a year earlier over the *Sun* debacle. Now his patience snapped. As far as he was concerned the board were losing control. He could bite his tongue no longer. He had had enough. If Souness wasn't going, then he certainly was. Ensor, a director for eight years, resigned at that meeting, although he agreed not to make any public announcement until the Souness matter had been resolved. But the resignation of Ensor only brought further confusion to a chaotic situation.

On Saturday 8 May Liverpool faced Tottenham at Anfield in the final match of their season. The club announced that Souness would still be in charge for the game, but come 3 p.m. there was no Graeme Souness. Instead, he was 100 miles down the M6 alongside Tom Saunders watching Coventry play Leeds United. He told journalists that he was on a scouting mission. His regular column in the Liverpool programme had been removed, and replaced with a piece by David Moores. There could be only one explanation: an announcement was imminent, Souness was going. Liverpool beat Tottenham 6–2 before an ecstatic Kop.

The following day, and just as his career at Anfield seemed to be at an end, Souness' ex-wife Danielle chose her moment to slap him in public, on the front page of the *Sunday People*. She was, no doubt, well paid for her efforts. It appeared under the grotesque headline 'You're a Dirty Rat Souness'.

'I must expose him for our children's sake,' she told the paper and then went on to catalogue his misdeeds. She told how Souness 'ordered her and their children to leave their farmhouse home by Christmas Eve; forced her to sign a bizarre "no men in the house" contract while she lived there; refused to pay school fees for their sons Frazer, 12, and Jordan, 8; failed to turn up at a court hearing to discuss maintenance for the boys'. And so it

went on, detailing how Souness had accused her of being
upset because he had £8 million in the bank and how he
had found the job of managing Liverpool more difficult
than he had ever imagined. Danielle could not understand his sudden change of attitude but did offer one
interesting thought. 'As far as I am concerned he has had
a personality change. Up to his operation he seemed OK,'
she said, 'but since then he has gone downright
ridiculous.'

'Graeme has always been the type of person who when
his team loses it affects him badly and being the closest
people to him at the time, the whole family suffered. He
had mood swings. He was either up or down – and very
difficult to live with.' One could imagine and she knew
where the blame lay. 'It was his temperament which was
more to blame because he would never accept defeat.'
Souness was obsessed with his job though it hardly
needed Danielle's public baring of her soul to the *Sunday
People* to confirm this.

As the *Sunday People* article hit the news stands the
Liverpool board convened yet again. They were not
exactly happy with what they read that morning but they
were now too far down the track of reinstating Souness
to do a further U-turn. The plan had by then been put to
Souness and Evans and at the board meeting that day
the final details were cobbled together. The board had
done a complete U-turn. Now they had to explain themselves to a waiting press. They knew it would be a public
humiliation. At 4 p.m. the assembled reporters were
called upstairs for a press conference.

Souness sat next to David Moores, Roy Evans on his
other side. Peter Robinson sat to the right of Moores with
Sir John Smith alongside him. Tony Ensor sat a few
feet away. Souness looked grim-faced; Evans bemused.
Robinson and Smith, the two men who had guided the
club throughout the glory years, simply looked fed up.

'The past few days at Anfield have probably been the most difficult in the club's history,' began David Moores. 'They started when Graeme Souness approached me to ask whether he still had the full support of the board. That sparked off a whole series of discussions . . . They went on rather longer than anyone would have wished, but for all of us the most important thing was to reach the best conclusion – not the quickest.'

Then he stunned just about every reporter in the room. 'Now it has all been sorted out and I am pleased to announce that Graeme Souness will be remaining as manager of Liverpool Football Club for the three years of his contract and I hope for much longer than that.' Some of those journalists, well versed in Liverpool affairs over the years, could scarcely believe it.

Moores then emphasised that at no time had Souness expressed any wish to leave Liverpool. 'At every stage he has said that he wanted to stay.' He then added that 'during our discussions we told him that if he wanted to leave we would pay out his contract in full. That would have represented a substantial sum. He told us very clearly he did not want the money, he wanted to stay.' Moores also pointed out that had they paid up it would have made 'only a fairly small dent in our financial resources'. Moores then announced that director Tony Ensor was resigning and that Tom Saunders was being co-opted to the board in his place.

Then came another dramatic announcement. 'With immediate effect,' announced Moores, 'Roy Evans is appointed assistant manager.' Everyone had wondered why Evans was sitting alongside Souness. Now they knew. Evans had just been made the first assistant manager in the club's history.

Then it was over to Tony Ensor. 'There were a number of matters relating to the way in which the club is being run with which I do not agree,' announced Ensor. He admitted that he had strongly held views and felt that they were no longer compatible with being a board member. But Ensor would elaborate no more. Although he had said that it was not a question of personalities, it clearly was. Ensor was hardly Graeme Souness' biggest fan.

Finally, Souness and Evans had their say. Souness was as commanding as ever. 'I'm relieved and delighted,' he said. 'At no time have I ever wanted to leave this club.' And yes, he was equally delighted that Roy Evans had been officially appointed as his number two. Then there was the question of whether he felt he had the full support of the board. 'There is no problem whatsoever between myself and any member of the board,' he insisted. But of course there was. The differences had merely been buried and it would not be long before they resurfaced again.

Souness and Evans then posed for photographs, arms around each other, smiles finally breaking out on their faces. Souness said that he would be spending the summer looking to add to his squad. Ten million pounds was said to be available for new players. 'Ideally I would like to get three top players for the start of the next season,' he announced.

And so ended one of the most extraordinary weeks in the history of the club, a boardroom battle that had ended in victory for David Moores and Graeme Souness. Twelve months earlier Souness had escaped a sacking by the skin of his teeth, now he had gone even closer. In effect, he had been sacked and then reinstated. The next time he would not be so lucky. What's more, the board had, in effect, now chosen his successor.

CHAPTER EIGHTEEN
The Revolution's Last Stand

The County Ground at Swindon is hardly the place where you would expect to see the ideals of a revolution fulfilled. It is a homely enough ground but hardly stately; drab rather than lordly. And yet there on Sunday 22 August 1993 Liverpool soared to the top of the Premier League for the first time since Kenny Dalglish's departure. It had taken two and a half years but for the thousands of Liverpool supporters crammed into the County Ground it was a treasured moment. It had been a long and often tortuous road. Graeme Souness' Liverpool were coming of age and what's more they were doing it with some style, overwhelming newly promoted Swindon by five goals to nil. The *Daily Telegraph* even described their performance as 'restrained', suggesting that Liverpool had been holding in reserve all their powers for the battles ahead. What mattered, however, was that Liverpool were back where they belonged at the top of the table.

Euphoria gripped the city. Another 42,000 turned out for the second home game of the season with talk of championship trophies on everyone's lips. But it was to be short-lived. Within ten days they had suffered a second defeat, been toppled from their perch at the top of the table and seen Manchester United draw clear of them. Then when Kenny Dalglish's Blackburn Rovers came to Anfield for a live BSkyB game, Liverpool crashed to their third defeat of the season and their second at home. Seven games played and three defeats already. It may have been too early to write off their title dreams, but it meant that they could not afford to lose more than a couple more games all season. In reality, it was all over. But what was perhaps more disturbing, and what was to be the talk of the city among older Kopites, was the team's attitude.

Commentators would argue, and most Kopites would agree, that while Liverpool have always been a determined side, they could never be described as a crude side, never a team committed to physical intimidation, never likely to get mixed up in punch-ups or red cards. Over the years they had had their iron men, players like Tommy Smith, Jimmy Case and even Graeme Souness himself, but they had never deliberately gone out to destroy their opponents with outright physical coercion. But suddenly all that had changed. Rob Jones had already been sent off a few weeks earlier and now he was being shown another yellow card after displaying the quality of his studs to an opponent. This was not the Liverpool style of old and, to make matters worse, against Blackburn new signing Neil Ruddock was dashing twenty yards to have his say and swing a punch. It all resulted in a major confrontation as players and officials measured up to each other, swapping insults and threats. Shirts were pulled, tongues wagged and everybody became overheated. Such scenes had not been witnessed at Anfield for decades. For old-time Kopites there was only one culprit. 'The word has to come from above,' they were telling the *Liverpool Echo* the next day, swelling its letters' page. It was the talk of the city and it had come under the close scrutiny of the TV cameras and its pundits.

Under Shankly, Paisley, Fagan and Dalglish such

behaviour would have been punished immediately and the players would have been left with no doubts that this was not the Liverpool style. But under Graeme Souness it almost seemed that the manager was encouraging his players to 'get stuck in' and show some mettle. It was partly frustration born out of their own failings. Liverpool were no longer invincible at Anfield and they did not like it.

Souness' solution should have been to calm his troops, slap them into line and punish a few culprits. Instead Kopites woke up days later to discover that their manager had put in a bid for Julian Dicks, the West Ham defender. Everyone was agog. Why did Liverpool need a defender when what was most needed was a quality midfielder and someone upfront to play alongside Rush? But there was another problem. Dicks might have been an effective addition but his disciplinary record was appalling. The punters might have questioned Ruddock's disciplinary record but Dicks' was even worse. He had been sent off on eight occasions and had collected at least twenty yellow cards, so many that nobody was quite sure of the exact number. And here were Liverpool, the side that only a few years ago boasted Hansen and Lawrenson in the heart of their defence, about to team up Neil Ruddock with Julian Dicks. The prospect might have frightened a few strikers but it only dismayed Liverpool supporters. The following day the deal was confirmed and, to make matters worse, if indeed that was possible, David Burrows and Mike Marsh were going in the opposite direction. It may have been necessary to unload players but eyebrows were raised that it should have been Burrows and Marsh.

Burrows had arrived at Anfield as a teenager, recruited by Dalglish from West Brom for £500,000. But he had never quite blossomed into the player he promised. He had a tendency to be impulsive, throwing in a boot when it was unnecessary although this now seemed to be the style of the new Liverpool. What's more, he had seemed to be an automatic choice under Souness. There was a good argument for keeping Burrows, at least as a utility player, and an even better argument for hanging on to Mike Marsh. The youngster had barely begun his first team career and had looked a bright prospect. He was a Liverpool lad, a Kop favourite, and had always played with commitment and effort though usually in an unfamiliar role. He was the future, yet Souness who had talked about needing a young team, was discarding him in favour of a 26-year-old. None of it made sense.

Dicks duly made his debut the following day at Goodison Park in the Merseyside derby as Liverpool faced an improving Everton side. They lost 2–0 with what was undoubtedly their most miserable performance so far that season. The midfield had been non-existent, like a soft boiled egg, easy to crack and messy in the middle. Time and again Tony Cottee cut through them. The new defence was left exposed and unable to counter Everton's penetrating attacks. Dicks escaped the referee's book but Ruddock found his name in there alongside that of Whelan. But there was worse. Two Liverpool players should have been sent off for fighting. And astonishingly they were fighting each other. After Everton's opening strike, goalkeeper Bruce Grobbelaar, somewhat unfairly, blamed midfielder Steve McManaman for failing to deal with a ball close to the edge of the area. Cottee had leapt on the ball and rifled it into the back of the net. It was hardly McManaman's fault but there was Grobbelaar telling him in no uncertain terms who was to blame. A punch was swung, McManaman retaliated and a disgraceful scene was captured for millions to watch later that evening on television.

The shameful episode was the gossip of Merseyside and much of the back pages the next day. Four defeats in five games. They would be lucky to get a UEFA place now and September was not even out. Outside Goodison, the Everton fans celebrated a rare victory over their neighbours with a chorus of 'Souness must stay'. It was hurtful but you could hardly blame them. On Radio Five's sports programme that evening the telephone lines buzzed as Liverpool supporters called in to demand Souness' resignation. It was the same vitriolic attack from everyone. Why the hard players, this was not the Liverpool style, where was the quality, millions spent and where were Liverpool?

But the pain did not stop there. Souness answered his critics with a vengeance. Ronnie Whelan, once the cultivated thinking man in Liverpool's midfield, found himself slapped on the transfer list while Steve Nicol, Steve McManaman and Mark Walters all joined him on the substitutes' bench. It was the night of the long knives. For Whelan it was a humiliation, after a long and distinguished Anfield career, and it seemed unfair that the blame should have been so emphatically placed on his shoulders. Over the years he had picked up a bagful of medals with the club and, although he was not always popular with the Liverpool crowd, the side had missed his tackling and scurrying back into defence during his enforced absence through injury. His return to the side in 1993 had sparked a mini-revival but now, at the age of 32, he was admittedly not performing with the same gusto and enthusiasm of his younger years and not too many people mourned his disappearance from the side. The wholesale changes seemed to do the trick as Liverpool travelled to London to take on Fulham in the Coca-Cola Cup. They won 3–1 although their victory had its fair share of anxious moments. The one success of Souness' purge was the introduction of the 18-year-old Robbie Fowler, who not only scored on his debut but gave a performance that showed much promise for the future.

The following Saturday, however, Liverpool came down to earth with a thud as they returned to the capital to take on a lively Chelsea side. The Londoners won 1–0 although in fairness Liverpool deserved at least a draw. But luck deserted them as they plunged into the lower half of the table.

It was the worst September in ninety years, not one league point to show for all their endeavours. With only nine games played they had already used twenty players. The goals had all but dried up and expensive new signing Nigel Clough was now looking distinctly anonymous; on the positive side the back four were beginning to look more secure than they had for years. The following week Liverpool entertained just about the last team they wanted, Arsenal, second in the league and always likely to steal the glory at Anfield. But it turned out to be not quite so bad. Arsenal came to defend and Liverpool might well have pinched the points, but in the end had to settle for a goalless draw. By now they had gone five league games without a goal, their worst run for forty years. The records were being broken thick and fast.

The deadlock was finally smashed two weeks later as they entertained relegation candidates Oldham at Anfield. 'If we don't score today, we'll never score,' was the word in the bars before the match. Although Liverpool were to win, it was thanks only to a couple of goals in the last three minutes, including an own goal. Earlier they had fallen behind to an Oldham goal and had given a performance that many rated the poorest Anfield had seen since the pre-Shankly days. The 2–1 win merely covered over the cracks and gave Souness another lease of life. Defeat might have meant another confrontation with the board. As it was, Souness responded by setting up a deal for Tim Flowers, the highly rated Southampton goalkeeper. The initial agreement was for David James and Don Hutchison to go as a direct swap. Unfortunately,

Hutchison wanted no part of it and the deal was resurrected as James plus £1 million. Southampton were happy, Flowers seemed happy but Flowers' agent was not. He had a whiff of interest from elsewhere. Flowers pulled out of the negotiations and a fortnight later was on his way to Ewood Park and a reported £8,000 a week.

It was a snub for Liverpool, and not the kind of snub they were used to. It was something which did not happen too often. Charlie Nicholas was the last man to reject their overtures, preferring the bright lights of London to the dark streets of Liverpool. It had never worked out for Nicholas and in hindsight he could reflect on the missed opportunity. But now it seemed to be happening with a regularity that was worrying. As in any other walk of life, word circulates and the word was that Liverpool were no longer the club they used to be. Souness' reputation travelled before him. The talk on the grapevine was that he was a difficult man to work for, exacting, impetuous and never quite sure of his policies, a politician being swayed this way one week, another way the next. Liverpool were no longer the attraction they had been in the seventies and eighties when any player would have gone to the club for a cut in salary, just to have the opportunity of winning trophies. Footballers may be castigated for their greed but the biggest incentive remains the winning of trophies. Now Liverpool were learning a painful new lesson, that other clubs were a greater attraction. Manchester United were the side everyone wanted to play for, while Blackburn Rovers were the club that could outbid all others.

But the protracted deal over Flowers also highlighted something else: Souness' inability to settle on his number one goalkeeper. Hooper, a perfectly adequate custodian though admittedly not outstanding, had been offloaded to Newcastle for £500,000. James, his £1.3 million recruit from Watford during the close season, had played only a handful of games before being expelled to the Siberia of reserve team football while Grobbelaar, ageing, sometimes brilliant but always prone to erratic behaviour, had been given a fresh lease of life. Had Flowers arrived, James would have been shown the door, with Grobbelaar no doubt being relegated to Pontins League football once more. Landing a top-flight goalkeeper hardly seemed Liverpool's priority when the midfield was scuffling wantonly most Saturday afternoons. It was the same sad story of Souness never being quite sure of what he wanted.

Although Liverpool were to make steady, though unspectacular, progress up the table during October and early November it was never really convincing. There always lurked the feeling that sooner or later their luck was going to run out. It finally did, at St James' Park, Newcastle, on a bitterly cold Sunday afternoon. Within five minutes they were a goal down to Kevin Keegan's emerging team and after thirty minutes had conceded three as Newcastle, producing one of their liveliest displays in years, tore Liverpool apart. It was embarrassing to watch. What's more, Newcastle boasted three ex-Liverpool players in their line-up – Barry Venison, Mike Hooper and Peter Beardsley – and all them Souness castoffs. On top of this the side was managed by two other former Liverpool stars of the seventies, Keegan and Terry McDermott. Six months earlier, Newcastle had been in the first division and now Keegan had shaped a side that could steamroller through the Liverpool defence. And, what's more, his side had cost a fraction of Souness'. There was surely a lesson to be learned somewhere.

Souness lay the blame on injuries. Admittedly, he was able to field only one of his normal back four. Jones, Dicks and Wright were all laid up with injuries of one kind or another. Dicks had only been at the club for a few weeks and already he was limping. It had a depressing familiarity about it.

288

'We have thirty-two professional players at Anfield injured,' he told reporters, adding that 'the only two fit players were sitting on the bench.' One might have wondered why they were sitting on the bench if they were fit. But at least one of those was John Barnes who came on for the second half, his first appearance in a Liverpool shirt for six months.

Two weeks later there was to be a repeat of the New-castle humiliation as Sheffield Wednesday ran in three goals at Hillsborough, and all thanks to the remarkable generosity of the Liverpool defence. Christmas had arrived early. Neil Ruddock converted Wednesday's first, Mark Wright the second and Grobbelaar, with a rash race out of goal, presented Wednesday with their third. There was little Souness could do or say about the gifts although there was much he could say about the rest of Liverpool's play. In the event he chose to bite his tongue.

Sandwiched in between the Newcastle and Sheffield defeats were an agonising victory over Aston Villa, which owed more to luck than anything else, and a fortuitous draw against Wimbledon in the Coca-Cola Cup at Anfield when Liverpool plumbed new depths. If their win over Oldham had been talked of as one of their most bankrupt performances in a quarter of a century, then the game against Wimbledon plunged Kopites into despairing gloom. In the second half Liverpool failed to create even a single opportunity. The inconsistency was incomprehensible. After the defeat at Sheffield they returned to Anfield and in a mid-week fixture played in driving rain and wind produced some of their best football of the season to notch up a 3–2 win over Queens Park Rangers. Four days later they lined up against bottom-of-the-table Swindon, the team they had crushed at the County Ground early in the season to take over at the top of the table. Swindon might still have been searching for their first away win in the Premier League but they showed few inhibitions at Anfield. Instead, they twice took the lead and only a looping Mark Wright header four minutes from time saved Liverpool from humiliation as they stole a draw. And steal was the appropriate word.

Souness was reported to be in despair. Throughout the month he had chopped and changed the line-up as he battled to find a solution. Rush, Clough, Stewart, Nicol, Redknapp and Matteo had all been dropped as he shuffled his pack around to find a winning hand. On the plus side, John Barnes had returned from his long lay-off but still the midfield seemed unable to create opportunities for the front runners. Steve McManaman had also returned from injury but with little conviction. The only outstanding injuries were now Julian Dicks and Michael Thomas, with both already knocking on the door for a return to the big time. But Souness had to admit that even their presence looked unlikely to turn the tide, though he insisted in one paper that 'it is unlike Liverpool to be inconsistent and it annoys me because I believe this is the best squad I have had'. The mood of despondency seemed to be catching. The reserves, once the elite of the Pontins League, were a shadow of the sides that had won nine consecutive titles back in the seventies. Former manager Bob Paisley always used to point out that if the reserves were winning they were putting pressure on the first team players. But this season they had won only five of their twelve fixtures. The problem seemed to permeate throughout the club. And yet it was a reserve side regularly boasting more quality players than it deserved, and certainly more than the likes of Bolton, Sunderland and Wolves who were getting the better of their aristocratic opposition. Ronny Rosenthal, Mark Walters, Torben Piechnik, Paul Stewart and Ronnie Whelan – all with years of first team experience and dozens of international caps between them – were regularly among the line-up. Yet the results remained little less than miserable.

It was hard to see where the solution could be found. A midfield general in the Souness/McMahon class was the obvious priority. But where to find one and, indeed, who? There was barely a candidate in the entire Premiership. David Batty, of Leeds United, was perhaps the one available man who could have brought some organisation to the midfield but Liverpool could not compete with Blackburn's hot money.

Predictably, Liverpool fell to Wimbledon in the replayed Coca-Cola Cup tie at Selhurst Park. And, ironically, it was penalties that again settled the tie as it had at Wembley years earlier. This time, with the teams level during extra time, John Barnes missed from the spot and then as the two teams faced a penalty shoot-out after drawing 2–2, it was Jamie Redknapp and Mark Walters who failed to make their spot-kicks count.

Out of the league and out of one cup competition and Christmas was still a fortnight away. Liverpool had only the FA Cup to play for now and with an away tie at Bristol City, even that was not a foregone conclusion. The previous year's encounter with Bolton had now put paid to any underestimating of clubs from the lower divisions.

Liverpool's dismissal from the Coca-Cola Cup initiated a further round of calls for Souness' resignation. The *Sun* even conducted a straw poll among Kopites and claimed that 75 per cent of Liverpool supporters wanted Souness out. But there were no signals from chairman David Moores that Souness' future might be in any doubt; in fact, the very opposite. Moores was unequivocal. 'Graeme Souness is the manager of the club and his position is not under review,' he insisted. Souness was equally determined. 'Our season is not over,' he stressed. 'We have the FA Cup coming up and are still very much within striking distance of second place in the league.' Gone were the days when a Liverpool manager would not have been proud of coming second. 'I knew the price on the ticket when I bought it,' he said. 'I knew what was expected of me and I have no intention of walking away from the challenge. I have never done that in my life.' You had to admire Souness' stubbornness and determination. It was the kind of attitude that usually brings success.

Former Liverpool star Mark Lawrenson offered one explanation. 'You've got to look at some of the players he's bought. Why haven't they done it? He's bought good players but they are not performing. He's sold quality players who are experienced. And there is no substitute for quality and experience.'

Lawrenson, who watched the Wimbledon game, went even further. 'His players looked to me like a bunch who have got too much, too early in their careers. They are fat cats who may not care what happens to the football club they are playing for. They are players without the pride and commitment to perform for Liverpool Football Club.'

Lawrenson was even prepared to finger the blame more specifically, adding that 'the ones at fault are the ones he has brought into the club. They should be asking themselves some serious questions. If they can't play for him, the man who has signed them and given them huge contracts, then they won't play for anyone. Where is the self-motivation, the respect?' But interestingly he was careful not to be too critical of the manager. 'Graeme has to take responsibility because he is the manager and they are his signings,' he argued, 'but he can't kick the ball for them.'

He had a point. You could hardly blame Souness for the inconsistency. On occasion, as at the beginning of the season and against QPR at Anfield, they had shown quality passing and determination. But it would be followed by the most depressing of performances as the side only faintly resembled the one that played the previous game. There was no denying that there were quality players at Anfield, brought in by him. The only signing that had really raised eyebrows was that of Julian Dicks, whose disciplinary record was not the sort that normally attracted Liverpool. Mark Wright, Saunders, Stewart and Nigel Clough had all looked intelligent signings, players who promised much and had excited Liverpool fans when they had joined the club. But somewhere along the line they had lost their appetite and desire to win.

Nigel Clough was typical. An England international, he had signed for Liverpool in between bouts of international duty. For years, fans had mentioned him as a potential Liverpool recruit, the kind of player who could shield and hold the ball while attackers scurried into openings. He began with great promise, scoring twice on his debut, and was heralded by more than one newspaper as Liverpool's saviour, the 'new Kenny Dalglish'. Anyone with the slightest insight however could have spotted that Clough, for all his abilities, was never going to be another Dalglish. But while Clough's early form promised much, it soon slumped. Media investigations into his father's financial dealings at Nottingham Forest might not have been public knowledge at that point, but the family was certainly aware of the Inland Revenue's interest. His father's resignation as manager of Forest and allegations in the press of his drinking problems must also have weighed heavily on the mind of the young Clough. The result was a serious loss of form, with Clough virtually anonymous at times. Eventually he was dropped and was talked of by more than one source as a possible figure in a swap transfer deal that would bring Derby County's Paul Kitson to Anfield. But early into the New Year Clough was suddenly to redeem himself as Liverpool staged one of the finest comebacks in their entire history.

The Liverpool–Manchester United clash of January 1994 was to go down as one of the most exciting games seen in Britain for years. Both sides could take satisfaction from the proceedings, if not the result, though Liverpool probably emerged the happier. The game was played in the tensest of atmospheres, the Kop putting on a display to rank with any in its long history and perhaps its last great stand. Points may have been at stake but, more importantly, pride was at honour. Liverpool, by now clearly out of contention for the league championship, twenty-one points adrift of United, with even a UEFA spot disappearing rapidly over the horizon, began confidently, Robbie Fowler spurning a golden opportunity in the first minute. And yet, despite their positive opening, Liverpool found themselves a goal behind after eight minutes as their limp-footed defence failed to deal with a corner kick. It was a devastating blow; shoulders drooped, chins dropped, fifteen minutes later Liverpool were three goals down as a rampant United, backed by their travelling army of cock-a-hoop supporters, began to fire in shots from every angle. Liverpool looked set to be engulfed in an avalanche of goals. Three down and less than half an hour gone. But in a remarkable comeback, Liverpool, urged on by the Kop and a grim-faced Souness in the dugout, suddenly found an extra yard of pace. They tackled with renewed vigour, scurried about and continued to take the game to United. The result was two splendid strikes by Nigel Clough and a half-time scoreline that looked far more respectable than many had imagined twenty minutes earlier. If the first half had belonged marginally to United, then the second half belonged to Liverpool as they stormed the United goal. An equaliser was inevitable and as it came Anfield erupted.

Liverpool had shown commendable courage and character to retrieve a three-goal deficit. United might have easily added to their score, but so too might Liverpool as chances fell every few minutes at either end. United manager Alex Ferguson labelled it the finest game of football he had ever seen, though he was not too happy that his side had thrown away a three-goal lead. Souness was equally euphoric and was able to take considerably more satisfaction from his side's fightback. Nigel Clough, who for so much of the season had looked dispirited and lethargic operating behind the front two, had emerged from his shell to give a performance that finally made him look value for money. The Kop went home happy, hopeful that events were about to turn their way. Souness had been given another stay of execution.

But it did not last long. After United came a flattering win at Ipswich and a last-gasp victory over Manchester City at Anfield. In between, Liverpool's third round Cup tie at Bristol City had been halted when the floodlights failed. But there were enough signs to hint that the first division outfit would be no pushovers. And, in the rearranged fixture, Liverpool were lucky to survive a City onslaught. Time and again Junior Bent, City's slippery winger, slithered beyond the Liverpool defence only to waste his opportunity. It should have been a warning. City were desperately unlucky, yet few would have put money on their chances in front of a packed Anfield. After all, lightning does not strike twice. But for once it did.

Twelve months earlier, having survived a third round battering at Bolton, Liverpool had returned to Anfield expecting some improvement. They had certainly seen a better performance, not from Liverpool but from Bolton, who had gone on to knock the Cup-holders out of the competition at the first hurdle. That had been humiliating enough and had been a crucial factor in the farce that followed in May when Souness' days at Anfield almost ended. But now history was about to repeat itself. At Anfield, Bristol City began where they had left off. Chances came begging, only to be wasted. Had Liverpool been beaten against the run of play or put up a stirring fight, then perhaps they might have been forgiven. As it was, they were simply run off their feet. City ripped the Liverpool defence apart. A goal was inevitable and when Brian Tinnion struck in the 67th minute Souness' days were numbered. It was the only goal of the game. Liverpool had the occasional chance, but had they won it would have been a reportable offence. It had been an abysmal performance from Liverpool, yet it was only twenty-one days since their stirring fightback against Manchester United.

At the end of the day, nothing lasts for ever. Liverpool had ridden their luck for years. Free of injury, free of boardroom squabbles and money worries, they had simply kept their heads down and got on with the job as professionally and doggedly as they knew. But suddenly in the nineties it had all gone wrong. First Dalglish had resigned, sending shock waves through Anfield. Then Souness arrived and the trusted system began to fall apart. It was almost as if someone had placed a curse on the club. There were injuries galore. Virtually every player in the squad at some point in Souness's first eighteen months had a long-term injury. In addition, every player they signed seemed to lose form as soon as they pulled on a red shirt while many of those sold found an extra lease of life elsewhere. Off the field there was a new chairman and worrying financial restraints. Liverpool found it increasingly difficult to compete in the transfer market. And the private rows that brew in every club had suddenly became public, splashed across the back pages. The board had dithered about sacking Souness after the LOVERPOOL photograph in the *Sun*, then dithered and dallied again as results continued to deteriorate the following year. It was all so unlike Liverpool. There seemed to be a lack of guidance both at the top and on the field. After twenty-five years of success, Liverpool fans were having to get used to being second best. Thirty miles down the M62 Manchester United were running away with the title.

The Kop's patience had finally run out. A second humiliating Cup defeat was too much. This time they could be neither understanding nor forgiving. They had had enough. Their venom was directed at one person – Graeme Souness. And in an unprecedented public display the chant of 'Souness out' resounded around the Kop. As the Liverpool team trooped off the field to a chorus of booing they must have known then that the Souness revolution was all but over. The people had spoken.

CHAPTER NINETEEN
The Power of the People

When the end came, it came swiftly. There was none of
the dithering that had muddled events the previous May
when the board, on the brink of sacking Souness, had
performed a spectacular U-turn that had more in common
with Parliamentary politics than football politics. On that
occasion the Liverpool board had been stung by press
criticism of their wavering. This time the directors faced
up to their responsibilities. They knew there could be
only one outcome. Souness knew too and the directors
were in no mood to try and dissuade him. The Kop had
spoken and it was clear to everyone that they reflected a
view commonly held throughout the club and the city.

As Souness watched on the touchline that Tuesday
evening, his head buried in his hands, listening to the
Kop baying for his blood he guessed the game was up.
The Kop had finally turned against him. No Liverpool
player or manager in the history of the club had ever
been subjected to so vitriolic a message; it rang out loud
and clear. Souness had to go. Even the directors sitting
in their plush seats in the directors' box in the Main
Stand were taken aback by the scorn that resounded from
the Kop. They had never heard anything like it before,

never had the Kop turned on its own. As the former
Liverpool defender Mark Lawrenson mentioned on the
night, 'If the directors weren't aware of the discontent
before, they certainly were after that. It will almost certainly have woken them up to the way the fans felt.'

And yet it was surprising that the fans had remained
loyal to Souness for so long. There had been one or two
half-hearted chants against him the previous season and
even at the 1992 Cup final he had hardly been given the
rapturous reception that a man who has just risen from
his sick bed surely deserved. But there had never been
anything that constituted a full-throated campaign
against Souness. Newspaper surveys had bleakly
revealed the astonishing level of discontent while the
letters page of the *Liverpool Football Echo* had told a
similar story. There was only ever one banner unfurled
against him and even that came in for much criticism
from Kopites. There were never any public taunts as
there were at other clubs when results did not go right.
But finally the patience of the Kop had snapped. Shankly
had always emphasised the importance of loyalty and
over the years at Anfield no one had demonstrated it
more so than Shankly, whose patience with players
usually proved right.

Even when Liverpool went a goal or two behind, there
were never any of the groans that normally accompany
losing sides. Instead, it was usually a case of the crowd
getting behind their favourites all the more. Liverpudlians have always been proud of their loyalty and like
nothing more than the chance to demonstrate it publicly.

Nor was it just one result, one humiliation, that gener-
ated the call for Souness' resignation. Rather it was a
catalogue of discontent. None of Souness' extravagant
signings had fired the Kop's imagination. Neither Stewart, Ruddock, Dicks, Walters, Saunders or Clough had
lived up to their expensive reputations. And nor had any

of the continental imports – Kozma, Piechnik and Bjornebye – shown much potential. The only signing to display
any promise had been the inexpensive Rob Jones. On top
of that, the traditions of the bootroom had been flagrantly
cast aside. Training, diet, personnel, attitude, it had all
been turned upside down. Souness' revolution had ripped
the heart out of Liverpool and it was that which counted
against him more than anything. Had the trophies rolled
in, then all would, no doubt, have been understood and
forgiven but one trophy in three years was not good
enough for Liverpool Football Club and its expectant fans.
The pride which Liverpudlians had in their club had
evaporated. And with the fall of pride, so too came an
end to loyalty. There was even a call from one of the
officials of the supporters' clubs for a boycott of Liverpool's
next home match. That was unprecedented in the club's
history.

After the defeat by Bristol City in the FA Cup there
were the inevitable questions. The papers had already
hinted that an early exit from the Cup would spell the
beginning of the end. It was clear that Liverpool's season
was, in effect, over. Knocked out of the League Cup by
Wimbledon, trailing Manchester United by a massive
twenty-one points and now out of the FA Cup, humiliated
three times by the lower division side. Liverpool's only
hope was a place in Europe but even that looked a hope-
less prospect with Kenny Dalglish's Blackburn disappearing into the distance, eight points ahead and with a game
in hand. The reality was that with January not even over
Liverpool had little left to play for. Thirty-five miles down
the East Lancs Road, rivals Manchester United were still
on target for a unique treble.

As the reporters swarmed around Souness after the
match, he admitted that he had to consider his future.
Yet even then he probably never guessed that the
end would come so quickly. Instead he sought out Peter

Robinson and asked for a few days' leave in order to think things over. Robinson agreed, suspecting what the outcome might be. The problem for Souness was where to go from here. He had tried just about everything. When he arrived at Anfield he had found a club overloaded with too many thirty-something players. He had set out to revolutionise the club and its facilities. Players had been unloaded, new players had been recruited, and young-sters had been drafted into the side. But still it had not worked. More than £21 million had been spent, only a couple of million pounds less than Kenny Dalglish at super-rich Blackburn. Dalglish could at least point to Alan Shearer, David Batty and Tim Flowers as well as second place in the league. Souness could take satisfac-tion from little.

Yet the inconsistencies remained, glaring and for every-one to see. They could play with passion and purpose against Manchester United one week but then weeks later against Bristol City could look as mediocre and flat-footed as any third division outfit. There were signs that results were picking up, only two defeats in twenty-two games, but the side was hardly playing with the style and flair of a traditional Liverpool team. Anywhere else that might have been acceptable and even a good case for a pay rise but not at Anfield. Victories had all too often been dug out of defeat in the dying seconds, goals were gifted to the opposition while the midfield looked constantly unsure of itself.

By 1994 Souness' spending had almost reached £22 million and although he might be able to persuade the board to make yet more money available he knew they would be reluctant. Players had to be sold but nobody seemed keen to invest and certainly not at the prices Liverpool were asking. Time and again he was being forced to lower the price tag on some of his reserves. Overpaid, most of them would not even leave the club.

Why should they? Some were earning as much as £5000 a week and they had contracts to prove it. Why go somewhere else for less money? There was no escaping the problem. The resolution lay with the players and they did not seem able to perform for him. There was simply no more that he could do. He could wait until the board sacked him but he had his pride. He would go before he was pushed.

Three days later he returned to Anfield, a decision made. You didn't need to have an earpiece into Souness' mind to know what the decision would be. Peter Robinson was informed beforehand and a meeting was set up to iron out the financial details. They met on the morning of Friday 28 January at a secret venue, secretary Peter Robinson and chairman David Moores representing the club on one side of the negotiating table, Graeme Souness and his advisers on the other. No attempt was made to dissuade Souness from his decision; it was doubtful anyhow that he could have been persuaded to change his mind. There was none of the determination to carry on as there had been the previous May. Everyone knew that it was the best course of action.

At five o'clock that evening, Moores and Robinson dashed back to Anfield. Outside the main entrance reporters and cameramen shivered in the gathering gloom waiting for the manager's car to sweep through the Shankly gates. It never came. At two minutes past six the waiting journalists were finally called inside for the expected press conference. But they were not ushered into the trophy room, the usual venue for such occasions. Instead they were taken to the new press room. Souness was absent, rumoured to be already aboard a flight to Spain with girlfriend Karen Levy. All but one member of the board was present, all dressed soberly, with the exception of David Moores who sported his usual tasteless style of jacket. Flanked by former chairman Sir John

303

Smith and directors Jack Cross and Tom Saunders, Moores read out a statement. He remained seated throughout. There was an air of gloom, no smiles, no jokes, no asides, no small chat.

'I am extremely sorry to announce that Graeme Souness has offered us his resignation as manager of Liverpool Football Club. By a unanimous decision of the board that has been accepted.'

Moores continued, his voice breaking slightly:

For all of us at Anfield this is a very sad day. Since Graeme returned to Anfield we have all enjoyed his enthusiasm and his friendship. We have also felt deeply for him over a number of personal difficulties including massive heart surgery and the death of his father. We have understood the difficulties he has faced over nearly three seasons with an unprecedented number of major injuries and the need to bring young players forward more quickly than is usual at Anfield. However, Liverpool Football Club is about winning things and being a source of pride to our fans. With the exception of winning the FA Cup in Graeme's first season, the results in the league and domestic and European cup competitions have been well below what is expected by the club and its supporters.

But it was in his next sentence that Moores revealed the real reasons that had brought about Souness' downfall when he admitted that: 'The fans have been unhappy with results and have not been slow to let us know.'

Moores ended his emotional statement with a pledge to return Liverpool to the top. 'What we want to say to our supporters and everyone else is this – for twenty-five years Liverpool was Britain's most successful and consistent football club. For four of those years we were also the most successful club in Europe. No one has an automatic right to success but we shall all be doing everything in our power to try and achieve those levels again.' Moores was almost in tears.

It had taken just a few moments to end a reign that had begun so positively thirty-three months before. A short statement from Graeme Souness was then handed out. It was to the point. It read:

> This is a sad day for me. After a great deal of soul searching I have reached the conclusion that the best thing for the club and I is that we should part company. I took this job believing that I could return the club to its former glory but this has proved to be more difficult than I anticipated. The fans have been very patient but I feel their patience is now running out. Liverpool Football Club has and always will have a very special place in my heart and I can only wish the club well and every success in the future.

He ended his statement by thanking 'the chairman, the board and everyone else associated with the club for the help and the support they have given me during my term as manager'.

Moores was not prepared to give any details about the financial settlement except to say that an amicable agreement had been reached. It soon leaked out, however, that amicable meant a pay-off of almost £400,000. Financially, Souness had done very well out of Liverpool, but Liverpool had not done well out of Souness. He had cost them a considerable sum of money. A £400,000 pay-off, £500,000 in compensation to Rangers when he joined plus a £250,000 a year salary that added up to £700,000 over his two and a half years. The total cost was £1.6 million, which worked out at £47,000 a month, or £11,700 a week.

And that was it. After nearly three years Souness'

revolution was over, overturned by people power. Graeme Souness had become the first Liverpool manager forced out of office since 1956 when Don Welsh was dismissed after Liverpool had plunged into the second division. Every other manager in the club's distinguished history had quit either by design or because of ill health. Technically speaking, Souness had not been fired but the board's unanimous acceptance of his resignation left little doubt that the parting was by mutual consent.

It was indeed a sad day for Moores who had befriended Souness throughout his reign. They had joked together, drunk together and enjoyed many an evening together. Had it been up to Moores alone, Souness might still have been manager but arguing a case for Souness with the board, as well as the Liverpool public, was a task even he shied from.

Tony Ensor, the former Liverpool director who had resigned in May 1993 as the board showed an amazing lack of conviction, did not share David Moores' sadness. He said:

It was always inevitable. Souness should have resigned back in May. He has not been able, even after spending £21 million in the transfer market to produce teams which in my opinion were capable of winning honours. He did his cause no good by his antics on the touchline in Europe and at home. His public criticism of players did not improve his relationship with them either. Personally I regret that it has taken him so long to see that his confrontational style of management has not been in accordance with Liverpool's tradition, where we previously earned a reputation for the way we conducted ourselves.

Ensor reckoned Souness should have resigned immedi-

306

ately after he had given his heart bypass story exclusively to the *Sun* back in the spring of 1992.

It wasn't a sad day for Tommy Smith either. For months the former Liverpool defender had been critical of Souness and his style. In his weekly column in the *Liverpool Football Echo* Smith's comments had fuelled the raging debate. When he went Smith was ruthless. 'Anybody who tries to be bigger than Liverpool – changing tried and trusted work practices – deserves to fall on his backside,' he wrote. 'Here's hoping it's not too late to get back to the sound and sensible principles that were a trade mark prior to his arrival. His treatment, not only of the club, but players and fans (the *Sun* affair) has not helped his cause.'

Smith had been accused by many loyal supporters of stoking the fires of discontent that had eventually led to Souness' downfall. But Smith defended his actions. 'The one thing I can say in my defence . . . is that I didn't sell any stories to the *Sun*; I didn't sell players who still had a lot to offer; I didn't buy others who were not in the Liverpool tradition; I didn't sack Phil Thompson. I did attend the testimonials of Bruce Grobbelaar and Steve Nicol. He didn't, which I find totally unacceptable. I could go on but it's enough to say the right decision has been taken.'

The former Liverpool favourite Alan Hansen summed up Souness' demise.

The standard which he helped to set as a player contributed to his downfall. At any other club his record would not have caused a problem but not at Liverpool.

Where did he go wrong? Well, he did not buy great players. Good players maybe, but not outstanding players. He also sold too many players too quickly. The old rule used to be two out, two in, with the two incoming players being better than the two outgoing players. Instead there were sweeping changes. More than the system could cope with.

But there was something else. It all boiled down to man-management. While managers cannot afford to be too friendly with their players, it was little use shouting and bawling either. That was not the way to win respect. Tony Ensor had summed it up with the word 'confrontational'. When Souness arrived at Anfield there were professionals with years of experience, international honours and medals galore, but they were to be treated much the same as anyone who had not yet proven themselves. It may have seemed egalitarian but you have to make allowances for experience. It was no way to deal with individuals who had distinguished themselves over the years. Rush, Grobbelaar, Whelan, Hysen and Barnes all had much-publicised rows with Souness that left a sour taste. The failure of some players to be willing to give as much as they once did was also down to poor basic man-management.

It was a tragedy that Souness' reign at Anfield should end in such tears and bitterness. He had genuinely set out to renew Liverpool's ambitions. He believed in the club and was as committed and single-minded in his pursuit of success as any Liverpool manager. If ever there was a born winner it was Graeme Souness. In the end he was probably too determined, too anxious to make his mark. He set out to stamp his own authority and his own imprint on Anfield. He forgot that Liverpool Football Club has prided itself on being bigger than any single person. His revolution had been too violent, too sweeping. The truth was that there had never really been any need for a revolution. And in the end it was the people who finally brought an end to Graeme Souness' revolution. The man who vowed he would never quit had finally been humbled.

But Liverpool Football Club also had to shoulder some of the blame. Souness had a revolutionary approach to soccer. At Ibrox his attitude had matched the moment as he helped bring Scottish football and Glasgow Rangers into the twentieth century. But it was different at Anfield. Liverpool did not need a revolution. They'd had their revolution the day Shankly arrived. What they needed was steady progress, a little more tinkering with that Rolls-Royce engine.

Liverpool is an insular city. Scousers don't take easily to change. They like things as they were, nostalgic rather than visionary. They can even be suspicious of their own kind, scornful of those with money, style or confidence. Anyone who is different is likely to be driven out, not just by the folk but by their own ambitions as well. Liverpool should have realised what they were getting the day they hired Graeme Souness. It was no good trying to change Souness. If Liverpool did not want a revolution then they should never have appointed him in the first place. The board had also failed to keep a tight rein on him. There had been too much drifting, not enough authority from those in charge. They had failed to fire him after the *Sun* affair, then a year later agreed to sack him only to perform a spectacular and humiliating U-turn. It had been another year before they finally plucked up the courage. As Ensor said, his departure was inevitable but the board slunk from the inevitable. The consequences would be catastrophic. Souness was allowed to spend far too extravagantly, particularly in his early years, with players earning so much that they were reluctant to move on. His legacy would be half a dozen players on long-term contracts and excessive wages, for sale at bargain prices, but not prepared to leave unless the wages matched those at Anfield. It had all the potential for a financial disaster.

Souness was gone and within twenty-four hours his replacement had been named. It came as no surprise when Liverpool called upon Roy Evans. It was a return to the old Liverpool style, evolutionary, not revolutionary. Evans, the bootroom apprentice, had served his time and was now ready to become a fully fledged journeyman. It was back to basics, a return to the principles of old. Nobody had any doubts that Evans was the man for the job. The only question was whether the old system could ever be recreated. Perhaps things had gone just too far.

CHAPTER TWENTY
Allegations

If 1994 had started badly for Graeme Souness, with his sacking by Liverpool Football Club, the year was to end even more disastrously. In December came a sensational claim from the *Mail on Sunday* alleging that Souness had received an 'under the table' payment on a transfer deal. The allegations surrounded some of Souness' transfer dealings in 1988 when he was manager at Rangers. The *Mail on Sunday* claimed that Souness had received a £30,000 'gift' from an agent and that his then wife Danielle had made a 750-mile round trip from Edinburgh to Heathrow Airport to collect the 'gift'. The allegations were so serious as to threaten any future role in the game for Souness, and he strongly denied them, immediately issuing a writ against the newspaper.

It was also revealed that Inland Revenue investigators had visited Liverpool Football Club a few months previously to look at some of the paperwork involving transfer deals negotiated by Souness during his period at Anfield. Liverpool Football Club secretary Peter Robinson insisted, however, that as far as the club was concerned the deals had been handled in a proper manner.

It was ironic that only days before the *Mail on Sunday*

story was published, Souness had made his first public comments since his sacking when he was a guest on a live Radio Five programme. He told listeners that he was happier now than he had ever been in his life, he was not missing football and had not even been to see a game in England since quitting Anfield. A week later, after the *Mail on Sunday*'s front page exclusive, Souness was no doubt feeling under pressure again.

Souness' successor at Anfield, Roy Evans, has remained honourably silent, refusing to join any stampede to criticise his predecessor. After Souness' departure the doors of Anfield were firmly slammed shut again. Tommy Smith summed up the attitude when he said: 'Souness has gone. We don't want to talk about him any more.' The only comment that Evans let slip was that 'some players were sold before their sell-by date while those coming in were not as good as those sold.' It may not have added up to much for the headline writers, but it spoke volumes for those knowledgeable of the Liverpool style. But if you were looking for a more public expression of the Souness days, you only had to look at the way the side was playing six months after Souness' departure.

The first three months of the post-Souness era at Anfield had continued uneasily. There were only a handful of victories; the side was never settled, never certain, nor confident. Evans promised to give everyone a chance. He was biding his time before he got tough. Nobody was shown the door and there were no major signings, though Evans did file a £2 million bid for Steve Staunton, a move that clearly showed his view of the sale of Staunton in the first place. But Staunton shrugged off the interest and instead contracted for a few more years with Aston Villa.

With so little activity in the transfer market, the omens did not look promising as the 1994/95 season kicked off. Liverpool had barely been linked with any of the major close season deals. The only addition to the squad was the young Danish goalkeeper Michael Stensgaard. What's more, hardly anyone had moved on. The legacy of Souness was proving expensive. Paul Stewart had been out on loan to Crystal Palace but had proved too expensive for a more permanent move. Although the London club made an inquiry, the £1 million-plus transfer tag was way beyond their means. As it was Liverpool stood to lose close on £1.5 million on the deal that had brought him to Anfield in the first place. There were no further inquiries for Stewart either until Wolves stepped in to take him on loan to Molineux later that year. By November the valuation of Stewart had slipped even further, with Liverpool finally agreeing to accept an £800,000 offer from Wolves only for the deal to fall through at the last minute as Stewart picked up another injury. Mark Walters was another priced out of the market. Bought by Souness for £1.25 million from his old club Glasgow Rangers, he made only a handful of appearances under new manager Roy Evans before being loaned out to Stoke City, but again the proposed fee proved too prohibitive for the Potteries club. Wolves also took him on loan, but returned him some months later without even making an offer to buy him.

The only absentees for the start of the new season were goalkeeper Bruce Grobbelaar, who had joined Southampton on a free transfer, and Torben Piechnik who had moved back to Denmark also on a free transfer. Piechnik, a Souness signing from Copenhagen for £500,000, had made fewer than 20 appearances for the club. There were later to be allegations surrounding the Piechnik transfer to Liverpool, with claims that the sums involved in the transfer deal did not add up. In particular the finger was pointed at the Danish soccer agent Rune Hauge who had negotiated the deal with Souness. Hauge was also at the centre of allegations surrounding the transfer of Danish midfielder John Jensen to Arsenal for £1.57 million. The

313

allegations immediately alerted the football authorities
and a Premier League inquiry was quickly set up to inves-
tigate a number of transfer deals involving Rune Hauge.

The transfer of Grobbelaar was not altogether unexpected. He was nearing the end of his career and with
David James returning to the side shortly after Souness'
departure to fill in for the injured Grobbelaar, the odds
were that he would retain his place once Grobbelaar was
fit again. Youth had to be given its chance. It was probably
just as well that he left given that even more unseemly
allegations were to surface in the national press that
autumn. This time they concerned match-fixing, with
Grobbelaar at the centre of an alleged syndicate. It was
a distraction Liverpool could have done without,
especially as one of the matches concerned took place at
Newcastle when Liverpool lost 3–0. There were certainly
no suggestions that Souness or Liverpool Football Club
had any knowledge of what had occurred. Indeed, it
would have been unthinkable and Souness was one of the
first to issue a public statement denying any knowledge
and condemning any attempts at match fixing.

As the new season approached, nobody was predicting
Liverpool for the championship. The bookmakers chalked
them up at 20–1, and on the back pages the name of
Liverpool was missing from the list of leading title contenders. This was something you would never have seen
in seasons past. But as kick-off day neared, Evans chose
his moment. The time for getting tough had arrived,
especially after a heavy pre-season defeat by Bolton Wanderers. Julian Dicks was slammed for his lack of fitness
and excess weight; Mark Wright was also told in no
uncertain terms that he was not up to scratch. These
criticisms quickly became public knowledge and,
although it may not have been the usual Liverpool style,
they did enough to shake up a few people around Anfield.
Evans was not going to be an easy ride. Both Dicks and

Wright were furious, complaining bitterly to the press. Within a few months Dicks was on his way back to his old club West Ham for £500,000, yet another Souness failure. As for Mark Wright, the former England international continued to languish in reserve team football. Don Hutchison, although not a Souness signing, was another who would soon move on. His poor disciplinary record, both on and off the field, finally brought matters to a head early into the new season and Hutchison was offloaded to West Ham United as well. It was a clear indication that Evans expected higher standards at Anfield and that anyone failing to comply would be shown the door.

It was to come as something of a surprise, then, that Liverpool should begin the season with a flourish as they slammed six goals past newly promoted Crystal Palace at Selhurst Park. Impressive, said the papers, though adding that almost any Premier League side could have put half a dozen past the Palace defence that day. The real test for Liverpool would come a week later. And so it would, as they faced Arsenal at Anfield. This time Liverpool won 3–0. Now here was something to take note of. This was not the Liverpool of Souness' days. There was a fresh enthusiasm. The players looked more confident, there were none of the usual cursory glances towards the bench for instructions or inspiration that had marked the Souness days. John Barnes, playing in a far deeper role, was relishing his new challenge. Jan Molby, given a second chance by the new manager, was rewarding him with the spraying passes that had once been his hallmark. And Steve McManaman, for so long a promising youngster but run off his feet by too much football, was now maturing into a quality marauder.

But the biggest revelation of all was Neil Ruddock. Under Souness, Ruddock had rarely shown any of the form that had once had his former manager Terry

Venables predicting an England career. He had looked hopelessly slow and clumsy, though he later put this down to living in a hotel and indulging in too much rich food. But a new house and a club dietician had him looking slim and fit for the start of the season. Molby and Barnes had also lost weight. Ruddock was a changed man. The Anfield faithful were suitably impressed. Football crowds may be fickle at times, but at Anfield they were not slow to revise their opinions of Ruddock, whose commitment and determination were about to make him a favourite.

After a third win, Liverpool again found themselves top of the table at the start of the season The doom merchants were quick to point out that it had been the same story the previous season – and look what had happened then. But this time the expected stumble was slow in arriving. Instead, they drew with West Ham before eventually losing their fifth game, at Old Trafford, though only after a spirited display against the champions that deserved some reward. Liverpool then drew with Premier League leaders Newcastle at St James' Park before losing at Blackburn. But there were also wins and by mid-November Liverpool were handily placed, just a few points off the top of the table. By then Evans had further publicly indicated the failings of Souness' side by spending £7 million on bringing Phil Babb from Coventry and John Scales from Wimbledon to strengthen the defence.

Admittedly, they still did not look like championship material, but there was no doubting there had been an improvement from the dark expressionless days of Graeme Souness. Nor were there the catalogue of injuries that had marred the Souness era. The side moved with purpose, passing with a pace and vision reminiscent of the Shankly/Paisley days and, although they lacked penetration in the final quarter of the field, they were still scoring at a hefty rate. In December, seven Liverpool players found themselves picked for the England 'B' against Ireland international, six of those players in the England side. It was public recognition that Liverpool were on the road back.

Meanwhile, little had been heard of Souness. After his marriage to Karen Levy in June, which had been splashed across numerous pages of the *Sun*, Souness had almost disappeared from public view. He had decided to bide his time, to reconsider his future. 'I may not even come back into the game,' he privately told one reporter. Roy Evans had a different view. 'He'll be back, the game's in his blood,' he argued.

It was inevitable that the out-of-work Souness would be linked with a number of clubs. Within months of leaving Anfield, there were rumours that he might be on his way back to Scotland. The Edinburgh club Hearts was up for sale and local-lad Souness was being talked of as a potential buyer, but nothing transpired. Then one of his former clubs, Middlesbrough, were in the market for a top name manager. The club, under new owners, were rumoured to be not averse to someone putting money into the club as well. Souness seemed an ideal candidate, but in the end Middlesbrough plumped for Bryan Robson of Manchester United, appointing him player-manager. Then, in October, the *Sunday Mirror* ran a story suggesting that Souness had been approached by Alan Sugar at Tottenham Hotspur, another of his former clubs. The story claimed that Souness had turned down the opportunity to succeed Ossie Ardiles as Spurs manager. Thoughts of Alan Sugar and Graeme Souness in the same room was enough to bring a smile to anyone's face. But Souness did actually contact Sugar to deny any involvement in the story. The following month Souness was being linked to the vacant managerial post at Aston Villa following the sacking of Ron Atkinson. Souness was reckoned to be seriously interested in this job and for some time he was clearly in th̲ ̲eckoning. But in the end the job went to Brian Little, the former Leicester City manager.

Souness was also occasionally spotted around the corridors of the media world, though he assiduously avoided any appearances on screen or radio. But he eventually surfaced in December, first as a pundit for Channel Four's coverage of Italian football, and then on Radio Five a week later to give a revealing and thoroughly honest interview.

He admitted to listeners that he had made mistakes at Liverpool, adding that the whole business had left 'a bad taste'. Yes, he agreed, he would do things differently if he had his time over again. But, perhaps more revealing, he believed that he had been let down by some players.

'I felt there were people who could have done more in the 90 minutes of football. There were people who could have done more to look after themselves during the week and there were people who could have done more when they were on the training ground. It wasn't so long ago that I was a player and nobody liked a night out and a glass of wine more than I did. But, as in every sport, there is a time and place for that and I just felt, for whatever reasons, I wasn't getting the professionalism from certain people that I felt they should have been giving.' It was all down to the lager and disco culture of English football.

It was a subtle but scathing attack on some of his former Liverpool colleagues, leaving you pondering exactly which players he was talking about. But it was always clear that there were certain players at Anfield who did not take to Souness' abrasive style of management and had not always given 100 per cent. There were faults on both sides. Some players, not the youngsters who always had the highest respect for him, refused to back his methods. There had been friction and not enough respect on both sides. In the end, Souness had probably at least come to understand this.

'There were enormous pressures,' he confessed in a statement that had a ring of his predecessor Kenny Dalglish's public unburdening. 'Going in to Anfield became difficult. I tried to make people as passionate about the game as I was. When that didn't happen I felt let down. That's maybe where some of my problems came. I wouldn't leave it at that. I couldn't accept that with my players. So I partly blame myself. I always said to the players that the first thing they should do when it has not gone well, is to stand in front of the mirror and in a quiet moment say "could I have done more today?" And if I'm honest I certainly got things wrong when I was manager at Liverpool, the same as I got things wrong when I was boss at Glasgow Rangers.'

Meanwhile, back at Anfield, they were still counting the cost of his managerial reign. Thousands of pounds were being paid out every week, not just to Souness, who will be receiving £25,000 a month until the summer of 1996, but to numerous of his signings languishing in reserve team football, while the transfer valuation of the two out on loan – Paul Stewart and Mark Walters – was being revalued, downwards, almost daily. Gone were four of his own multi-million pound signings – Dean Saunders, Julian Dicks, Torben Piechnik and Istvan Kozma – while there was no regular spot in the side for three of his other signings – Nigel Clough, Michael Thomas and Mark Wright, worth a combined £6.5 million. Of Souness' fifteen signings at Liverpool only David James, Stig Bjornebye, Rob Jones and Neil Ruddock looked to be part of Roy Evans' immediate plans, with Michael Thomas and Nigel Clough part of the squad but having to bide their time in the hope that an injury to someone might offer them a lifeline into first team football.

As for Souness, despite the back page rumours linking

him with various clubs, there appeared to be no great urge to rejoin the managerial merry-go-round. It was hardly surprising given the money he was still picking up from his former employers. In his Radio Five interview Souness claimed that he was not missing football. In fact, he revealed that he had only just seen his first game since leaving Liverpool and that was in Italy. In the past months, he said that he had stepped back and realised the pressures he was under. 'I think I'm a better person now. I see more of the children, I'm enjoying my life like I've never done before.' All that was before the *Mail on Sunday* bombshell dropped.

But you did begin to get the feeling that perhaps Graeme Souness was better off without football and its appalling pressures, and that he now recognised it. Yet there were also plenty on Merseyside and Clydeside prepared to stand up and argue that football was better off without Souness. Millions of pounds had filtered through his hands with a total of 109 transfer deals worth £55 million. He had brought success to Rangers and a brief change of attitude, but at Liverpool there remains only a painful and bitter memory. There is still much to be told, and no doubt the jigsaw of transfer deals and dressing room rows will be slowly pieced together. And with the door to a football future looking increasingly closed, Graeme Souness' future remains as uncertain as it was the day he left Anfield.

APPENDIX ONE
Graeme Souness: Career Record

May 1970. Signs professional forms for Tottenham Hotspur. One appearance, UEFA Cup, 14 September 1971.
FA Youth Cup winner, 1970.

January 1973. Signs for Middlesbrough FC, £32,000.
League debut v. Fulham 26 January 1973.
202/2 appearances, 23 goals.

January 1978. Signs for Liverpool for £352,000.
First division debut v. West Bromwich Albion
14 January 1978.
350/2 appearances, 56 goals.

July 1984. Signs for Sampdoria, £650,000.
56 appearances, 8 goals.

April 1986. Appointed player-manager Glasgow Rangers.
Scottish League debut v. Hibernian 9 August 1986.
55/17 appearances, 5 goals.

17 April 1991. Appointed manager Liverpool Football Club.

28 January 1994. Resigns as manager of Liverpool FC.

APPENDIX TWO
Honours as a Player

1973/74 (Middlesbrough)
Division Two champions

1977/78 (Liverpool)
European Cup winners
League Cup finalist

1978/79
League champions

1979/80
League champions

1980/81
European Cup winners
League Cup winners

1981/82
League champions
League Cup winners

1982/83
League champions
League Cup winners

1983/84
European Cup winners
League champions
League Cup winners

1984/85 (Sampdoria)
Italian Cup winners

International Honours

International debut 30 October 1974 Scotland v. East
Germany.
Three caps with Middlesbrough.
37 caps with Liverpool.
14 caps with Sampdoria.

APPENDIX THREE
Honours as a Manager

GLASGOW RANGERS

1986/87
Scottish League champions
Scottish League Cup winners

1987/88
Scottish League Cup winners

1988/89
Scottish League champions
Scottish League Cup winners

1989/90
Scottish League champions

1990/91
Scottish League Cup winners

LIVERPOOL

1991/92
FA Cup winners

APPENDIX FOUR
Dealings in the Transfer Market

GLASGOW RANGERS

Players signed

1986/87 season

Colin West (Watford) June 86	£200,000
Chris Woods (Norwich) July 86	£600,000
Terry Butcher (Ipswich) August 86	£725,000
Jimmy Nicholl (WBA) August 86	£70,000
Lindsay Hamilton (Stenhousemuir) November 86	£25,000
Graham Roberts (Spurs) December 86	£450,000
Neil Woods (Doncaster) December 86	£100,000
Jimmy Phillips (Bolton) March 87	£75,000
David Kirkwood (East Fife) March 87	£30,000
9 players signed. Total	£2,275,000

1987/88 season

Avi Cohen (Maccabi) June 87	£100,000
John McGregor (Liverpool) June 87	FREE
Mark Falco (Watford) July 87	£270,000
Trevor Francis (Atalanta) August 87	£75,000
Ian McCall (Dunfermline) August 87	£200,000
Richard Gough (Spurs) October 87	£1,100,000
Ray Wilkins (Paris St Germain) November 87	£150,000
Mark Walters (Aston Villa) December 87	£500,000
John Brown (Dundee) January 88	£350,000
Jan Bartram (Silkeborg) January 88	£180,000
Ian Ferguson (St Mirren) February 88	£850,000
11 players signed. Total	£3,775,000

1988/89 season

Kevin Drinkell (Norwich) June 88	£500,000
Gary Stevens (Everton) July 88	£1,000,000
Andy Gray (WBA) September 88	£25,000
Neale Cooper (Aston Villa) October 88	£250,000
Tom Cowan (Clyde) February 89	£100,000
Mel Sterland (Sheffield Wed) March 89	£800,000
6 players signed. Total	£2,675,000

1989/90 season

Trevor Steven (Everton) June 89	£1,525,000
Mo Johnston (Nantes) July 89	£1,250,000
Bonni Ginzberg (Maccabi) August 89	£200,000
Davie Dodds (Aberdeen) August 89	£100,000
Chris Vinnicombe (Exeter) November 89	£500,000
Nigel Spackman (QPR) November 89	£500,000

6 players signed. Total   £4,075,000

1990/91 season

Mark Hateley (Monaco) June 90	£500,000
Oleg Kuznetsov (Dynamo Kiev) June 90	£1,200,000
Pieter Huistra (FC Twente) August 90	£250,000
Terry Hurlock (Millwall) August 90	£325,000
Brian Reid (Morton) August 90	£300,000

5 players signed. Total   £2,575,000

Grand total spent on signing 37 players   £15,375,000

Players transferred

1986/87 season

Derek Johnstone (Partick) June 86	FREE
David MacKinnon (Airdrie) June 86	FREE
Andy Bruce (Hearts) June 86	FREE
Billy Davies (Elfsborg) June 86	FREE
Eric Ferguson (Dunfermline) June 86	FREE
Iain Ferguson (Dundee) August 86	£125,000
Bobby Williamson (WBA) August 86	£70,000
John MacDonald (Barnsley) October 86	FREE
Colin Miller (Doncaster) December 86	£30,000
Dougie Bell (Hibs) December 86	£30,000
Craig Paterson (Motherwell) December 86	£20,000
Stuart Beattie (Doncaster) December 86	£30,000
Ted McMinn (Seville) January 87	£225,000
Bobby Russell (Motherwell) May 87	FREE
Cammie Fraser (Raith) May 87	FREE

15 players sold. Total   £530,000

1987/88 season

David McPherson (Hearts) July 87	£325,000
Hugh Burns (Hearts) July 87	£75,000
Neil Woods (Ipswich) July 87	£125,000
Ally Dawson (Blackburn) August 87	£50,000
Colin West (Sheffield Wed) August 87	£150,000
Mark Falco (QPR) December 87	£350,000
Robert Fleck (Norwich) December 87	£580,000
Trevor Francis (QPR) March 88	FREE
8 players sold. Total	£1,655,000

1988/89 season

Jan Bartram (Brondby) July 88	£315,000
Graham Roberts (Chelsea) August 88	£475,000
Jimmy Phillips (Oxford) August 88	£150,000
Dave MacFarlane (Kilmarnock) October 88	£100,000
Andy Gray (Cheltenham) May 89	FREE
Avi Cohen (Maccabi) June 89	FREE
6 players sold. Total	£1,040,000

1989/90 season

Mel Sterland (Leeds) July 89	£600,000
Jimmy Nicholl (Dunfermline) July 89	£25,000
Dave Kirkwood (Hearts) August 89	£100,000
Davie Cooper (Motherwell) August 89	£50,000

Dealings in the Transfer Market

Nicky Walter (Hearts) August 89   £125,000
Kevin Drinkell (Coventry) October 90   £800,000
Ray Wilkins (QPR) November 90   FREE
Ian McCall (Bradford) January 90   £200,000

8 players sold. Total   £1,900,000

1990/91 season

Derek Ferguson (Hearts) July 90   £750,000
Terry Butcher (Coventry) November 90   £500,000

2 players sold. Total   £1,250,000

Grand total from sale of 39 players over
five seasons   £6,375,000

Grand total spent on signing 37 players   £15,375,000
Grand total from sale of 39 players   £6,375,000
Net amount spent on transfers   £9,000,000

NOTE
Of the 37 players signed by Graeme Souness, 17 of them
were sold again. Of these, 5 lasted for less than a year at
Ibrox. Mel Sterland, Mark Falco and Jan Bartram lasted
for six months or less.

20 players were signed from English clubs.
8 players were signed from Scottish clubs.
9 players were signed from continental clubs.

331

LIVERPOOL

Players signed

1991/92 season

Mark Wright (Derby) July 91	£2,200,000
Dean Saunders (Derby) July 91	£2,900,000
Mark Walters (Rangers) August 91	£1,250,000
Rob Jones (Crewe) September 91	£300,000
Michael Thomas (Arsenal) December 91	£1,500,000
Istvan Kozma (Dunfermline) January 92	£300,000
Lee Jones (Wrexham) March 92	£300,000
Scott Patterson (Cove Rangers) March 92	£25,000
8 players signed. Total	**£8,775,000**

1992/93 season

David James (Watford) June 92	£1,300,000
Paul Stewart (Spurs) July 92	£2,300,000
Torben Piechnik (Copenhagen) September 92	£500,000
Stig Bjornebye (Rosenberg) December 92	£600,000
4 players signed. Total	**£4,700,000**

1993/94 season

Nigel Clough (Nottingham Forest) June 93	£2,750,000
Neil Ruddock (Spurs) July 93	£2,500,000
Julian Dicks (West Ham) September 93	£2,500,000

3 players signed. Total	£7,750,000
Grand total spent on signing 15 players	£21,225,000

Players transferred

1991/92 season

Peter Beardsley (Everton) August 91	£1,000,000
Steve Staunton (Aston Villa) August 91	£1,100,000
Gary Gillespie (Celtic) August 91	£900,000
David Speedie (Blackburn) August 91	£500,000
Jimmy Carter (Arsenal) October 91	£500,000
Steve McMahon (Manchester City) December 91	£900,000
Gary Ablett (Everton) January 92	£750,000
Glenn Hysen (GAIS) January 92	FREE
8 players sold. Total	£5,650,000

1992/93 season

David Collins (Oxford) July 92	FREE
Barry Venison (Newcastle) July 92	£250,000
Ray Houghton (Aston Villa) July 92	£825,000
Dean Saunders (Aston Villa) October 92	£2,300,000
Michael Fox (Runcorn) November 92	FREE
5 players sold. Total	£3,375,000

1993/94 season

Istvan Kozma (Ujpest) August 93	FREE

David Burrows (West Ham) September 93	£1,250,000
Mike Marsh (West Ham) September 93	£1,000,000
Mike Hooper (Newcastle) September 93	£550,000
Ronny Rosenthal (Spurs) January 94	£250,000
5 players sold. Total	£3,050,000
18 players sold for a grand total of	£12,075,000

15 players signed for a grand total of	£21,225,000
18 players sold for a grand total of	£12,075,000
Net expenditure on transfers	£9,150,000

NOTE
Two Souness signings for Liverpool were subsequently sold by him. They were Dean Saunders who was sold for a loss of £600,000 and Istvan Kozma who was sold for a loss of £300,000.

Total amount spent on signing 52 players at Rangers and Liverpool	£36,600,000
Total amount raised from sale of 57 players at Rangers and Liverpool	£18,450,000
Net loss on transfers at both clubs	£18,150,000

Index

335

Index

INDEX

Index

Index

troubles 35–6, 114–15, 177–91; manager of GR 43–55, 57–71, 73–82, 83–101, 103–06, 114–19, 185–8, 194–201, 222–32, 242–4, 311; approached by LFC 111–14, 116–19; manager of LFC 124–6, 136–7, 139–55, 159–75, 188–91, 198–211, 213–18, 220–24, 232–43, 249–64, 318–19; *1993* negotiations with LFC 272–80; *1994* 281–97; resigns from LFC 299–310; after leaving LFC 311–20; managerial honours *listed* 325–6; transfer dealings *listed* 327–34; media relations 193–211; first marriage 7–8, 47–8, 91, 216–17, 277–8; heart troubles 205–09, 213–18; second marriage 211, 317; allegations 311, 313–14; career record 321–2; *A Manager's Diary* 111; *No Half Measures* 177

Souness, Jimmy (father of GS) 11, 181–2; death 263

Souness, Karen (second wife of GS) *see* Levy

Spackman, Nigel 67, 118–19, 328

Speedie, David 164–5, 173, 174, 333

St Johnstone 115, 243–4

Star newspaper 204

Stark, Billy 114, 183

Staunton, Steve 163, 168, 312, 333

Stavin, Mary 36

Stein, Jock 6, 49

Stensgaard, Michael 313

Sterland, Mel 66, 67, 69, 328, 330, 331

Steven, Trevor 66, 328

Stevens, Gary 65–6, 326

Stewart, Paul 149–50, 153, 155, 233, 261, 262, 332; *1994* 313, 319

Stielike, Ulrike 35

Stoke City 313

Struth, Bill 37, 85, 87–9

Sugar, Alan 317

Sun newspaper 178, 201, 291, 307; on GS's second marriage 211, 317; on Hillsborough 203–05; on Johnston 94; 'Loverpool' 205–08, 210–11, 216–17, 296

Sunday Mirror 317

Sunday People 277

Sunday Times 159

Sunderland 260–61

Swindon 281, 289–90

Symon, Scot 89

Szymanski, Stefan 246

Taylor, Graham 145

Taylor Report 131, 264

television 201, 241–2, 318; *see also* Scottish Television; Sky Television

Texaco Cup 18

Thatcher, Margaret 126

Thomas, Michael 147, 261, 262, 290, 319, 332

Thompson, Phil 30, 123, 174, 215, 222, 238–41, 256, 257, 307

Times, The 204

Today 204

Toshack, John 111, 215, 256

Tottenham Hotspur 12, 60–61, 149, 153, 223; GS signed for 13–19, 321; matches 31, 37, 221, 277; *1994* 317

training 250–53

transfer deals 57–71, 139–55, 255–7, 319, 320; *listed* (GR 327–31) (LFC 332–4); investigated 311, 313–14

Twentyman, Geoff 238

Tynecastle Boys Club 12

UEFA 59, 172, 189; Cup 18, 105–06

Venables, Terry 149, 316

Venison, Barry 168, 172, 261, 288, 333

Vinnicombe, Chris 67, 328

Waddell, Willie 89

Walfrid, Brother 85

Walker, Jack 74

Walker, John 99

Wallace, Jock 44, 48–50, 186

Walter, Nicky 331

Walters, Mark 65, 99–100, 117, 144–6, 187, 285, 290, 291, 328, 332; *1994* 313, 319

Watson, Tom 158

Webb, Neil 268–9

Welsh, Don 306

Welton, Pat 16

341

INDEX